STREET SPEAK 2

THE COMPLETE COURSE IN AMERICAN SLANG & IDIOMS

D1612247

Front cover:

scare the pants off someone (to) *exp.* to frighten a
person so intensely that even the pants are scared.

SLANGMAN DAVID BURKE

Book Design and Production: Slangman Publishing
Managing Partner/Brand & Marketing Director: Jason Reese
Design (Logo/Web): Jennifer Reese
Editor: Lee Murphy
Illustrator – Outside cover & Contributing artist: Ty Semaka
Icon Design: Sharon Kim
Contributing artist: Ty Semaka

ISBN 1891888064

Printed in the United States of America
10 9 8 7 6 5 4

LEGEND

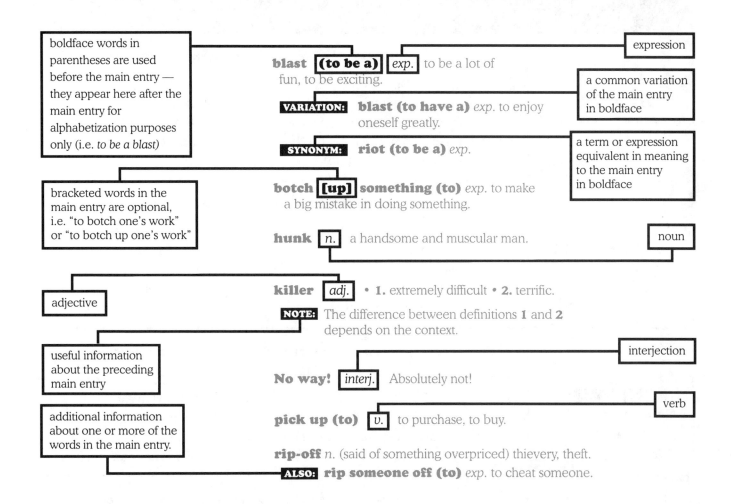

boldface words in parentheses are used before the main entry — they appear here after the main entry for alphabetization purposes only (i.e. *to be a blast*)

expression

blast **(to be a)** *exp.* to be a lot of fun, to be exciting.

a common variation of the main entry in boldface

VARIATION: **blast (to have a)** *exp.* to enjoy oneself greatly.

SYNONYM: **riot (to be a)** *exp.*

a term or expression equivalent in meaning to the main entry in boldface

bracketed words in the main entry are optional, i.e. "to botch one's work" or "to botch up one's work"

botch **[up]** **something (to)** *exp.* to make a big mistake in doing something.

hunk *n.* a handsome and muscular man.

noun

adjective

killer *adj.* • **1.** extremely difficult • **2.** terrific.

NOTE: The difference between definitions **1** and **2** depends on the context.

interjection

useful information about the preceding main entry

No way! *interj.* Absolutely not!

verb

additional information about one or more of the words in the main entry.

pick up (to) *v.* to purchase, to buy.

rip-off *n.* (said of something overpriced) thievery, theft.

ALSO: **rip someone off (to)** *exp.* to cheat someone.

EXPLANATION OF ICONS

These exercises reinforce visual recognition of the slang terms and idioms presented throughout this book.

These exercises include fill-ins, crossword puzzles, word matches and many other fun word games to help you use the new terms in context.

One of the most important parts of any language is to be able to understand what you hear. These exercises can all be found on the audio program. (*See coupon on back page for details*)

These oral exercises are designed to help you to begin speaking and thinking like a native.

TABLE OF CONTENTS

ACTIVITIES	FROM THE SLANGMAN FILES
LET'S WARM UP! `READING` **LET'S TALK!** `LISTENING/SPEAKING` A. Dialogue (*Slang & Idioms*) B. Dialogue (*Translated*) C. Dialogue (*in "Real Speak"*) **LET'S PRACTICE!** `READING` A. Choose The Right Word `READING` B. Context Exercise `SPEAKING` C. Create Your Own Sentence `WRITING` D. Complete the Phrase	Fruits & Vegetables Used in Slang
LET'S WARM UP! `READING` **LET'S TALK!** `LISTENING/SPEAKING` A. Dialogue (*Slang & Idioms*) B. Dialogue (*Translated*) C. Dialogue (*in "Real Speak"*) **LET'S PRACTICE!** `READING` A. Find the Missing Words `WRITING` B. Create Your Own Newspaper Column `SPEAKING` C. Match the Sentences	Food Used in Slang Expressions
LET'S WARM UP! `READING` **LET'S TALK!** `LISTENING/SPEAKING` A. Dialogue (*Slang & Idioms*) B. Dialogue (*Translated*) C. Dialogue (*in "Real Speak"*) **LET'S PRACTICE!** `READING` A. What Does it Mean? `WRITING` B. Complete the Fairy Tale `READING` C. Context Exercise `WRITING` D. Complete the Phrase	Car and On-the-Road Slang
LET'S WARM UP! `READING` **LET'S TALK!** `LISTENING/SPEAKING` A. Dialogue (*Slang & Idioms*) B. Dialogue (*Translated*) C. Dialogue (*in "Real Speak"*) **LET'S PRACTICE!** `WRITING` A. Choose the Right Word `READING` B. Crossword Puzzle `READING` C. Match the Column	Clothing Used in Slang Expressions
LET'S WARM UP! `READING` **LET'S TALK!** `LISTENING/SPEAKING` A. Dialogue (*Slang & Idioms*) B. Dialogue (*Translated*) C. Dialogue (*in "Real Speak"*) **LET'S PRACTICE!** `WRITING` A. You're the Author `READING` B. I Know the Answer, But What's the Question? `SPEAKING` C. Find Your Perfect Match `WRITING` D. Imagine That...	Body Parts Used in Slang Expressions

TABLE OF CONTENTS *(CONTINUED)*

ACTIVITIES		FROM THE SLANGMAN FILES

LET'S WARM UP! `READING`
 	
LET'S TALK! `LISTENING/SPEAKING`
A. Dialogue *(Slang & Idioms)*
B. Dialogue *(Translated)*
C. Dialogue *(in "Real Speak")*
	LET'S PRACTICE! `WRITING`
	A. The Unfinished Conversation
	`READING`
	B. Choose the Right Word
	`WRITING`
	C. Complete the Story
	`SPEAKING`
	D. Create Your Own Sentence
		Proper Names Used in Slang

LET'S WARM UP! `READING`
 	
LET'S TALK! `LISTENING/SPEAKING`
A. Dialogue *(Slang & Idioms)*
B. Dialogue *(Translated)*
C. Dialogue *(in "Real Speak")*
	LET'S PRACTICE! `SPEAKING`
	A. You're the Author
	`READING`
	B. Crossword Puzzle
	`WRITING`
	C. True or False
	`READING`
	D. Create Your Own Sentence
		Initials Used in Slang Expressions

LET'S WARM UP! `READING` **LET'S TALK!** `LISTENING/SPEAKING` A. Dialogue *(Slang & Idioms)* B. Dialogue *(Translated)* C. Dialogue *(in "Real Speak")*	**LET'S PRACTICE!** `READING` A. Truth or Lie `WRITING` B. Find the Definition `WRITING` C. Find-the-Word Grid	Fish, Insects, & Animals Used in Slang

LET'S WARM UP! `READING`
 	
LET'S TALK! `LISTENING/SPEAKING`
A. Dialogue *(Slang & Idioms)*
B. Dialogue *(Translated)*
C. Dialogue *(in "Real Speak")*
	LET'S PRACTICE! `WRITING`
	A. Create Your Own Story *(Part 1)*
	`SPEAKING`
	B. Create Your Own Story *(Part 2)*
	`READING`
	C. What Would You Do...?
	`WRITING`
	D. "Across" Word Puzzle
		Numbers Used in Slang

LET'S WARM UP! `READING`
 	
LET'S TALK! `LISTENING/SPEAKING`
A. Dialogue *(Slang & Idioms)*
B. Dialogue *(Translated)*
C. Dialogue *(in "Real Speak")*
	LET'S PRACTICE! `READING`
	A. Correct or Incorrect?
	`WRITING`
	B. Blank-Blank
	`READING`
	C. True or False
		Colors Used in Slang Expressions

"Carl got called on the carpet!"

LET'S WARM UP!

MATCH THE PICTURES *(Answers on p. 219)*

As a fun way to get started, see if you can guess the meaning of the new slang words and expressions on the opposite page by using the pictures below and following the context of the sentences.

READING

1. Earl got reprimanded by the boss for ***falling asleep at the wheel***.
   "*falling asleep at the wheel*" means: ❑ doing a great job . . . . ❑ failing to do his job

2. The boss ***called me on the carpet*** for arriving late to work this morning.
   "*called on the carpet*" means: . . . . ❑ reprimanded me . . . . ❑ called me bad names

3. The new employee keeps talking to himself. I think he's a ***wacko***!
   "*wacko*" means: . . . . ❑ talkative person. . . . . . ❑ lunatic

4. My boss and I never ***see eye to eye*** on anything. Frankly, I think he's just stubborn.
   "*see eye to eye*" means: . . . . . . ❑ agree . . . . ❑ see poorly

5. Jerry didn't know the answer to that simple math problem? He needs to ***get a clue***!
   "*get a clue*" means: . . . . ❑ get smarter and more aware . ❑ go on vacation

6. Stop ***goofing off*** and help me?
   "*goofing off*" means: . . . . ❑ working hard . . . . ❑ playing instead of working

7. How did the boss know you came in late? Did someone ***blow the whistle on*** you?
   "*blow the whistle on*" means: . . . . ❑ compliment . . . . ❑ report

8. If Bob thinks he going to have a peaceful morning, he's going to have ***a rude awakening***!
   "*a rude awakening*" means: . . . . . ❑ an undesirable surprise . . . . ❑ a wonderful surprise

9. Fido was ***caught in the act*** of stealing!
   "*caught in the act*" means: . . . . . ❑ seen doing something wrong . ❑ seen in a movie or play

10. Tom ***botched up*** the simple job I gave him to do! It was horrible!
    "*botched up*" means: . . . . ❑ made mistakes with . . . . . . ❑ excelled in

LET'S TALK!

A. DIALOGUE USING SLANG & IDIOMS

The words introduced on the first two pages are used in the dialogue below. See if you can understand the conversation. *Note:* The translation of the words in boldface is on the right-hand page.

CD-A: TRACK 2

Mike is telling David some news about work.

Mike: Did you hear the news about Carl? He was **called on the carpet** for **falling asleep at the wheel**!

David: You're kidding! Who **blew the whistle on** him?

Mike: No one. The boss **caught him in the act**. Most of the day, he does nothing but **goof off**. Then when he does finally work, he **botches it [up]**. If he doesn't **get a clue** and start working harder, he's going **to have a rude awakening**.

David: I've never been able **to see eye to eye** with him. Frankly, I think he's kind of a **wacko**!

B. DIALOGUE TRANSLATED INTO STANDARD ENGLISH

LET'S SEE HOW MUCH YOU REMEMBER!
Just for fun, bounce around in random order to the words
and expressions in boldface below. See if you can remember
their slang equivalents without looking at the left-hand page!

Mike is telling David some news about work.

Mike: Did you hear the news about Carl? He was **reprimanded** for **failing to do his work**!

David: You're kidding! Who **reported** him?

Mike: No one. The boss **saw him in the process of doing something wrong**. Most of the day, he does nothing but **play instead of work**. Then when he does finally work, he **makes big mistakes**. If he doesn't **get smarter** and start working harder, he's going **to get an undesirable surprise**.

David: I've never been able **to understand** him. Frankly, I think he's kind of a **lunatic**!

C. DIALOGUE USING "REAL SPEAK"

The dialogue below demonstrates how the slang conversation on the previous page would *really* be spoken by native speakers!

Mike's telling David s'm news about work.

Mike: Did'ja hear the news about Carl? He w'z **called on the carpet** fer **falling asleep 'it the wheel**!

David: Y'r kidding! Who **blew the whistle on** 'im?

Mike: No one. The boss **cod 'im in the act**. Most 'a the day, he does nothing b't **goof off**. Then when 'e does fin'lly work, he **botches id [up]**. If 'e doesn't **ged a clue** 'n start working harder, he's gonna **have a rude awakening**.

David: I've never been able **da see eye da eye** with 'im. Frankly, I think 'e's kind of a **wacko**!

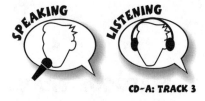

CD-A: TRACK 3

VOCABULARY

The following words and expressions were used in the previous dialogues. Let's take a closer look at what they mean.

blow the whistle on someone (to) *exp.* to report someone for doing something wrong.

EXAMPLE:	Steve **blew the whistle** on me for leaving work early.
TRANSLATION:	Steve **reported** me for leaving work early.
"REAL SPEAK:"	Steve **blew the whistle** on me fer leaving work early.

Note: This expression comes from the world of crime, describing a police officer who blows his whistle in order to stop an offender.

Also: **whistle blower** *n.* one who reports back to an official.

Synonym 1:   **fink on someone (to)** *exp.*

Synonym 2:   **rat on someone (to)** *exp.*

Synonym 3:   **snitch on someone (to)** *exp.*

NOW DO IT. COMPLETE THE PHRASE ALOUD:

I'd blow the whistle on someone who...

botch [up] something (to) *exp.* to make a big mistake in doing something.

EXAMPLE: Howard tried to put his new bicycle together himself but he **botched it [up]**!

TRANSLATION: Howard tried to put his new bicycle together himself but he **made a big mistake**!

"REAL SPEAK:" Howard tried ta pud 'is new bike tagether 'imself bud 'e **botched id [up]**!

Also: **botch-job** *n.* a job poorly done.

Synonym: **screw up something (to)** *exp.*

NOW YOU DO IT:
(Use "botch [up]" in a sentence)

called on the carpet (to get) *exp.* to get reprimanded (by one's parents, boss, etc.).

EXAMPLE: Norman **got called on the carpet** for wasting time at work.

TRANSLATION: Norman **got reprimanded** for wasting time at work.

"REAL SPEAK:" Norman **got called on the carpet** fer wasting time 'it work.

Synonym 1: **bawl someone out (to)** *exp.*

Synonym 2: **chew someone out (to)** *exp.*

NOW YOU DO IT. COMPLETE THE PHRASE ALOUD:
The boss called me on the carpet when I...

fall asleep at the wheel (to) *exp.* to fail to do one's job.

EXAMPLE: Ralph was supposed to contact all the clients but he completely forgot! He **fell asleep at the wheel** again.

TRANSLATION: Ralph was supposed to contact all the clients but he completely forgot! He **failed to do his job** again.

"REAL SPEAK:" Ralph was sapposta contact all the clients bud 'e c'mpletely fergot! He **fell asleep 'it the wheel** again.

Synonym 1: **fall asleep at the switch (to)** *exp.*

Synonym 2: **fall down on the job (to)** *exp.*

NOW YOU DO IT. COMPLETE THE PHRASE ALOUD:
...fell asleep at the wheel! He/she forgot to...

get caught in the act (to) *exp.* to be seen in the process of doing something wrong.

EXAMPLE: Fido is in big trouble. He was **caught in the act** stealing food.

TRANSLATION: Fido is in big trouble. He was **seen in the process of** stealing food.

"REAL SPEAK:" Fido's 'n big trouble. He w'z **cod in the act** stealing food.

Synonym: **get caught red-handed (to)** *exp.*

NOW YOU DO IT. COMPLETE THE PHRASE ALOUD:
The police caught Bob in the act of...

get a clue (to) *exp.* to get smarter and more aware.

> **EXAMPLE:** You loaned a stranger money because he said he'd pay you back? You'll never see that money again! **Get a clue**!
>
> **TRANSLATION:** You loaned a stranger money because he said he'd pay you back? You'll never see that money again! **Get smarter and more aware**!
>
> **"REAL SPEAK:"** You loaned a stranger money 'cause 'e said 'e'd pay ya back? You'll never see that money again! **Ged a clue**!
>
> *Note:* **clueless (to be)** *adj.* to be completely unaware.
>
> **NOW YOU DO IT. COMPLETE THE PHRASE ALOUD:**
> *You just ....?! Get a clue!*

goof off (to) *exp.* to play when one is supposed to be working.

> **EXAMPLE:** I hired my best friend to help me at my office. Instead, he just **goofed off**.
>
> **TRANSLATION:** I hired my best friend to help me at my office. Instead, he just **played instead of worked**.
>
> **"REAL SPEAK:"** I hired my best frien' da help me 'it my office. Instead, 'e jus' **goofed off**.
>
> *Also 1:* **goof** *n.* fool / **goofy** *adj.* foolish.
>
> *Also 2:* **goof around (to)** *exp.* to play.
>
> *Also 3:* **goof up (to)** *exp.* to make a mistake.
>
> **NOW YOU DO IT. COMPLETE THE PHRASE ALOUD:**
> *Stop goofing off and help me to...*

rude awakening (to have a) *exp.* to get an undesirable surprise.

> **EXAMPLE:** If Pat thinks he can keep cheating on his taxes, he's going **to have a rude awakening**.
>
> **TRANSLATION:** If Pat thinks he can keep cheating on his taxes, he's going **to get an undesirable surprise**.
>
> **"REAL SPEAK:"** If Pat thinks 'e c'n keep cheading on 'is taxes, he's gonna **have a rude awakening**.
>
> **NOW YOU DO IT. COMPLETE THE PHRASE ALOUD:**
> *Susan's going to have a rude awakening if she thinks she can...*

see eye to eye (to) *exp.* said of two or more people who agree on the same matter.

> **EXAMPLE:** Rob and I never **see eye to eye** on anything. Sometimes I think he disagrees with me just to be difficult.
>
> **TRANSLATION:** Rob and I never **agree** on anything. Sometimes I think he disagrees with me just to be difficult.
>
> **"REAL SPEAK:"** Rob 'n I never **see eye da eye** on anything. Sometimes I think 'e disagrees with me jus' ta be difficult.
>
> **NOW YOU DO IT. COMPLETE THE PHRASE ALOUD:**
> *I never see eye to eye with...*

wacko *n.* crazy person, lunatic.

EXAMPLE:	My uncle is a real **wacko**. He has names for all the objects in his house and even talks to them!
TRANSLATION:	My uncle is a real **lunatic**. He has names for all the objects in his house and even talks to them!
"REAL SPEAK:"	My uncle's a real **wacko**. He has names fer all the objec's in 'is house an' even talks to 'em!

Variation: **wack job** *exp.*

Synonyms: **nuts** *adj.* / **nutty** *adj.* / **to be a nut case** *exp.* to be crazy.

NOW YOU DO IT. COMPLETE THE PHRASE ALOUD:
I think... is a wacko because...

LET'S PRACTICE!

READING

CD-A: TRACK 4

A. CHOOSE THE RIGHT WORD *(Answers on p. 219)*
Underline the appropriate word(s) that best complete(s) the phrase.

1. I don't agree with you. I guess we'll never see (**toe to toe**, **head to head**, **eye to eye**).

2. If Bob thinks he can get away with cheating people, he's going to have a (**polite**, **rude**, **discourteous**) awakening!

3. The boss called Ed on the (**floor**, **carpet**, **rug**) for not working hard.

4. Gina got fired for stealing office supplies? Who (**blew**, **inhaled**, **exhaled**) the whistle on her?

5. The boss gave Jim a simple assignment and he totally botched it (**up**, **down**, **over**).

6. My grandmother thinks she's Cleopatra. She's definitely a (**wrinkle**, **wacko**, **wheez**)!

7. You loaned your brother your car?! Get a (**flue**, **glue**, **clue**)! He'll probably wreck it!

8. Bill doesn't do anything at work but goof (**off**, **on**, **in**). I hope he gets fired soon.

9. The boss finally caught Greg in the (**scene**, **act**, **play**) stealing. He'll probably go to jail!

10. If you don't stop falling asleep at the (**meal**, **wheels**, **wheel**), you're going to get fired!

B. CONTEXT EXERCISE *(Answers on p. 219)*
Read the short conversations. Decide whether the slang used makes sense or doesn't make sense. Circle your answer.

CD-A: TRACK 5

– Al fell asleep at the wheel again!
– I know. He's a great worker.

MAKES SENSE   DOESN'T MAKE SENSE

– Bob got fired for stealing!
– Who blew the whistle on him?

MAKES SENSE   DOESN'T MAKE SENSE

– I got called on the carpet today.
– Did the boss give you a raise?

MAKES SENSE   DOESN'T MAKE SENSE

– Ron and I agree on everything.
– You must always see eye to eye.

MAKES SENSE   DOESN'T MAKE SENSE

– Chris loves to goof off.
– I know. He's a great worker!

MAKES SENSE   DOESN'T MAKE SENSE

– Norman botched [up] his work.
– He can't do anything right.

MAKES SENSE   DOESN'T MAKE SENSE

– Timmy stole something from Bill.
– Was he caught in the act?

MAKES SENSE   DOESN'T MAKE SENSE

– Mark is so smart.
– I know. He needs to get a clue.

MAKES SENSE   DOESN'T MAKE SENSE

– My uncle thinks he can fly.
– He must really be a wacko!

MAKES SENSE   DOESN'T MAKE SENSE

C. *CREATE YOUR OWN SENTENCE* (Answers on p. 219)

Read Person A's questions or statements aloud and use the suggested words to create your response for Person B.

SPEAKING

PERSON A	PERSON B

1. Where's Joe? I haven't seen him this morning.   [use: **called on the carpet**]

2. Why did Arnold get in trouble at work?   [use: **fell asleep at the wheel**]

3. How did the boss find out you left early yesterday?   [use: **blew the whistle**]

4. Are you positive that Janet stole your purse?   [use: **caught in the act**]

5. Why do you think Peggy got fired?   [use: **goofing off**]

6. How is Anne doing on her job assignment?   [use: **botched**]

7. Chris asked the boss for a raise his second day here?   [use: **get a clue**]

8. Tina tells lies constantly!   [use: **rude awakening**]

9. Are Jane and Lisa still arguing?   [use: **eye to eye**]

10. Did you meet the new employee?   [use: **wacko**]

D. COMPLETE THE PHRASE *(Answers on p. 219)*
Complete the phrase by choosing the appropriate
words from the list below.

CD-A: TRACK 6

wheel	get a clue	rude
called on the carpet	act	blow the whistle
goofing off	eye to eye	wacko

1. Pat got _____ for coming to work late for the third
   time this week.

2. Tom and I never see _____ on any subject. We always disagree with
   each other.

3. You left food in your tent when you went camping? _____ ! You could have been
   attacked by bears!

4. My car was almost stolen last night! Luckily, there was a policeman standing on the corner who
   caught the thief in the _____ .

5. You're going to start a company with that _____? Everyone knows he's insane! He even
   makes psychiatrists nervous!

6. Morgan leaves work early every day and I'm left to do his work. Well, if he does that again
   today, I'm going to _____ on him!

7. Michelle lied on her job application. When the boss find outs, she's going to have a _____
   awakening.

8. Don forgot to file all these papers. He's falling asleep at the _____ again!

9. Would you stop _____ and help me?!

Fruits & Vegetables Used in Slang

If you're starting **to go bananas** (*become crazy*) because you **don't know beans** (*don't know anything*) about expressions containing fruits and vegetables, this section will help you keep **as cool as a cucumber** (*extremely calm*)!

Fruits and vegetables have given rise to a number of colorful slang expressions in American-English as demonstrated in the following list:

APPLES

"An apple a day keeps the doctor away" *exp.* "If you eat a piece of fruit every day, you'll stay healthy and not need to go to the doctor."

   EXAMPLE: You need to eat more fruit. Remember, **an apple a day keeps the doctor away**.

   TRANSLATION: You need to eat more fruit. Remember, **if you eat a piece of fruit every day, you'll stay healthy and not need to go to the doctor.**

   "REAL SPEAK": Ya need ta eat more fruit. Remember, **an apple a day keeps the docter away**.

as American as apple pie (to be) *exp.* to have traditional American values.

   EXAMPLE: Our new president is **as American as apple pie**.

   TRANSLATION: Our new president **has traditional American values**.

   "REAL SPEAK": 'Are new president's **'ez American 'ez apple pie**.

Big Apple (the) *exp.* New York City (because it represents temptation as did the apple from the Garden of Eden).

   EXAMPLE: I'm moving to **the Big Apple** to be in a Broadway play!

   TRANSLATION: I'm moving to **New York City** to be in a Broadway play!

   "REAL SPEAK": I'm moving ta **the Big Apple** ta be in a Broadway play!

compare apples to oranges (to) *exp.* to make a comparison between two things which are completely different.

   EXAMPLE: You can't compare those two situations. You're **comparing apples to oranges**!

   TRANSLATION: You can't compare those two situations. You're **making a comparison between two things which are completely different**!

   "REAL SPEAK": Ya can't c'mpare those two situations. Y'r **c'mparing apples ta oranges**!

"How do you like them apples?!" *exp.*
- 1. (*said in astonishment*) "Can you believe it?!"
- 2. (*in anger*) "What do you think of that?!"

   EXAMPLE 1: My boss wants to lower my salary and I've been working overtime every week for three months! **How do you like them apples**?!

   TRANSLATION: My boss wants to lower my salary and I've been working overtime every week for three months! **Can you believe it**?!

"REAL SPEAK": My boss wants ta lower my salary 'n I've b'n working overtime ev'ry week fer three months! **How do ya like them apples**?!

EXAMPLE 2: Since you stole money from my company, I'm firing you immediately. **How do you like them apples**?!

TRANSLATION: Since you stole money from my company, I'm firing you immediately. **What do you think of that**?!

"REAL SPEAK": Since ya stole money fr'm my company, I'm firing you immediately. **Howdy ya like them apples**?!

Note: There are two important details to note in this expression. First, this sentence is actually grammatically incorrect! It *should* be: *How do you like **those** apples.* "Those" is intentionally used incorrectly to add emphasis to "*apples*" which, in this expression, represents anything astonishing or intriguing. Second, the word "them" is emphasized by raising the voice. In fact, this is so important that not to stress this term would actually sound strange to the native speaker of English!

BANANAS

bananas (to be) *exp.* to be insane, crazy.

EXAMPLE: That woman is talking to her car. She's **bananas**!

TRANSLATION: That woman is talking to her car. She's **crazy**!

"REAL SPEAK": That woman's talking to 'er car. She's **b'nanas**!

Note: **go bananas (to)** *exp.* • **1.** to go crazy • *In her old age, my aunt went bananas. She thinks she's Cleopatra!;* In her old age, my aunt went crazy.

She thinks she's Cleopatra! • **2.** to get extremely angry • *When I told my father that I ruined his car, he went bananas!;* When I told my father that I ruined his car, he got extremely angry! • **3.** to become very excited • *The crowd went bananas when their favorite singer walked on stage;* The crowd went wild when their favorite singer walked on stage.

play second banana to someone (to) *exp.* to be secondary to someone

EXAMPLE: The employees only listen to Carl and not me because I'm the vice president and Carl is the president. I'm tired of **playing second banana to him**!

TRANSLATION: The employees only listen to Carl and not me because I'm the vice president and Carl is the president. I'm tired of **being secondary to him**!

"REAL SPEAK": The employees only listen ta Carl 'n not me b'cause I'm the vice president 'n Carl's the president. I'm tired 'ev **playing secon' banana da him**!

top banana *m.* the person with the most authority.

EXAMPLE: If you want a raise, you'd better talk to the **top banana** about it, not me

TRANSLATION: If you want a raise, you'd better talk to the **person with the most authority** about it, not me.

"REAL SPEAK": If ya wanna raise, ya bedder talk ta the **top banana** aboud it, not me.

BEANS

bean counter *exp.* accountant

EXAMPLE: My father is a **bean counter**. He's always been great at math.

TRANSLATION: My father is an **accountant**. He's always been great at math.

"REAL SPEAK": My father's a **bean counter**. He's always been grade 'it math.

bean pole *exp.* a very tall and thin person

> EXAMPLE: Carla is a **bean pole** but everyone else in her family is short and fat.
>
> TRANSLATION: Carla is **tall and thin** but everyone else in her family is short and fat.
>
> "REAL SPEAK": Carla's a **bean pole** b'd ev'ryone else in 'er fam'ly 's short 'n fat.

Bean Town *exp.* a nickname for Boston, Massachusetts, which is popular for its baked beans.

> EXAMPLE: I'm going to begin school in **Bean Town** next year
>
> TRANSLATION: I'm going to begin school in **Boston** next year.
>
> "REAL SPEAK": I'm gonna b'gin school 'n **Bean Town** next year.

beans about something (not to know)
exp. not to know anything about something.

> EXAMPLE: I'm afraid I can't help you with your algebra homework. I **don't know beans about** math!
>
> TRANSLATION: I'm afraid I can't help you with your algebra homework. I **don't know anything about** math!
>
> "REAL SPEAK": I'm afraid I can't help ya with yer algebra homework. I **dunno beans about** math!
>
> *Note:* This expression only works in the negative: **not to know beans about something**. The expression does not work in the positive. For example, the following example is incorrect and would actually sound strange to the native-speaker: *I'd be glad to help you with your algebra homework. I know beans about math.*

spill the beans (to) *exp.* to reveal a secret.

> EXAMPLE: I told you not to tell Helen that we were planning a surprise party for her. Why did you **spill the beans**?
>
> TRANSLATION: I told you not to tell Helen that we were planning a surprise party for her. Why did you **reveal the secret**?
>
> "REAL SPEAK": I told 'ja not ta tell Helen th't we were planning a serprise pardy fer her. Why'dja **spill the beans**?

BEETS

beet red (to be/to turn) *exp.* to be/to become extremely red (due to a sunburn, embarrassment, anger, etc.).

> EXAMPLE: When Cecily's wig came off at the party, she turned **beet red**!
>
> TRANSLATION: When Cecily's wig came off at the party, she **blushed**!
>
> "REAL SPEAK": When Cecily's wig came off 'it the pardy, she turned **beet red**!

CARROTS

carrot in front of someone (to dangle a)
exp. to tempt someone with something.

> EXAMPLE: The boss wants me to work in our New York office, so he **dangled a carrot in front of me**. He's offering me twice my salary if I accept!
>
> TRANSLATION: The boss wants me to work in our New York office, so he **tempted me with something**. He's offering me twice my salary if I accept!
>
> "REAL SPEAK": The boss wants me da work 'n 'ar New York office, so 'e **dangled a carrod in fronna me**. He's offering me twice my salary if I accept!

CHERRIES

bowl of cherries (to be a) *exp.* (used in reference to someone's life) wonderful, fantastic.

> EXAMPLE: I had such a bad week. Well, I guess life isn't always **a bowl of cherries**.
>
> TRANSLATION: I had such a bad week. Well, I guess life isn't always **wonderful**.
>
> "REAL SPEAK": I had such a bad week. Well, I guess life isn' always **a bowl 'a cherries**.

CORN

corny *adj.* overly sentimental

EXAMPLE: In the movie, every time the two lovers spoke to each other, their voices shook as the music swelled. It was so **corny**!

TRANSLATION: In the movie, every time the two lovers spoke to each other, their voices shook as the music swelled. It was so **overly sentimental**.

"REAL SPEAK": In the movie, ev'ry time the two lovers spoke to each other, their voices shook 'ez the music swelled. It w'z so **corny**!

Variation: **cornball** *adj.*

"For corn sake!" *interj.* an interjection of surprise.

EXAMPLE: John is your brother? **For corn sake**! I didn't know that!

TRANSLATION: John is your brother? **I'm really surprised**! I didn't know that!

"REAL SPEAK": John's yer brother? **Fer corn sake**! I didn' know that!

Note: Although this expression is outdated, it is still occasionally used by older generations or in jest.

CUCUMBERS

cool as a cucumber (to be as) *exp.* to be calm and collected.

EXAMPLE: When the thief was interrogated by the police, he was **as cool as a cucumber**.

TRANSLATION: When the thief was interrogated by the police, he was **calm and collected**.

"REAL SPEAK": When the thief w'z interragaded by the police, he w'z **'ez cool 'ez a cucumber**.

FRUIT

fruit *n.* (derogatory) gay, homosexual.

EXAMPLE: Just because Steve is gay is no reason to call him a **fruit**!

TRANSLATION: Just because Steve is gay is no reason to call him a **derogatory name for homosexual**!

"REAL SPEAK": Just b'cause Steve is gay is no reason ta call 'im a **fruit**!

Note 1: **fruity** *adj.* (derogatory) effeminate • *If John wants to be a serious actor, he's going to have to stop acting so fruity!;* If John wants to be a serious actor, he's going to have to stop acting so effeminate!

Note 2: This term is extremely derogatory and offensive to homosexuals. The accepted term in the homosexual community is "gay."

Variation 1: **fruitcake** *n.* (see next entry).

Variation 2: **fruit loop** *exp.* (from a popular brand of cereal).

fruitcake *n.* • **1.** crazy person • **2.** derogatory for "homosexual."

EXAMPLE 1: My piano teacher thinks he's really Mozart! The guy is a total **fruitcake**!

TRANSLATION: My piano teacher thinks he's really Mozart! The guy is total **lunatic**!

"REAL SPEAK": My piano teacher thinks 'e's really Mozart! The guy's a tod'l **fruitcake**!

EXAMPLE: My piano teacher wears makeup every day. The guy's a total **fruitcake**!

TRANSLATION: My piano teacher wears makeup every day. The guy's extremely **effeminate**!

"REAL SPEAK": My piano teacher wears makeup ev'ry day. The guy's a tod'l **fruitcake**!

Note: The difference between definitions **1.** and **2.** simply depends on the context.

GRAPES

grapevine (to hear something through the) *exp.* to hear some news through informal conversation or gossip.

> **EXAMPLE:** – How do you know Al inherited a million dollars?
> – I **heard it through the grapevine**.

> **TRANSLATION:** – How do you know Al inherited a million dollars?
> – I **heard it through some gossip**.

> **"REAL SPEAK":** – Howdy'ya know Al inherided a million dollers?
> – I **heard it through the grapevine**.

sour grapes *exp.* jealousy or bitterness due to something one cannot have for oneself.

> **EXAMPLE:** Carol was really angry that Nancy won the prize and not her. It's just **sour grapes**, but Carol needs to grow up!

> **TRANSLATION:** Carol was really angry that Nancy won the prize and not her. It's just **due to jealousy**, but Carol needs to grow up!

> **"REAL SPEAK":** Carol w'z really angry th't Nancy won the prize 'n not her. It's jus' **sour grapes**, b't Carol needs ta grow up!

LEMONS

lemon *n.* worthless thing, junk

> **EXAMPLE:** I bought a new car yesterday and it already broke down! What a **lemon**!

> **TRANSLATION:** I bought a new car yesterday and it already broke down! What a **worthless thing**!

> **"REAL SPEAK":** I bod a new car yesterday 'n id already broke down! Whad a **lemon**!

ORANGES

compare apples to oranges (to) *exp.* – see: *Apples – compare apples to oranges (to), p. 12.*

PEAS

as thick as pea soup (to be) *exp.* said of extremely dense fog.

> **EXAMPLE:** It was impossible to drive. The fog was **as thick as pea soup**!

> **TRANSLATION:** It was impossible to drive. The fog was **extremely thick**!

> **"REAL SPEAK":** It w'z impossible ta drive. The fog w'z **'ez thick 'ez pea soup**!

like two peas in a pod (to be) *exp.* to be very much alike

> **EXAMPLE:** Carl and Wendy have all the same interests. They're **like two peas in a pod**.

> **TRANSLATION:** Carl and Wendy have all the same interests. They're **very much alike**.

> **"REAL SPEAK":** Carl 'n Wendy have all the same int'rests. They're **like two peas 'n a pod**.

pea brain exp. fool, idiot

> **EXAMPLE:** I'm such a **pea brain**. I completely forgot about my doctor's appointment today!

> **TRANSLATION:** I'm such a **fool**. I completely forgot about my doctor's appointment today!

> **"REAL SPEAK":** I'm such a **pea brain**. I c'mpletely fergod about my docter's appointment taday!

PEACHES

a real peach (to be) *exp.* said of a very pleasant or exceptional person.

> **EXAMPLE:** The new secretary is a **real peach**. She sounds annoyed every time she answers the phone!
>
> **TRANSLATION:** The new secretary is **terrible**. She sounds annoyed every time she answers the phone!
>
> **"REAL SPEAK":** The new secretary's a **real peach**. She soun'z annoyed ev'ry time she answers the phone!
>
> *Note:* As defined above, this expression is somewhat outdated though still occasionally used by the older generations or in jest. It is actually more commonly used in a sarcastic way as demonstrated in the example.

peach of a... (to be a) *exp.* to be a wonderful... (but typically used sarcastically to mean "a terrible...").

> **EXAMPLE:** He's a **peach of an** employee. He arrives to work late and leaves early every day!
>
> **TRANSLATION:** He's a **terrible** employee. He arrives to work late and leaves early every day!
>
> **"REAL SPEAK":** He's a **peach 'ev 'n** employee. He arrives ta work late 'n leaves early ev'ry day!

peachy (to be) *adj.* to be terrific (but typically used sarcastically to mean "terrible").

> **EXAMPLE:** Well, that's just **peachy**. I'm supposed to be at the airport in thirty minutes and my taxi still hasn't arrived!
>
> **TRANSLATION:** Well, that's just **terrible**. I'm supposed to be at the airport in thirty minutes and my taxi still hasn't arrived!
>
> **"REAL SPEAK":** Well, that's just **peachy**. I'm sappozta be 'it the airpord in thirdy minutes 'n my taxi still hasn' arrived!
>
> *Note:* This expression is somewhat outdated though still occasionally used by the older generations or in jest.

PICKLES

pickle (to be in a) *exp.* to be in a predicament.

> **EXAMPLE:** I'm in a real **pickle**. I promised my mother that I'd pick her up at the airport, but my boss needs me to work late tonight! Could you pick her up for me?
>
> **TRANSLATION:** I'm in a real **predicament**. I promised my mother that I'd pick her up at the airport, but my boss needs me to work late tonight! Could you pick her up for me?
>
> **"REAL SPEAK":** I'm 'n a real **pickle**. I promised my mother th'd I'd pick 'er up 'it the airport, b't my boss needs me da work late tanight! Could'ju pick 'er up fer me?

pickled (to be) *adj.* to be drunk.

> **EXAMPLE:** I don't think you should have anything else to drink. You're already **pickled**.
>
> **TRANSLATION:** I don't think you should have anything else to drink. You're already **drunk**.
>
> **"REAL SPEAK":** I don't think you should have anything else ta drink. Y'r already **pickled**.

POTATOES

couch potato (to be a) *exp.* said of a lazy person who does nothing but lie on the couch.

> **EXAMPLE:** Joe is such a **couch potato**. All he does is watch television all day.
>
> **TRANSLATION:** Joe is such a **lazy person**. All he does is lie on the couch and watch television all day.
>
> **"REAL SPEAK":** Joe's such a **couch patado**. All 'e does 'ez watch TV all day.

hot potato *exp.* said of something potentially dangerous, unpredictable, volatile.

> **EXAMPLE:** Are you sure you want to date the boss's daughter? That could be a **hot potato**!
>
> **TRANSLATION:** Are you sure you want to date the boss's daughter? That could be a **potentially volatile situation**!
>
> **"REAL SPEAK":** Are ya sher ya wanna date the boss's dawder? That could be a **hot patado**!

meat and potatoes (the) *exp.* the essence.

> **EXAMPLE:** You're talking around the subject. You're not dealing with the **meat and potatoes** of the problem.
>
> **TRANSLATION:** You're talking around the subject. You're not dealing with the **essence** of the problem.
>
> **"REAL SPEAK":** Y'r talking aroun' the subject. Y'r not dealing with the **meat 'n patadoes** 'ev the problem.

small potatoes *exp.* trivial, unimportant.

> **EXAMPLE:** I don't want to work for that company. They're **small potatoes**. I want to work for a larger corporation.
>
> **TRANSLATION:** I don't want to work for that company. They're **unimportant**. I want to work for a larger corporation.
>
> **"REAL SPEAK":** I don't wanna work fer that company. They're **small patadoes**. I wanna work fer a larger corperation.

PRUNES

prune face *exp.* a very wrinkled face

> **EXAMPLE:** If you don't stop spending hours in the sun, you're going to turn into a **prune face**.
>
> **TRANSLATION:** If you don't stop spending hours in the sun, you're going to turn into a **person with a wrinkled face**.
>
> **"REAL SPEAK":** If ya don't stop spending hours in the sun, y'r gonna turn into a **prune face**.

pruney *adj.* wrinkled (like a prune)

> **EXAMPLE:** My hands got all **pruney** from washing the dishes.

> **TRANSLATION:** My hands got all **wrinkled** from washing the dishes.
>
> **"REAL SPEAK":** My hands god all **pruney** fr'm washing the dishes.

wrinkled as a prune (to be as) *exp.* to be extremely wrinkled.

> **EXAMPLE:** After soaking in the bathtub for an hour, I was as **wrinkled as a prune**!
>
> **TRANSLATION:** After soaking in the bathtub for an hour, I was **extremely wrinkled**!
>
> **"REAL SPEAK":** After soaking in the bathtub fer 'n hour, I w'z 'ez **wrinkled as a prune**!

PUMPKINS

pumpkin *n.* (*term of endearment*) sweetheart, darling, honey.

> **EXAMPLE:** Hi, **pumpkin**. How are you?
>
> **TRANSLATION:** Hi, **darling**! How are you?
>
> **"REAL SPEAK":** Hi, **pungkin**. How are you?

> *Note:* When used as a term of endearment, "pumpkin" may occasionally be heard pronounced "*pung-kin.*"

TOMATOS

tomato *n.* girl, woman, "chick."

> **EXAMPLE:** What's a nice **tomato** like you doing in a place like this?
>
> **TRANSLATION:** What's a nice **girl** like you doing in a place like this?
>
> **"REAL SPEAK":** What's a nice **tomado** like you doing in a place like this?

> *Note:* This term is outdated. However, it is still heard in old movies or used in jest. In fact, in many old movies taking place in New York, "tomato" is heard pronounced "*ta-may-da.*"

"My computer is on the fritz!"

LET'S WARM UP!

MATCH THE PICTURES *(Answers on p. 219)*

As a fun way to get started, see if you can guess the meaning of the new slang words and expressions on the opposite page by using the pictures below and following the context of the sentences.

1. May I use your computer? Mine is **on the fritz**.
   ❏ broken
   ❏ too slow

2. Do you have any aspirin? I have a **splitting headache**.
   ❏ mild headache
   ❏ severe headache

3. I don't trust that salesperson. He's really **slimy**.
   ❏ dishonest
   ❏ honest

4. I've **had it**! I'm never coming here again!
   ❏ had all I can tolerate
   ❏ won

5. He thinks he knows the answer to every question the teacher asks. What a **know-it-all**!
   ❏ intellectually arrogant person
   ❏ stupid person

6. You paid two hundred dollars for a shirt? I think you got **burned**!
   ❏ a bargain
   ❏ cheated

7. I lost my car keys for the third time this week! I'm such a **birdbrain**!
   ❏ genius
   ❏ fool

8. I don't believe her. Something seems **fishy**.
   ❏ suspicious
   ❏ normal

9. When I lost my wallet, I was **beside myself**.
   ❏ extremely happy
   ❏ very upset

10. I can't afford these prices. They're **through the roof**!
    ❏ excessively high
    ❏ extremely low

LET'S TALK!

A. DIALOGUE USING SLANG & IDIOMS

The words introduced on the first two pages are used in the dialogue below. See if you can understand the conversation. *Note:* The translation of the words in boldface is on the right-hand page.

SPEAKING LISTENING

CD-A: TRACK 7

Tessa: I wonder why this computer is so cheap!

Nick: That's kind of **fishy**. It's probably old and slow.

Tessa: I feel like such a **birdbrain** when it comes to buying a computer. The last computer I bought broke after a week. I was **beside myself**. The salesperson assured me that it would last for years. I believed him because he was such a **know-it-all**. I'm so tired of getting **burned** by these **slimy** salespeople!

Nick: Me, too. **I've had it** with paying prices that are **through the roof** for merchandise that **goes on the fritz** the second you bring it home.

Tessa: Frankly, shopping for a computer gives me a **splitting headache**!

B. DIALOGUE TRANSLATED INTO STANDARD ENGLISH

LET'S SEE HOW MUCH YOU REMEMBER!
Just for fun, bounce around in random order to the words
and expressions in boldface below. See if you can remember
their slang equivalents without looking at the left-hand page!

Tessa: I wonder why this computer is so cheap!

Nick: That's kind of **suspicious**. It's probably old and slow.

Tessa: I feel like such a **fool** when it comes to buying a computer. The last computer I bought broke after a week. I was **extremely upset**. The salesperson assured me that it would last for years. I believed him because he was a **person who arrogantly claimed to know everything**. I'm so tired of getting **cheated** by these **dishonest** salespeople!

Nick: Me, too. **I've had all I can tolerate** with paying prices that are **excessive** for merchandise that **becomes inoperable** the second you bring it home.

Tessa: Frankly, shopping for a computer gives me a **very painful headache**!

C. DIALOGUE USING "REAL SPEAK"

The dialogue below demonstrates how the slang conversation on the previous page would *really* be spoken by native speakers!

Tessa: I wonder why this computer's so cheap!

Nick: That's kind 'a **fishy**. It's prob'ly old 'n slow.

Tessa: I feel like such a **birdbrain** when it comes ta buying a compuder. The last compuder I bought broke after a week. I w'z **beside myself**. The salesperson assured me thad it would last fer years. I believed 'im because 'e w'z such a **know-id-all**. I'm so tired of gedding **burned** by these **slimy** salespeople!

Nick: Me, too. **I've had it** with paying prices thad'er **through the roof** fer merchandise that **goes on the fritz** the secon' ya bring it home.

Tessa: Frankly, shopping fer a c'mpuder gives me a **splidding headache**!

LET'S LEARN!

CD-A: TRACK 8

VOCABULARY

The following words and expressions were used in the previous dialogues. Let's take a closer look at what they mean.

beside oneself (to be) *exp.* to be extremely upset (with anger, worry, grief, or any strong emotion).

EXAMPLE:	When Anthony found out his car was stolen this morning, he was **beside himself**!
TRANSLATION:	When Anthony found out his car was stolen this morning, he was **extremely upset**!
"REAL SPEAK:"	When Anthony found oud 'is car w'z stolen this morning, he w'z **beside 'imself**!

Synonym 1: **at the end of one's rope (to be)** *exp.*

Synonym 2: **flipped out (to be) / flipping out (to be)** *exp.*

Synonym 3: **freaked out (to be) / freaking out (to be)** *exp.*

Synonym 4: **lose it (to)** *exp.* (Here "it" refers to "one's composure").

NOW YOU DO IT. COMPLETE THE PHRASE ALOUD:

I was beside myself when I found out that...

birdbrain (to be a) *n.* said of someone who is a moron; imbecile.

EXAMPLE: I'm such a **birdbrain**! I totally forgot that I had a doctor's appointment yesterday!

TRANSLATION: I'm such a **moron**! I totally forgot that I had a doctor's appointment yesterday!

"REAL SPEAK:" I'm such a **birdbrain**! I todally fergot th'd I had a doctor's appointment yesderday!

Synonyms: Since there are so many synonyms for the term "imbecile," I'll list many of the most common ones here: **airhead, bonehead, dimwit, dipstick, dork, dumbbell, geek, lamebrain, loser, nitwit, not all there, out to lunch, peabrain, scatterbrain**, etc.

NOW YOU DO IT. COMPLETE THE PHRASE ALOUD:
... is such a birdbrain because...

burned (to get) *adj.* to get cheated.

EXAMPLE: You paid three thousand dollars for your computer and it doesn't work?! You really got **burned**.

TRANSLATION: You paid three thousand dollars for your computer and it doesn't work?! You really got **cheated**.

"REAL SPEAK:" You paid three thousan' dollers fer yer c'mpuder an' it doesn' work?! Ya really got **burned**.

Synonym 1: **get ripped [off] (to)** *exp.* (extremely popular).
Synonym 2: **get taken [for a ride] (to)** *exp.*

NOW YOU DO IT. COMPLETE THE PHRASE ALOUD:
The got burned was...

fishy (to be) *adj.* said of something suspicious.

EXAMPLE: Norm said he was going to work late tonight, but Albert saw him at the gym. I wonder why he lied to me. Something is a little **fishy**.

TRANSLATION: Norm said he was going to work late tonight, but Albert saw him at the gym. I wonder why he lied to me. Something is a little **suspicious**.

"REAL SPEAK:" Norm said 'e w'z gonna work late tanight, bud Albert saw 'im at the gym. I wonder why 'e lied ta me. Something's a liddle **fishy**.

Synonym 1: **something doesn't smell right** *exp.*
Synonym 2: **something isn't kosher** *exp.*
Synonym 3: **there's some funny business going on here** *exp.*

NOW YOU DO IT. COMPLETE THE PHRASE ALOUD:
I think something is fishy because...

had it (to have) *exp.* to be all one can tolerate.

> **EXAMPLE:** The neighbors are playing their loud music again and it's two o'clock in the morning! **I've had it**!
>
> **TRANSLATION:** The neighbors are playing their loud music again and it's two o'clock in the morning! **This is all I can tolerate**!
>
> **"REAL SPEAK:"** The neighbors'er playing their loud music again an' it's two a'clock 'n the morning! **I've had it**!
>
> *Variation:* **had it up to here (to have)** *exp.* / **up to here with something (to be)** *exp.* (In these expressions, the speaker usually makes a gesture below the chin or above the head indicating where "here" is).
>
> *Synonym 1:* **at the end of one's rope (to be) exp.**
>
> *Synonym 2:* **over something (to be)** *exp.* (*extremely popular*) • *I'm over this!*; I'm tired of this!
>
> *Synonym 3:* **sick and tired of something (to be) exp.**
>
> **NOW YOU DO IT. COMPLETE THE PHRASE ALOUD:**
> *I've had it with...*

know-it-all (to be a) *adj.* a person who arrogantly claims to know everything.

> **EXAMPLE:** John is a **know-it-all**. He talks nonstop about every subject imaginable. He's so annoying!
>
> **TRANSLATION:** John is a **person who arrogantly claims to know everything**. He talks nonstop about every subject imaginable. He's so annoying!
>
> **"REAL SPEAK:"** John's a **know-id-all**. He talks nonstop about ev'ry subject imaginable. He's so annoying!
>
> *Synonym:* **showoff** *exp.* said of someone who pretentiously demonstrates something he/she is proud of such as knowledge, clothing, wealth, etc.
>
> **NOW YOU DO IT. COMPLETE THE PHRASE ALOUD:**
> *...is such a know-it-all.*

on the fritz (to be/go) *exp.* said of a piece of machinery that is broken.

> **EXAMPLE:** May I borrow your computer? Mine is **on the fritz**.
>
> **TRANSLATION:** May I borrow your computer? Mine is **broken**.
>
> **"REAL SPEAK:"** May I borrow yer c'mpuder? Mine's **on the fritz**.
>
> *Synonym 1:* **conked out (to be)** *adj.*
>
> *Synonym 2:* **down (to be)** *adj.*
>
> *Synonym 3:* **on the blink (to be)** *exp.*
>
> *Synonym 4:* **out of commission (to be)** *exp.*
>
> *Synonym 5:* **out of whack (to be)** *exp.*
>
> **NOW YOU DO IT. COMPLETE THE PHRASE ALOUD:**
> *...just went on the fritz again.*

slimy *adj.* deceitful, dishonest • (lit.): greasy, slippery.

EXAMPLE:	I just don't trust that car salesman. He seems **slimy**.
TRANSLATION:	I just don't trust that car salesman. He seems **dishonest**.
"REAL SPEAK:"	I jus' don't trust that car salesman. He seems **slimy**.
Note:	The illustration shows the salesman with his fingers crossed. In America, as long as a person has two fingers crossed while lying, he/she is cleared of any guilt.
Synonym 1:	**crooked** *adj.* (pronounced as two syllables: *crook-ed*).
Synonym 2:	**shady** *adj.*
Synonym 3:	**snake** *n.* a dishonest and deceitful person.
Synonym 4:	**two-faced** *adj.* said of someone who appears to be very helpful and friendly but who is actually deceitful.

NOW YOU DO IT. COMPLETE THE PHRASE ALOUD:
I think the salesperson at... is slimy.

splitting headache (to have a) *exp.* to have an extremely painful headache (so much that one's head feels as if it has been split open).

EXAMPLE:	I'd like to go out with you to dinner tonight, but I have a **splitting headache**.
TRANSLATION:	I'd like to go out with you to dinner tonight, but I have an **extremely painful headache**.
"REAL SPEAK:"	I'd like ta go out with ya da dinner d'night, bud I have a **splidding headache**.
Synonym:	**whopper of a headache (to have a)** *exp.*

NOW YOU DO IT. COMPLETE THE PHRASE ALOUD:
The last time I had a splitting headache was...

through the roof (to be / to go) *exp.* said of prices that are excessive.

EXAMPLE:	It wasn't very expensive shopping here last week, but today the prices are **through the roof**!
TRANSLATION:	It wasn't very expensive shopping here last week, but today the prices are **excessive**!
"REAL SPEAK:"	It wasn't very expensive shopping here last week, but taday the prices 'er **through the roof**!
Also:	**through the roof (to go)** *exp.* to get extremely angry • *When I discovered Norm had lied to me, I went through the roof!*; When I discovered Norm had lied to me, I got extremely angry!
Synonym 1:	**steep (to be)** *adj.* Those prices are steep!
Synonym 2:	**up there (to be)** *exp.*
Synonym 3:	**way out there (to be)** *exp.*

NOW YOU DO IT. COMPLETE THE PHRASE ALOUD:
The prices at... are through the roof!

LET'S PRACTICE!

A. FIND THE MISSING WORDS *(Answers on p. 219)*
Complete the dialogue by filling in the blanks with the
correct word(s) using the list below.

CD-A: TRACK 9

KNOW-IT-ALL	BURNED
SPLITTING	BIRDBRAIN
ROOF	SLIMY
MYSELF	HAD
FISHY	FRITZ

Tom: I hate car shopping. It always gives me a _____ headache.

Pat: Me, too I hate having to talk with those _____ car salespeople who try to cheat you.

Tom: And some of them talk to you like you're a moron. I've really _____ it with being treated like a _____ just because I don't know a lot about cars.

Pat: I know what you mean. Also, there's something I don't understand. The prices are all through the _____ on the cars on the other side of the lot. But the cars over here are all relatively inexpensive. Doesn't that seem _____?

Tom: That's probably because the cars on this side are all used and will go on the _____ within a week.

Pat: If that happens to my new car, I'm going to be beside _____! I'm so tired of being _____ every time I buy something. No matter what price you pay for something, it should work!

Tom: Oh, no. Here comes a salesperson. Great. He'll probably give us a lecture all about cars and act like a total _____.

B. CREATE YOUR OWN NEWSPAPER COLUMN *(Answers on p. 220)*

Fill in the spaces then transfer your answers to the newspaper column below. Make sure to match the number of your answer with the numbered space. Next, read your column aloud. Remember: The funnier your answers, the funnier your column will be!

1. Write down a "thing" *(pencil, potato, toothbrush, etc.)*: _____

2. Write down a "thing" *(pencil, potato, toothbrush, etc.)*: _____

3. Write down a "thing" *(pencil, potato, toothbrush, etc.)*: _____

4. Write down an "adverb" *(strangely, quickly, sickeningly, etc.)*: _____

5. Write down a "thing" *(pencil, potato, toothbrush, etc.)*: _____

6. Write down a "verb" in the first person *(drink, run, type, etc.)*:_____

7. Write down an "occupation" *(mechanic, doctor, janitor, etc.)*: _____

8. Write down a "thing" *(pencil, potato, toothbrush, etc.)*: _____

9. Write down an "insulting name" *(idiot, jerk, nerd, etc.)*:_____

10. Write down an "adverb" *(strangely, quickly, sickeningly, etc.)*: _____

11. Write down a "thing" *(pencil, potato, toothbrush, etc.)*: _____

12. Write down a "thing" in plural form *(pencils, potatoes, toothbrushes, etc.)*:_____

THE WEEKLY
BICHON-MOAN GAZETTE

THE WEEKLY NEWSPAPER THAT LETS YOU LET IT ALL OUT

"Dear Blabby..."

by Blabby Bichon-Moan
Advice Columnist

Dear Blabby...

I'm **beside myself**! I just bought a new [1.] and it's already **on the fritz**.

When I plugged it into the [2.], nothing happened. I read the entire instruction [3.] very [4.] but every time I press the [5.] to turn it on, it won't [6.]. I'm not a **birdbrain**, so I know I'm following the instructions correctly. Finally, I tried calling the **know-it-all** [7.] several times,

but I can never get him on the [8.]. I think that's **fishy**. I think that **slimy** [9.] is [10.] ignoring my [11.] This is giving me a **splitting headache**. The prices were **through the roof**, too! I paid two thousand [12.] for this and it should work. Well, I've **had it**!

Signed... **BURNED**

C. **MATCH THE SENTENCES** (Answers on p. 220)

Match the numbered sentences below with the lettered sentences on the opposite page. Write your answers in the boxes at the bottom of the pages.

CD-A: TRACK 10

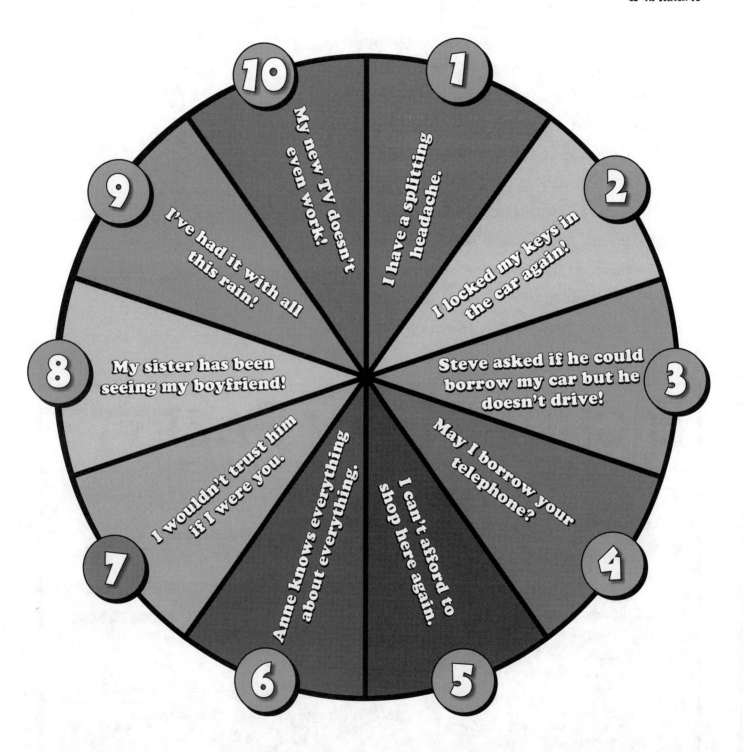

NUMBERS	1	2	3	4	5
LETTERS					

C. MATCH THE SENTENCES - *(continued)*

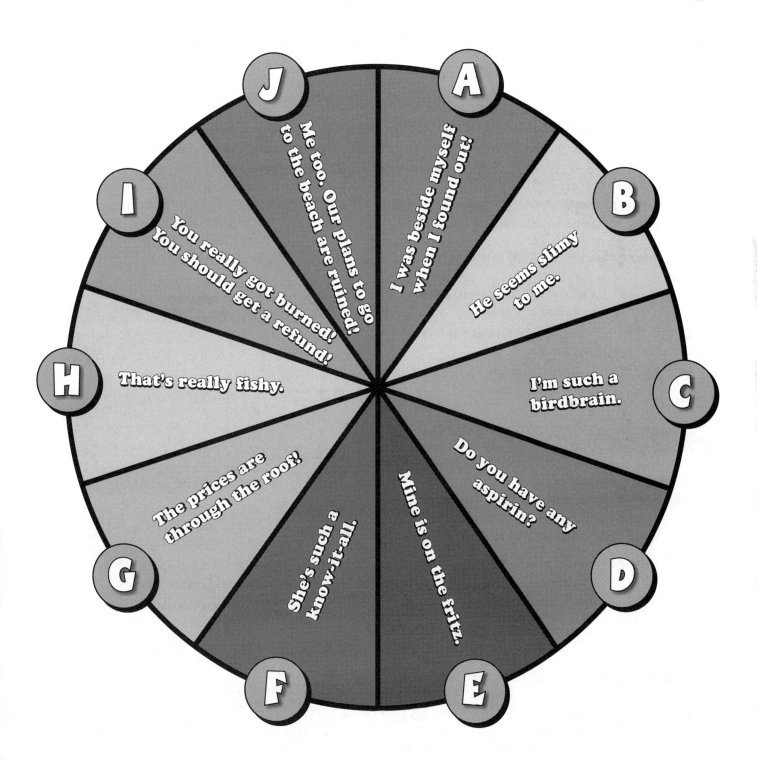

NUMBERS	6	7	8	9	10
LETTERS					

THE SLANGMAN FILES
Food Used in Slang Expressions

Any **smart cookie** (*clever person*) will see right away that this next section on food used in slang expressions is **a piece of cake** (*extremely easy*)! Since food is certainly a daily topic of conversation, it's no wonder that different foods have made their way into many of our most imaginative expressions. In the following list, you should find **the whole enchilada** (*the whole story*)!

BACON

bring home the bacon (to) *exp.* to earn a living.

> **EXAMPLE:** My wife and I both **bring home the bacon** in our family.

> **TRANSLATION:** My wife and I both **earn a living** in our family.

> **"REAL SPEAK":** My wife 'n I both **bring home the bacon** 'n 'ar family.

BALONEY

baloney *n.* nonsense.

> **EXAMPLE:** Peggy said she got a promotion? What a bunch of **baloney**! The boss almost fired her today!

> **TRANSLATION:** Peggy said she got a promotion? What a bunch of **nonsense**! The boss almost fired her today!

> **"REAL SPEAK":** Peggy said she god a pruhmotion? Whad a bunch 'a **baloney**! The boss almost fired 'er taday!

phoney baloney *exp.* said of someone who is not genuine.

> **EXAMPLE:** Anne was always mean to me until she found out I won the lottery. Now she's so sweet! I've never met anyone so **phoney baloney**.

> **TRANSLATION:** Anne was always mean to me until she found out I won the lottery. Now she's so sweet! I've never met anyone so **fake**!

> **"REAL SPEAK":** Anne w'z always mean ta me until she found oud I won the loddery. Now she's so sweet! I've never med anyone so **phoney baloney**.

BEEF

beef *n.* • **1.** quarrel • **2.** a complaint, an objection • **3.** substance.

> **EXAMPLE 1:** My best friend and I had a **beef** about something stupid, but I'm sure we'll make up tomorrow.

> **TRANSLATION:** My best friend and I had a **quarrel** about something stupid, but I'm sure we'll make up tomorrow

> **"REAL SPEAK":** My best friend 'n I had a **beef** about something stupid, b'd I'm sher we'll make up tamorrow.

> **EXAMPLE 2:** I have a **beef** about the way you treated Steve yesterday.

> **TRANSLATION:** I have an **objection** about the way you treated Steve yesterday.

> **"REAL SPEAK":** I have a **beef** about the way you treeded Steve yesterday.

> **EXAMPLE 3:** Your report is weak. Where's the **beef**?

> **TRANSLATION:** Your report is weak. Where's the **substance**?

> **"REAL SPEAK":** Yer repord is weak. Where's the **beef**?

beef up something (to) *exp.* to improve something.

EXAMPLE: I bought a new stereo and **beefed it up** by attaching new speakers to it.

TRANSLATION: I bought a new stereo and **improved it** by attaching new speakers to it.

"REAL SPEAK": I bod a new stereo 'n **beefed id up** by attaching new speakers to it.

beefy *adj.* big and muscular.

EXAMPLE: Nick has been working out for years. That's why he's so **beefy**.

TRANSLATION: Nick has been working out for years. That's why he's so **big and muscular**.

"REAL SPEAK": Nick's been working out fer years. That's why 'e's so **beefy**.

BITE

bite (to) *v.* (used commonly by the younger generation) to be horribly unpleasant.

EXAMPLE: My history class really **bites**!

TRANSLATION: My history class is really **horrible**!

"REAL SPEAK": My histery class really **bites**!

"Bite me!" *exp.* "Go to hell!"

EXAMPLE:
– Hey, baby. Would you like to come home with me today?
– **Bite me**!

TRANSLATION:
– Hey, baby. Would you like to come home with me today?
– **Go to hell**!

"REAL SPEAK":
– Hey, baby. Would'ja like ta come home with me taday?
– **Bite me**!

bite off more than one can chew (to) *exp.* to take on a task larger than one can accomplish.

EXAMPLE: I volunteered my time to two different charities, plus I have my full-time job. I've **bitten off more than I can chew**.

TRANSLATION: I volunteered my time to two different charities, plus I have my full-time job. I've **taken on more tasks than I can accomplish**.

"REAL SPEAK": I volunteered my time ta two diff'rent charidies, plus I have my full-time job. I've **bitten off more th'n I c'n chew**.

bite someone's head off (to) *exp.* to explode with anger toward someone.

EXAMPLE: When I asked Gene about his vacation, he **bit my head off** and said it was none of my business! I wonder what's really bothering him

TRANSLATION: When I asked Gene about his vacation, he **exploded with anger** toward me and said it was none of my business! I wonder what's really bothering him.

"REAL SPEAK": When I ast' Gene about 'is vacation, he **bit my head off** 'n said it w'z none 'a my business! I wonder what's really bothering 'im.

bite the bullet (to) *exp.* to accept something unpleasant.

EXAMPLE: I know you don't want to go to Carol's party, but you promised her. You're just going to have to **bite the bullet**.

TRANSLATION: I know you don't want to go to Carol's party, but you promised her. You're just going to have to **accept it**.

"REAL SPEAK": I know ya don't wanna go da Carol's pardy, but'cha promised 'er. Y'r jus' gonna hafta **bite the bullet**.

bite the dust (to) *exp.* to die.

EXAMPLE: My next door neighbor was mowing the lawn when he suddenly **bit the dust**!

TRANSLATION: My next door neighbor was mowing the lawn when he suddenly **died**!

"REAL SPEAK": My nex' door neighbor w'z mowing the lawn when 'e suddenly **bit the dust**!

Variation: **bite it (to)** *exp.*

bite the hand that feeds one (to) *exp.* to offend the person that one depends on for survival.

> **EXAMPLE:** Tony insulted the boss today? That's not very smart. He's **biting the hand that feeds him**.

> **TRANSLATION:** Tony insulted the boss today? That's not very smart. He's **offending the person that he needs for survival**.

> **"REAL SPEAK":** Tony insulted the boss taday? That's not very smart. He's **biding the han' th't feeds 'im**.

"Bite your tongue!" *exp.* "Stop talking like that!" ("Punish your tongue by biting it!").

> **EXAMPLE:** – I hope Bob's new company fails.
> – **Bite your tongue!** I know that you two aren't friends anymore, but you shouldn't say those kinds of things.

> **TRANSLATION:** – I hope Bob's new company fails.
> – **Stop talking like that!** I know that you two aren't friends anymore, but you shouldn't say those kinds of things.

> **"REAL SPEAK":** – I hope Bob's new company fails.
> – **Bite cher tongue!** I know th't you two aren't friends anymore, but you shouldn't say those kinds of things.

grab a bite (to) *exp.* to get something quick to eat.

> **EXAMPLE:** Let's **grab a bite** before the movie.

> **TRANSLATION:** Let's **get something quick to eat** before the movie.

> **"REAL SPEAK":** Let's **grab a bite** b'fore the movie.

one's bark is worse than one's bite *exp.* one's threats are worse than one's actions.

> **EXAMPLE:** Don't worry about Ralph threatening you. His **bark is worse than his bite**.

> **TRANSLATION:** Don't worry about Ralph threatening you. His **threats are worse than his actions**.

> **"REAL SPEAK":** Don't worry about Ralph threat'ning you. His **bark's worse th'n 'is bite**.

put the bite on someone (to) *exp.* to ask someone for a loan.

> **EXAMPLE:** Karen **put the bite on me** for five dollars. She never has enough money on her.

> **TRANSLATION:** Karen **asked me for a loan** of five dollars. She never has enough money on her.

> **"REAL SPEAK":** Karen **put the bide on me** fer five dollers. She never has anough money on 'er.

BREAD

best thing since sliced bread (to be the) *exp.* to be the absolute best.

> **EXAMPLE:** I love my cell phone. It's **the best thing since sliced bread**!

> **TRANSLATION:** I love my cell phone. It's **the absolute best**!

> **"REAL SPEAK":** I love my cell phone. It's **the bes' thing since sliced bread**!

bread and butter (to be one's) *exp.* one's means of survival.

> **EXAMPLE:** I can't quit my job. It's my **bread and butter**.

> **TRANSLATION:** I can't quit my job. It's my **means of survival**.

> **"REAL SPEAK":** I can't quit my job. It's my **bread 'n budder**.

bread winner *exp.* the member of the family who supports the family monetarily.

> **EXAMPLE:** Brenda is the **bread winner** of the family and Dirk takes care of the children.

> **TRANSLATION:** Brenda **supports the family monetarily** and Dirk takes care of the children.

> **"REAL SPEAK":** Brenda's the **bread winner** 'a the fam'ly 'n Dirk takes care 'a the children.

> *Note:* It's interesting to note that though the term "*bread*" is no longer used in American slang to mean "money," the term "*bread winner*" is!

BUN

bun in the oven (to have a) *exp.* to be pregnant.

EXAMPLE:	I saw Kathy at the market yesterday. **She has a bun in the oven!**
TRANSLATION:	I saw Kathy at the market yesterday. **She's pregnant!**
"REAL SPEAK":	I saw Kathy 'it the market yesterday. **She has a bun 'n the oven!**

buns *n.pl.* buttocks, rear end.

EXAMPLE:	Tony has great **buns**! He must be a dancer.
TRANSLATION:	Tony has a great **rear end**! He must be a dancer.
"REAL SPEAK":	Tony has great **buns**! He mus' be a dancer.

freeze one's buns off (to) *exp.* to be very cold.

EXAMPLE:	I went to Chicago over the Christmas holiday and **froze my buns off!**
TRANSLATION:	I went to Chicago over the Christmas holiday and **totally froze!**
"REAL SPEAK":	I went to Chicago over the Christmas holiday and **froze my buns off!**

CAKE

cakewalk *n.* said of something very easy to do.

EXAMPLE:	This book report I have to write is going to be a **cakewalk**.
TRANSLATION:	This book report I have to write is going to be **easy**.
"REAL SPEAK":	This book r'pord I hafta wride is gonna be a **cakewalk**.

have one's cake and eat it, too (to) *exp.* to have it both ways.

| EXAMPLE: | I want to go on vacation next week, but I also want to be in town to meet the new president of our company. I guess I can't **have my cake and eat it, too.** |

| TRANSLATION: | I want to go on vacation next week, but I also want to be in town to meet the new president of our company. I guess I can't **have it both ways**. |
| "REAL SPEAK": | I wanna go on vacation next week, bud I also wanna be 'n town ta meet the new president 'ev 'are company. I guess I can't **have my cake 'n eat it, too.** |

piece of cake (a) *exp.* said of something extremely easy to do.

EXAMPLE:	Learning English isn't hard. It's **a piece of cake!**
TRANSLATION:	Learning English isn't hard. It's **really easy!**
"REAL SPEAK":	Learning English isn't hard. It's **a piece 'a cake!**

Variation: **cake** *adj.* • *It's cake!;* It's easy!

take the cake (to) *exp.* • **1.** to be the best • **2.** to be extreme.

EXAMPLE 1:	What a great party! It really **takes the cake!**
TRANSLATION:	What a great party! It's really **the best!**
"REAL SPEAK":	Whad a great pardy! It really **takes the cake!**
EXAMPLE 2:	Can you believe the stupid thing Ron did? **It really takes the cake.**
TRANSLATION:	Can you believe the stupid thing Ron did? **It's the most stupid thing he could have done.**
"REAL SPEAK":	C'n you b'lieve the stupid thing Ron did? **It really takes the cake.**

CHEESE

big cheese *exp.* the boss.

| EXAMPLE: | If you have a suggestion for the company, talk to Jason. He's the **big cheese** here. |
| TRANSLATION: | If you have a suggestion for the company, talk to Jason. He's the **boss** here. |

"REAL SPEAK": If ya have a suggestion fer the company, talk ta Jason. He's the **big cheese** here.

cheesecake *n.* sexually suggestive material involving women.

EXAMPLE: Your son is too young to look at that magazine. It's full of **cheesecake**.

TRANSLATION: Your son is too young to look at that magazine. It's full of **sexually suggestive material involving women**.

"REAL SPEAK": Yer son's too young ta look 'it that magazine. It's full 'a **cheesecake**.

Also: **beefcake** *n.* sexually suggestive material involving men.

cheesy *adj.* (*as introduced in Lesson Three, p. 87*) said of something cheap-looking and of poor taste.

EXAMPLE: How can Emily wear that dress. It looks so **cheesy**!

TRANSLATION: How can Emily wear that dress. It looks so **cheap and ugly**!

"REAL SPEAK": How c'n Emily wear that dress. It looks so **cheesy**!

cut the cheese (to) *exp.* to pass gas.

EXAMPLE: What stinks? Did someone **cut the cheese**?

TRANSLATION: What stinks? Did someone **pass gas**?

"REAL SPEAK": [no change]

CHEW

"Chew on that for a while!" *exp.* "Think about *that* for a while!"

EXAMPLE: If you ever lie to me again, I'm leaving you forever. **Chew on that for a while**!

TRANSLATION: If you ever lie to me again, I'm leaving you forever. **Think about that for a while!**"

"REAL SPEAK": If ya ever lie da me again, I'm leaving you forever. **Chew on that fer a while**!

chew someone out (to) *exp.* to reprimand someone.

EXAMPLE: My mother **chewed me out** for coming home late.

TRANSLATION: My mother **reprimanded me** for coming home late.

"REAL SPEAK": My mother **chewed me out** fer coming home late.

chew the fat (to) *exp.* to have a chat.

EXAMPLE: Bill and I **chewed the fat** for an hour at his house.

TRANSLATION: Bill and I **had a chat** for an hour at his house.

"REAL SPEAK": Bill 'n I **chewed the fat** fer 'n hour ad 'is house.

CLAM

clam *n.* dollar.

EXAMPLE: That guy stole a hundred **clams** from me!

TRANSLATION: That guy stole a hundred **dollars** from me!

"REAL SPEAK": That guy stole a hundred **clams** fr'm me!

Note: This term is outdated but is still occasionally heard in old gangster movies or in jest.

clam up (to) *exp.* to stop talking.

EXAMPLE: Becky is usually very talkative, but as soon as Dan walked into the room, she **clammed up**.

TRANSLATION: Becky is usually very talkative, but as soon as Dan walked into the room, she **stopped talking**.

"REAL SPEAK": Becky's ujally very talkadive, bud 'ez soon 'ez Dan walked inta the room, she **clammed up**.

happy as a clam (to be as) *exp.* to be extremely happy.

EXAMPLE: Ever since Dana met Noah, she's been **as happy as a clam**.

TRANSLATION: Ever since Dana met Noah, she's been **extremely happy**.

"REAL SPEAK": Ever since Dana met Noah, she's been **'ez happy 'ez a clam**.

COFFEE

wake up and smell the coffee (to) *exp.* to become aware of what's really happening.

> **EXAMPLE:** You don't think Ken is going to cheat on you even though he cheated on all his other girlfriends? **Wake up and smell the coffee!**
>
> **TRANSLATION:** You don't think Ken is going to cheat on you even though he cheated on all his other girlfriends? **Become aware of what's really happening!**
>
> **"REAL SPEAK":** Ya don't think Ken's gonna chead on you even though he cheated on all 'is other girlfriends? **Wake up 'n smell the coffee!**

COOK

cook something up (to) *exp.* to scheme, to do something suspicious.

> **EXAMPLE:** What **are you two cooking up** in there?
>
> **TRANSLATION:** What **suspicious thing are you two doing** in there?
>
> **"REAL SPEAK":** Whad**'er you two cooking up** 'n there?

cook with gas (to) *exp.* said of a person who is performing a task very well.

> **EXAMPLE:** I knew you'd eventually learn how to use a computer. Now you're **cooking with gas!**
>
> **TRANSLATION:** I knew you'd eventually learn how to use a computer. Now you're **doing great!**
>
> **"REAL SPEAK":** I knew you'd evenchally learn how da use a c'mpuder. Now y'r **cooking with gas!**

cooking on all four burners (not to be) *exp.* said of someone who is mentally unbalanced.

> **EXAMPLE:** I **don't think our new neighbor is cooking on all four burners.** He likes to dress up like Napoleon Bonaparte.
>
> **TRANSLATION:** I **don't think our new neighbor is mentally balanced.** He likes to dress up like Napoleon Bonaparte.
>
> **"REAL SPEAK":** I **don't think 'ar new neighbor is cooking on all four burners.** He likes ta dress up like Napoleon Bonaparte.

goose cooked (to have one's) *exp.* to be in a great deal of trouble.

> **EXAMPLE:** There's my boss! If he sees me here during office hours, **my goose is cooked!**
>
> **TRANSLATION:** There's my boss! If he sees me here during office hours, **I'm going to be in big trouble!**
>
> **"REAL SPEAK":** There's my boss! If 'e sees me here during office hours, **my goose 'ez cooked!**

"Too many cooks spoil the broth" *proverb*
• "Too many people in charge with different ideas end up ruining everything."

> **EXAMPLE:** There are too many people in charge of this project. **Too many cooks spoil the broth.**
>
> **TRANSLATION:** There are too many people in charge of this project. **Too many people in charge with different ideas end up ruining everything.**
>
> **"REAL SPEAK":** There're too many people 'n charge 'a this project. **Too many cooks spoil the broth.**

"What's cooking?" *exp.* a greeting meaning "What's happening (in your life)?"

> **EXAMPLE:** Hi, Tom. **What's cooking?**
>
> **TRANSLATION:** Hi, Tom. **What's happening in your life?**
>
> **"REAL SPEAK":** Hi, Tom. **What's cookin'?**
>
> *Note:* In this expression, the verb "cooking" is commonly shortened to "cookin'."

COOKIE

caught with one's hand in the cookie jar (to be) *exp.* to be caught in the act of taking something.

EXAMPLE: I told Bonnie never to take money from my purse, but I **caught her with her hand in the cookie jar**.

TRANSLATION: I told Bonnie never to take money from my purse, but I **caught her in the act of taking it**.

"REAL SPEAK": I told Bonnie never da take money fr'm my purse, b'd I **cod 'er with 'er hand in the cookie jar**.

smart cookie (to be a) *exp.* to be a very smart and clever person.

EXAMPLE: You can't fool Michelle. She's a **smart cookie**.

TRANSLATION: You can't fool Michelle. She's a **very smart and clever person**.

"REAL SPEAK": Ya can't fool Michelle. She's a **smart cookie**.

"That's the way the cookie crumbles" *exp.* "That's just the way things are."

EXAMPLE: I'm sorry you didn't get the job you wanted. But **that's the way the cookie crumbles**.

TRANSLATION: I'm sorry you didn't get the job you wanted. But **that's just how things are**.

"REAL SPEAK": I'm sorry ya didn't get the job ya wan'ed. B't **that's the way the cookie crumbles**.

Variation: **"That's how the cookie crumbles"** *exp.*

toss one's cookies (to) *exp.* to vomit.

EXAMPLE: I **tossed my cookies** all night. I've never been so sick in my life.

TRANSLATION: I **vomited** all night. I've never been so sick in my life.

"REAL SPEAK": I **tossed my cookies** all night. I've never been so sick 'n my life.

tough cookie *exp.* a stubborn and strict person.

EXAMPLE: My new boss is a **tough cookie**. I used to be able to take an hour and a half for lunch. Now I'm allowed exactly one hour.

TRANSLATION: My new boss is a **stubborn and strict person**. I used to be able to take an hour and a half for lunch. Now I'm allowed exactly one hour.

"REAL SPEAK": My new boss 'ez a **tough cookie**. I usta be able da take 'n hour an' a half fer lunch. Now I'm allowed exactly one hour.

DOUGH

dough *n.* money.

EXAMPLE: I don't have enough **dough** to buy that shirt.

TRANSLATION: I don't have enough **money** to buy that shirt.

"REAL SPEAK": I don't have anough **dough** da buy that shirt.

Note: This term is outdated though it is still occasionally heard in old movies or in jest.

EAT

dog-eat-dog *adj.* a situation where one has to be ruthless in order to succeed.

EXAMPLE: In business it's often **dog-eat-dog**.

TRANSLATION: In business it's often **ruthless**.

"REAL SPEAK": In bizness it's often **dog-eat-dog**.

eat and run (to) *exp.* to eat quickly and leave.

EXAMPLE: I hate to **eat and run** but I have a meeting in ten minutes.

TRANSLATION: I hate to **eat quickly and leave** but I have a meeting in ten minutes.

"REAL SPEAK": I hate ta **eat 'n run** b'd I have a meeding 'n ten minutes.

eat away at someone (to) *exp.* to upset someone greatly.

EXAMPLE: I can't believe John cheated me. It's been **eating away at me** for months.

TRANSLATION: I can't believe John cheated me. It's been **upsetting me** for months.

"REAL SPEAK": I can't believe John cheated me. It's been **eading away 'it me** fer months.

eat crow (to) *exp.* to be forced to admit a mistake.

EXAMPLE: Betty said that I'd never become a movie star. Well, when she finds out that I'm starring in a new movie, she'll **eat crow**.

TRANSLATION: Betty said that I'd never become a movie star. Well, when she finds out that I'm starring in a new movie, she'll **be forced to admit she was wrong**.

"REAL SPEAK": Betty said th'd I'd never become a movie star. Well, when she fin'z out th'd I'm starring in a new movie, she'll **eat crow**.

eat high on the hog (to) *exp.* to eat expensive food.

EXAMPLE: You should have seen the food my sister prepared for Christmas. We **ate high on the hog** at her house!

TRANSLATION: You should have seen the food my sister prepared for Christmas. We **ate expensive food** at her house!

"REAL SPEAK": Ya shouldn'ev seen the food my sister pruhpared fer Chris'mas. We **ate high on the hog** 'it her house!

eat it (to) *exp.* • **1.** to crash • **2.** to fail.

EXAMPLE 1: That driver went around the curve too fast and **ate it**.

TRANSLATION: That driver went around the curve too fast and **crashed**.

"REAL SPEAK": That driver wen' aroun' the curve too fast 'n **ade it**.

EXAMPLE 2: I **ate it** on the biology test. I should have studied more

TRANSLATION: I **failed** the biology test. I should have studied more.

"REAL SPEAK": I **ade it** on the biology test. I should'ev studied more.

eat like a bird (to) *exp.* to eat very little.

EXAMPLE: Kim **eats like a bird**. That's why she's so thin.

TRANSLATION: Kim **eats very little**. That's why she's so thin.

"REAL SPEAK": [no change]

eat like a horse (to) *exp.* to eat a lot.

EXAMPLE: David **eats like a horse** because he's a bodybuilder.

TRANSLATION: David **eats a lot** because he's a bodybuilder.

"REAL SPEAK": David **eats like a horse** b'cause 'e's a bodybuilder.

eat one up (to) *exp.* to torment one emotionally.

EXAMPLE: I trusted Rob but he cheated me. It's really **eating me up**.

TRANSLATION: I trusted Rob but he cheated me. It's really **tormenting me**.

"REAL SPEAK": I trusted Rob bud 'e cheated me. It's really **eading me up**.

eat one's words (to) *exp.* to be forced to admit a mistake, to take back one's words.

EXAMPLE: – I don't think your new company will be very successful.
– You'll **eat your words** some day. You'll see!

TRANSLATION: – I don't think your new company will be very successful.
– You'll **take back your words** some day. You'll see!

"REAL SPEAK": – I don't think yer new company'll be very successful.
– You'll **eat cher words** some day. You'll see!

eat someone out of house and home (to) *exp.* said of someone who eats so much food that the only way to keep that person fed would be to sell one's house and personal belongings.

EXAMPLE: Our houseguest is **eating us out of house and home**!

TRANSLATION: Our houseguest is **eating everything to the point of making us poor**!

"REAL SPEAK": Our houseguest 'ez **eading us oud 'ev house 'n home**!

"Eat your heart out!" *exp.* "You should be very envious!"

EXAMPLE: Take a look at my new car! **Eat your heart out**!

TRANSLATION: Take a look at my new car! **You should be very envious**!

"REAL SPEAK":	Take a look 'it my new car! **Eat cher hard out!**

ENCHILADA

big enchilada *exp.* the boss.

EXAMPLE:	The company president is retiring next week and I'm taking over. Now it'll be my turn to be the **big enchilada** around here.
TRANSLATION:	The company president is retiring next week and I'm taking over. Now it'll be my turn to be the **boss** around here.
"REAL SPEAK":	The company president's retiring next week 'n I'm taking over. Now id'll be my turn ta be the **big enchilada** around here.

whole enchilada (the) *exp.* the whole story.

EXAMPLE:	Bernie got fired because he stole money from the company. That's **the whole enchilada**.
TRANSLATION:	Bernie got fired because he stole money from the company. That's **the whole story**.
"REAL SPEAK":	Bernie got fired b'cause 'e stole money fr'm the company. That's **the whole enchilada**.

FEED

chicken feed *exp.* a trivial amount of money.

EXAMPLE:	It will only cost twenty dollars to place an advertisement in the newspaper. That's **chicken feed**.
TRANSLATION:	It will only cost twenty dollars to place an advertisement in the newspaper. That's **a trivial amount of money**.
"REAL SPEAK":	It'll only cost twen'y dollers ta place 'n ad 'n the newspaper. That's **chicken feed**.

feed one's face (to) *exp.* to eat.

EXAMPLE:	I'm hungry. Let's go **feed our faces**.
TRANSLATION:	I'm hungry. Let's **go eat**.
"REAL SPEAK":	I'm hungry. Let's go **feed 'ar faces**.

put on the feed bag (to) *exp.* to eat.

EXAMPLE:	Let's **put on the feedbag**. I'm starving!
TRANSLATION:	Let's **eat**. I'm starving!
"REAL SPEAK":	Let's **pud on the feedbag**. I'm starving!

spoon-feed someone (to) *exp.* to feed someone information very slowly and carefully as one feeds a little baby.

EXAMPLE:	Melissa isn't very bright. You have to **spoon-feed her everything**.
TRANSLATION:	Melissa isn't very bright. You have to **explain everything to her slowly and carefully**.
"REAL SPEAK":	Melissa isn't very bright. Ya hafta **spoon-feed 'er ev'rything**.

FRUITCAKE

nutty as a fruitcake (to be as) *exp.* to be totally crazy.

EXAMPLE:	My uncle Albert is **as nutty as a fruitcake**. He told me that he had a tea party on the ceiling.
TRANSLATION:	My uncle Albert is **really crazy**. He told me that he had a tea party on the ceiling.
"REAL SPEAK":	My uncle Alberd is **'ez nuddy 'ez a fruitcake**. He told me thad 'e had a tea pardy on the ceiling.

Variation: **nuttier than a fruitcake (to be)** *exp.*

Note: These two expressions are a play on words since "*nutty*" means "crazy" in slang but literally means "filled with nuts" as is a holiday fruitcake.

FUDGE

fudge around with something (to) *exp.* to attempt to fix something, to tamper with something.

| EXAMPLE: | You've been **fudging around with** that television for an hour. Why don't you just call a professional to repair it? |

| TRANSLATION: | You've been **tampering with** that television for an hour. Why don't you just call a professional to repair it? |

| "REAL SPEAK": | You've been **fudging aroun' with** that TV fer 'n hour. Why doncha just call a pruhfessional ta repair it? |

fudge it (to) exp. • **1.** to improvise • **2.** to falsify.

| EXAMPLE 1: | I wasn't sure how to fix my computer properly, so I just **fudged it**. It should work for a while. |

| TRANSLATION: | I wasn't sure how to fix my computer properly, so I just **improvised**. It should work for a while. |

| "REAL SPEAK": | I wasn't sher how da fix my c'mpuder properly, so I just **fudged it**. It should work fer a while. |

| EXAMPLE 2: | Larry **fudged** the numbers on his tax report so that he wouldn't have to pay anything at the end of the year. |

| TRANSLATION: | Larry **falsified** the numbers on his tax report so that he wouldn't have to pay anything at the end of the year. |

| "REAL SPEAK": | Larry **fudged** the numbers on 'is tax report so thad 'e wouldn' hafta pay anything 'it the end 'a the year. |

GRAVY

gravy n. profit.

| EXAMPLE: | It cost us a thousand dollars to make these dolls. Once we've made our initial investment, the rest will be **gravy**. |

| TRANSLATION: | It cost us a thousand dollars to make these dolls. Once we've made our initial investment, the rest will be **profit**. |

| "REAL SPEAK": | It cost us a thousan' dollers ta make these dolls. Once we've made 'ar initial investment, the rest'll be **gravy**. |

gravy train exp. a job that makes a lot of money with little effort.

| EXAMPLE: | I'm never going to quit this job. It's a real **gravy train**. |

| TRANSLATION: | I'm never going to quit this job. It's a real **easy job that makes a lot of money**. |

| "REAL SPEAK": | I'm never gonna quit this job. It's a real **gravy train**. |

HAM

ham n. • **1.** a performer who overacts • **2.** said of an extroverted person who loves to perform any chance he/she can get.

| EXAMPLE 1: | His performance was horrible. He's a **ham**! |

| TRANSLATION: | His performance was horrible. He's a **performer who overacts**! |

| "REAL SPEAK": | His performance w'z horr'ble. He's a **ham**! |

| EXAMPLE 2: | At the party, Debbie started singing for everyone. She's such a **ham**. |

| TRANSLATION: | At the party, Debbie started singing for everyone. She's such an **extrovert**. |

| "REAL SPEAK": | At the pardy, Debbie starded singing fer ev'ryone. She's such a **ham**. |

Variation: **hambone (to be a)** exp.

ham it up (to) exp. to overact.

| EXAMPLE: | Let's call in sick today and go to the movies. Just make sure that when you call your boss to tell him you're not feeling well, don't **ham it up**. |

| TRANSLATION: | Let's call in sick today and go to the movies. Just make sure that when you call your boss to tell him you're not feeling well, don't **overact**. |

| "REAL SPEAK": | Let's call in sick taday 'n go da the movies. Jus' make sher th't when ya call yer boss ta tell 'im y'r not feeling well, don't **ham it up**. |

HOTCAKE

sell like hot cakes (to) exp. to sell exceptionally well.

EXAMPLE:	Our books are **selling like hot cakes**!
TRANSLATION:	Our books are **selling exceptionally well**!
"REAL SPEAK":	'Ar books'er **selling like hot cakes**!

MUSTARD

cut the mustard (not to) *exp.* not to perform to the desired standard.

EXAMPLE:	I'm afraid we're going to have to fire Shawn because he **can't cut the mustard**.
TRANSLATION:	I'm afraid we're going to have to fire Shawn because he's **not doing a good enough job**.
"REAL SPEAK":	I'm afraid w'r gonna hafta fire Shawn b'cause 'e **can't cut the mustard**.

NOODLE

limp as a noodle (to be as) *exp.* to be totally relaxed.

EXAMPLE:	After my massage, I was as **limp as a noodle**.
TRANSLATION:	After my massage, I was **totally relaxed**.
"REAL SPEAK":	After my massage, I w'z 'ez **limp 'ez a noodle**.

noodle *n.* brain.

EXAMPLE:	You'll find the answer to the problem. Just use your **noodle**.
TRANSLATION:	You'll find the answer to the problem. Just use your **brain**.
"REAL SPEAK":	You'll find the answer da the problem. Just use yer **noodle**.

off one's noodle (to be) *exp.* to be crazy.

EXAMPLE:	That woman is screaming at her umbrella. She must be **off her noodle**.
TRANSLATION:	That woman is screaming at her umbrella. She must be **crazy**.
"REAL SPEAK":	That woman's screaming ad 'er umbrella. She mus' be **off 'er noodle**.

wet noodle *exp.* a dull or tiresome person who spoils other people's enjoyment.

EXAMPLE:	Why did you invite John to the party? He's such a **wet noodle**!
TRANSLATION:	Why did you invite John to the party? He's such a **tiresome person**!
"REAL SPEAK":	Why'dja invite John ta the pardy? He's such a **wet noodle**!

PIE

easy as pie (to be as) *exp.* to be extremely easy.

EXAMPLE:	Don't let the computer scare you. Learning it is **as easy as pie**.
TRANSLATION:	Don't let the computer scare you. Learning it is **extremely easy**.
"REAL SPEAK":	Don't let the c'mpuder scare you. Learning it's **'ez easy 'ez pie**.

eat humble pie (to) *exp.* to be forced to admit being wrong.

EXAMPLE:	When I proved that Don was wrong, I made him **eat humble pie**.
TRANSLATION:	When I proved that Don was wrong, I made him **admit he was wrong**.
"REAL SPEAK":	When I proved th't Don w'z wrong, I made 'im **eat humble pie**.

sweetie-pie *n. (a term of endearment).*

EXAMPLE:	Hi, **sweetie-pie**! How are you?
TRANSLATION:	Hi, **darling**. How are you?
"REAL SPEAK":	Hi, **sweetie-pie**! How'er you?

Variation: **sweetie** *n.*

SANDWICH

knuckle sandwich *exp.* a punch to the face.

EXAMPLE: If you don't stop bothering me, I'm going to give you a **knuckle sandwich**.

TRANSLATION: If you don't stop bothering me, I'm going to give you a **punch in the face**.

"REAL SPEAK": If ya don't stop bothering me, I'm gonna give you a **knuckle sandwich**.

sandwiched *adj.* trapped between two objects.

EXAMPLE: I couldn't get out of my parking place because I got **sandwiched** by two other cars!

TRANSLATION: I couldn't get out of my parking place because I got **trapped between** two other cars!

"REAL SPEAK": I couldn' ged oudda my parking place b'cause I got **sandwiched** by two other cars!

STEW

in a stew (to be) *exp.* to be upset or worried.

EXAMPLE: Don't get **in a stew** about it. We'll find a solution to the problem.

TRANSLATION: Don't get **upset** about it. We'll find a solution to the problem.

"REAL SPEAK": Don't ged **in a stew** aboud it. We'll find a solution ta the problem.

stew in one's own juices (to) *exp.* to suffer the consequences of one's own actions.

EXAMPLE: Tom invested his money in a company that was already failing and now he's lost everything. It's too bad, but now he has to **stew in his own juices**.

TRANSLATION: Tom invested his money in a company that was already failing and now he's lost everything. It's too bad, but now he has to **suffer the consequences of his own actions**.

"REAL SPEAK": Tom invesded 'is money in a company that w'z already failing 'n now 'e's lost ev'rything. It's too bad, but now 'e hasta **stew 'n 'is own juices**.

SUGAR

sugar *n.* a term of endearment.

EXAMPLE: Hi there, **sugar**!

TRANSLATION: Hi there, **darling**!

"REAL SPEAK": [no change]

sugar-coat something (to) *exp.* to describe something as less pleasant than it really is.

EXAMPLE: – We've decided that your talents aren't used to their fullest in this job. All of us here believe that you have a lot of important qualities to offer a company.
– Don't **sugar-coat it**. Just tell me. Am I being fired?

TRANSLATION: – We've decided that your talents aren't used to their fullest in this job. All of us here believe that you have a lot of important qualities to offer a company.
– Don't **make it seem less pleasant than it is**. Just tell me. Am I being fired?

"REAL SPEAK": – We've decided th't cher talents aren't used ta their fullest in this job. All 'ev us here believe that chu have a lot 'ev important qualidies ta offer a company.
– Don't **sugar-code it**. Jus' tell me. Am I being fired?

sugar daddy *exp.* a man who provides money to someone in exchange for romantic/sexual companionship.

EXAMPLE: That rich guy must be forty years older than she is. I guess that's her **sugar daddy**.

TRANSLATION: That rich guy must be forty years older than she is. I guess that guy pays her in exchange for **romantic/sexual companionship**.

"REAL SPEAK": That rich guy must be fordy years older th'n she is. I guess that's 'er **sugar daddy**.

LESSON 3 HOUSEGUEST

"Earl is in for a shocker!"

LET'S WARM UP!

MATCH THE PICTURES *(Answers on p. 220)*

As a fun way to get started, see if you can guess the meaning of the new slang words and expressions on the opposite page by using the pictures below and following the context of the sentences. Each answer can only be used once!

1. Bill's health has been ***going downhill***. I hope he gets better soon!

2. Ted has been rich all his life. He ***has it made***.

3. My houseguest is ***eating me out of house and home***!

4. Ernie is calm now, but I think he's ***in for a shocker***.

5. I'm ***a nervous wreck*** today. I just can't relax.

6. I have to ***beat it*** or I'm going to be late for the movie.

7. If I have just one beer, I'll get ***plastered***.

8. I'm starving. Let's go ***wolf down*** a hamburger before the movie.

9. Tom has a huge appetite. At the restaurant, he ordered ***everything but the kitchen sink***!

10. I'm exhausted. I'm going home to ***crash***.

A. has an easy life

B. an overanxious person

C. eat quickly

D. leave quickly

E. collapse

F. going to be surprised

G. everything imaginable

H. getting worse

I. extremely drunk

J. eating everything I have

LET'S TALK!

A. DIALOGUE USING SLANG & IDIOMS

The words introduced on the first two pages are used in the dialogue below. See if you can understand the conversation.
Note: The translation of the words in boldface is on the right-hand page.

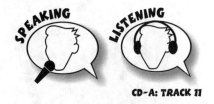

CD-A: TRACK 11

Cecily: How is it going with your houseguest?

Lee: It's **going downhill**. Every day he **crashes** in front of the television for hours. All he ever does is sleep and **eat us out of house and home**. You should have seen the sandwich he **wolfed down** this morning. He put **everything on it but the kitchen sink**. He **has it made** here.

Cecily: Why don't you just tell him to **beat it**?

Lee: He was my roommate in college and it's only for another two days. I just hope that I don't turn into a **nervous wreck** by the time he leaves. He even came home **plastered** last night.

Cecily: Maybe you should just lock the front door so he can't come back in! Wouldn't he be **in for a shocker**?!

B. DIALOGUE TRANSLATED INTO STANDARD ENGLISH

LET'S SEE HOW MUCH YOU REMEMBER!
Just for fun, bounce around in random order to the words
and expressions in boldface below. See if you can remember
their slang equivalents without looking at the left-hand page!

Cecily: How is it going with your houseguest?

Lee: It's **getting worse**. Every day he **collapses** in front of the television for hours. All he ever does is sleep and **eat everything I have**. You should have seen the sandwich he **ate** this morning. He put **everything imaginable on it**. He **has an easy life** here.

Cecily: Why don't you just tell him to **leave immediately**?

Lee: He was my roommate in college and it's only for another two days. I just hope that I don't turn into an **overanxious person** by the time he leaves. He even came home **extremely drunk** last night.

Cecily: Maybe you should just lock the front door so he can't come back in! Wouldn't that **give him a surprise**?!

C. DIALOGUE USING "REAL SPEAK"

The dialogue below demonstrates how the slang conversation on the previous page would *really* be spoken by native speakers!

Cecily: How's it going with yer houseguest?

Lee: It's **going downhill**. Ev'ry day 'e **crashes** 'n fronna the TV fer hours. All 'e ever does is sleep 'n **ead us oudda house 'n home**. You should'a seen the sandwich 'e **wolf' down** this morning. He pud **ev'rything on it b't the kitchen sink**. He **has it made** here.

Cecily: Why doncha jus' tell 'im da **beat it**?

Lee: He w'z my roommate 'n college an' it's only fer another two days. I just hope thad I don't turn into a **nervous wreck** by the time 'e leaves. He even came home **plasdered** las' night.

Cecily: Maybe you should jus' lock the front door so 'e can't come back in! Wouldn't 'e be **in fer a shocker**?!

LET'S LEARN!

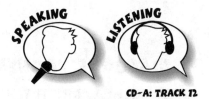

CD-A: TRACK 12

VOCABULARY

The following words and expressions were used in the previous dialogues. Let's take a closer look at what they mean.

beat it (to) *v.* to leave quickly.

EXAMPLE:	Our airplane leaves in ten minutes. We'd better **beat it**!
TRANSLATION:	Our airplane leaves in ten minutes. We'd better **leave quickly**!
"REAL SPEAK:"	Are plane leaves 'n ten minutes. We 'better **bead it**!

Synonym 1:   **get going (to)** *exp.*

Synonym 2:   **get out of here (to)** *exp.*

Synonym 3:   **hit the road (to)** *exp.*

Synonym 4:   **scram (to)** *v.*

Synonym 5:   **split (to)** *v.*

NOW YOU DO IT. COMPLETE THE PHRASE ALOUD:
I have to beat it or I'll be late for...

crash (to) *v.* to collapse (since "crashing" refers to a hard impact as would happen when someone who is extremely tired falls into bed, on the couch, into a chair, etc.).

> **EXAMPLE:** All the hotels in the city are full. I need to find a place to **crash** tonight!
>
> **TRANSLATION:** All the hotels in the city are full. I need to find a place to **collapse** tonight!
>
> **"REAL SPEAK:"** All the hotels 'n the cidy'er full. I need da find a place ta **crash** tanight!
>
> *Also 1:* **catch some Z's (to)** *exp.* (originated because in comic books, a series of "Z's" are shown over a character's head to indicate sleep).
>
> *Also 2:* **get some shut-eye (to)** *exp.*
>
> *Also 3:* **sack out (to)** *exp.*
>
> **NOW YOU DO IT. COMPLETE THE PHRASE ALOUD:**
>
> *I need to crash for a while before I go to...*

downhill (to go) *exp.* to get worse.

> **EXAMPLE:** I'm afraid Tina's health isn't improving. It keeps **going downhill**.
>
> **TRANSLATION:** I'm afraid Tina's health isn't improving. It keeps **getting worse**.
>
> **"REAL SPEAK:"** I'm afraid Tina's health isn't improving. It keeps **going downhill**.
>
> *Synonym 1:* **down the toilet (to go)** *exp.*
>
> *Synonym 2:* **down the tubes (to go)** *exp.* (Here, "*tubes*" represents "plumbing").
>
> **NOW YOU DO IT. COMPLETE THE PHRASE ALOUD:**
>
> *... has been going downhill since...*

eat someone out of house and home (to) *exp.* to eat everything someone has.

> **EXAMPLE:** Tina and Bruce have a daughter who eats constantly. She's **eating them out of house and home**!
>
> **TRANSLATION:** Tina and Bruce have a daughter who eats constantly. She's **eating to the point where they're going to have nothing left**!
>
> **"REAL SPEAK:"** Tina 'n Bruce have a dawder who eats constantly. She's **eating 'em oudda house 'n home**!
>
> *Synonym:* **eat someone into the poorhouse (to)** *exp.*
>
> **NOW YOU DO IT. COMPLETE THE PHRASE ALOUD:**
>
> *... is eating his family out of house and home!*

everything but the kitchen sink *exp.* everything and anything.

> **EXAMPLE:** You should have seen all the items Don bought at the store. He bought **everything but the kitchen sink**!
>
> **TRANSLATION:** You should have seen all the items Don bought at the store. He bought **everything and anything**!
>
> **"REAL SPEAK:"** You should've seen all the items Don bawd 'it the store. He bawd **ev'rything b't the kitchen sink**!
>
> **NOW YOU DO IT. COMPLETE THE PHRASE ALOUD:**
> *...ate everything but the kitchen sink!*

have it made (to) *exp.* to have an easy life.

> **EXAMPLE:** Stan's parents buy him anything he wants because they're so rich. He sure **has it made**.
>
> **TRANSLATION:** Stan's parents buy him anything he wants because they're so rich. He sure **has an easy life**.
>
> **"REAL SPEAK:"** Stan's parents buy 'im anything 'e wants cuz they're so rich. He sher **has it made**.
>
> *Synonym:* **easy street (to be on)** *exp.*
>
> **NOW YOU DO IT. COMPLETE THE PHRASE ALOUD:**
> *...has it made because...*

nervous wreck (to be a) *n.* to be extremely anxious.

> **EXAMPLE:** I hope I win. The judges should have announced the winner an hour ago. I'm a **nervous wreck**!
>
> **TRANSLATION:** I hope I win. The judges should have announced the winner an hour ago. I'm **extremely anxious**!
>
> **"REAL SPEAK:"** I hope I win. The judges should've announced the winner 'n hour ago. I'm a **nervous wreck**!
>
> *Synonym 1:* **basket case (to be a)** *exp.*
>
> *Synonym 2:* **bundle of nerves (to be a)** *exp.*
>
> *Synonym 3:* **falling apart (to be)** *exp.*
>
> **NOW YOU DO IT. COMPLETE THE PHRASE ALOUD:**
> *I was a nervous wreck when...*

plastered (to be) *adj.* to be extremely drunk.

> **EXAMPLE:** If I drink one glass of vodka, I get **plastered**!
>
> **TRANSLATION:** If I drink one glass of vodka, I get **extremely drunk**!
>
> **"REAL SPEAK:"** If I drink one glass 'a vodka, I get **plastered**!
>
> *Synonyms:* Since there is such a large number of synonyms for the adjective "drunk," I'll list many of the most common ones here: **bombed, bombed out of one's skull, crocked, dead drunk, drunk as a skunk, feeling no pain, hammered, ripped, roaring drunk, sloshed, smashed, stinking drunk**, etc.
>
> **NOW YOU DO IT. COMPLETE THE PHRASE ALOUD:**
> *If you drink too much... you'll get plastered!*

shocker (to be in for a) *exp.* to get a big surprise.

> **EXAMPLE:** My children have really grown since you last saw them. You're **in for a shocker**!
>
> **TRANSLATION:** My children have really grown since you last saw them. You're **about to be extremely surprised**!
>
> **"REAL SPEAK:"** My children've really grown since you las' saw th'm. Y'r **in fer a shocker**!
>
> *Synonym 1:* **blown away (to be)** *exp.*
>
> *Synonym 2:* **floored (to be)** *exp.*
>
> **NOW YOU DO IT. COMPLETE THE PHRASE ALOUD:**
>
> *You're going to be in for a shocker when you...*

wolf down something (to) *exp.* to eat something quickly.

> **EXAMPLE:** I'm hungry. I think we have some time **to wolf down** a sandwich before we leave.
>
> **TRANSLATION:** I'm hungry. I think we have some time **to eat** a sandwich **quickly** before we leave.
>
> **"REAL SPEAK:"** I'm hungry. I think we have some time **ta wolf down** a sandwich before we leave.
>
> *Synonyms:* **polish off (to), power down (to), scarf down (to), thrown down (to), chow down (to)**, etc.
>
> **NOW YOU DO IT. COMPLETE THE PHRASE ALOUD:**
>
> *I only have ten minutes to wolf down this...*

LET'S PRACTICE!

READING

CD-A: TRACK 13

A. WHAT DOES IT MEAN? *(Answers on p. 220)*
Choose the correct definition of the words in boldface.

1. **a shocker**: ☐ a surprise ☐ good news

2. **to be a nervous wreck**: ☐ extremely nervous ☐ extremely happy

3. **to beat it**: ☐ to die ☐ to leave quickly

4. **to go downhill**: ☐ to get worse ☐ to get stronger

5. **everything but the kitchen sink**: ☐ everything imaginable ☐ nothing at all

6. **to have it made**: ☐ to have an easy life ☐ to have a hard life

7. **to crash**: ☐ to laugh ☐ to collapse

8. **plastered**: ☐ extremely drunk ☐ very scared

9. **to eat someone out of house and home**: ☐ to eat everything ☐ to eat very little

10. **to wolf down something**: ☐ to eat quickly ☐ to eat slowly

B. COMPLETE THE FAIRY TALE

(Answers on p. 220)

Fill in the blanks by choosing the correct words from the list below. Note that two extra words are in the list from the previous lesson!

WRITING

CD-A: TRACK 14

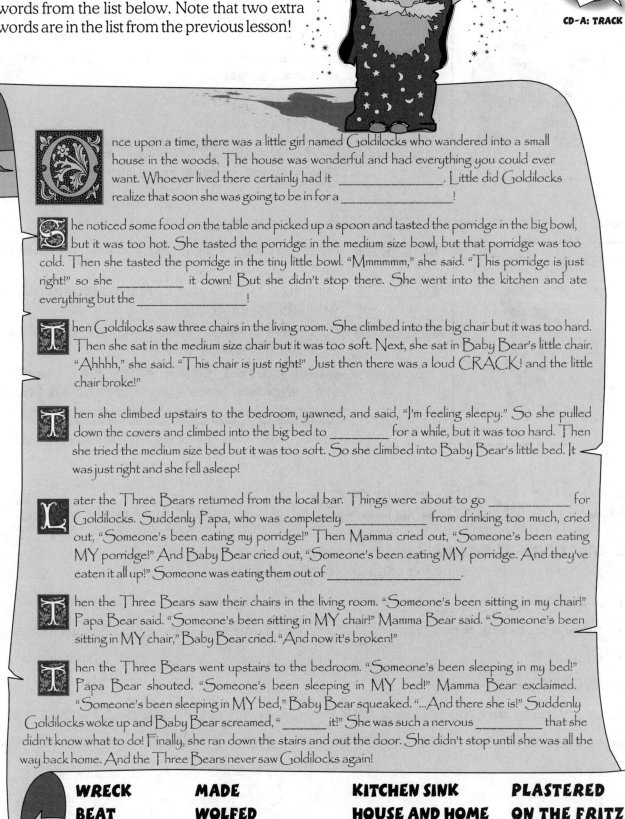

Once upon a time, there was a little girl named Goldilocks who wandered into a small house in the woods. The house was wonderful and had everything you could ever want. Whoever lived there certainly had it _____. Little did Goldilocks realize that soon she was going to be in for a _____!

She noticed some food on the table and picked up a spoon and tasted the porridge in the big bowl, but it was too hot. She tasted the porridge in the medium size bowl, but that porridge was too cold. Then she tasted the porridge in the tiny little bowl. "Mmmmmm," she said. "This porridge is just right!" so she _____ it down! But she didn't stop there. She went into the kitchen and ate everything but the _____!

Then Goldilocks saw three chairs in the living room. She climbed into the big chair but it was too hard. Then she sat in the medium size chair but it was too soft. Next, she sat in Baby Bear's little chair. "Ahhhh," she said. "This chair is just right!" Just then there was a loud CRACK! and the little chair broke!"

Then she climbed upstairs to the bedroom, yawned, and said, "I'm feeling sleepy." So she pulled down the covers and climbed into the big bed to _____ for a while, but it was too hard. Then she tried the medium size bed but it was too soft. So she climbed into Baby Bear's little bed. It was just right and she fell asleep!

Later the Three Bears returned from the local bar. Things were about to go _____ for Goldilocks. Suddenly Papa, who was completely _____ from drinking too much, cried out, "Someone's been eating my porridge!" Then Mamma cried out, "Someone's been eating MY porridge!" And Baby Bear cried out, "Someone's been eating MY porridge. And they've eaten it all up!" Someone was eating them out of _____.

Then the Three Bears saw their chairs in the living room. "Someone's been sitting in my chair!" Papa Bear said. "Someone's been sitting in MY chair!" Mamma Bear said. "Someone's been sitting in MY chair," Baby Bear cried. "And now it's broken!"

Then the Three Bears went upstairs to the bedroom. "Someone's been sleeping in my bed!" Papa Bear shouted. "Someone's been sleeping in MY bed!" Mamma Bear exclaimed. "Someone's been sleeping in MY bed," Baby Bear squeaked. "...And there she is!" Suddenly Goldilocks woke up and Baby Bear screamed, " _____ it!" She was such a nervous _____ that she didn't know what to do! Finally, she ran down the stairs and out the door. She didn't stop until she was all the way back home. And the Three Bears never saw Goldilocks again!

WRECK	**MADE**	**KITCHEN SINK**	**PLASTERED**
BEAT	**WOLFED**	**HOUSE AND HOME**	**ON THE FRITZ**
CRASH	**SHOCKER**	**DOWNHILL**	**FISHY**

C. CONTEXT EXERCISE *(Answers on p. 220)*
Look at the phrase in the left column, then find the best
match in the right column. Write the appropriate letter
in the box.

CD-A: TRACK 15

☐ 1. Have you seen Bob? He doesn't look very well.

A. Are you serious? You're going to eat **everything but the kitchen sink**!

☐ 2. Tony thinks he passed the history test but I just found out that he failed! He has no idea because he wasn't in school today.

B. **Beat it**!

☐ 3. Why are you following me everywhere?!

C. I'm a **nervous wreck**!

☐ 4. I'm exhausted.

D. I know. His health has been **going downhill** for a week.

☐ 5. I'm so hungry! I'm going to order a hamburger, fries, salad, onion rings, milk shake, chicken sandwich, and dessert.

E. He **wolfed down** that pie in about a minute!

☐ 6. My husband is two hours late coming home and he hasn't called!

F. They're **eating us out of house and home**!

☐ 7. I've never seen anyone eat so fast!

G. He has it **made**.

☐ 8. You're in no condition to drive!

H. You're **plastered**!

☐ 9. Our houseguests eat constantly! I hope they leave soon!

I. I'm going to go home and **crash** for a while.

☐ 10. Ron's parents are extremely rich and pay for anything he wants.

J. When he gets back, he's **in for a shocker**.

D. COMPLETE THE PHRASE *(Answers on p. 220)*
Complete the opening dialogue using the list below. Try not to look at the dialogue at the beginning of the lesson until you're done!

SHOCKER	**KITCHEN SINK**
MADE	**PLASTERED**
BEAT IT	**DOWNHILL**
WRECK	**WOLFED**
CRASHES	**HOUSE AND HOME**

Cecily: How is it going with your houseguest?

Lee: It's going _____. Every day he _____ in front of the

television for hours. All he ever does is sleep and eat us out of _____. You

should have seen the sandwich he _____ down this morning. He put everything

on it but the _____. He has it _____ here.

Cecily: Why don't you just tell him to _____?

Lee: He was my roommate in college and it's only for another two days. I just hope that I don't

turn into a nervous _____ by the time he leaves. He even came home

late last night totally _____!

Cecily: Maybe you should just lock the front door so he can't come back in! Wouldn't he be in for

a _____?!

Car and On-the-Road Slang

As many Americans spend hours a day in their cars, it was only a matter of time before the category of car and on-the-road slang was created. Whether you're out **taking a spin** (*taking a drive*) or buying a new **set of wheels** (*car*), you're sure to encounter many of the following terms and expressions. So, **stop spinning your wheels** (*wasting time*) and **put it in high gear** (*hurry*) in order to familiarize yourself with this list right away!

automatic *n.* short for "a car with automatic transmission."

> **EXAMPLE:** My mother can't understand why anyone would want to drive a car with a stick shift ever since the **automatic** was invented!

> **TRANSLATION:** My mother can't understand why anyone would want to drive a car with a stick shift ever since the **car with automatic transmission** was invented!

> **"REAL SPEAK":** My mother can' understand why anyone would wanna drive a car with a stick shift ever since the **audamatic** was invented!

blow a tire (to) *exp.* to get a ruptured tire.

> **EXAMPLE:** I'm sorry I'm late. I **blew a tire** on the way over here.

> **TRANSLATION:** I'm sorry I'm late. I **got a ruptured tire** on the way over here.

> **"REAL SPEAK":** [no change]

blowout *n.* ruptured tire.

> **EXAMPLE:** Something is wrong with your car. I think you just got a **blowout**.

> **TRANSLATION:** Something is wrong with your car. I think you just got a **ruptured tire**.

> **"REAL SPEAK":** Something's wrong with yer car. I think ya jus' god a **blowout**.

broadside (to) *v.* to hit the side of another car with the front of one's own car.

> **EXAMPLE:** That driver went through the intersection on a red light and **broadsided me**! Luckily, no one was hurt.

> **TRANSLATION:** That driver went through the intersection on a red light and **smashed into the side of my car**! Luckily, no one was hurt.

> **"REAL SPEAK":** That driver went through the intersection on a red light 'n **broadsided me**! Luckily, no one w'z hurt.

bumper-to-bumper traffic *exp.* traffic that is so heavy that the cars are extremely close to each other.

> **EXAMPLE:** It took me two hours to get home because of the **bumper-to-bumper traffic**.

> **TRANSLATION:** It took me two hours to get home because of the **heavy and slow traffic**.

> **"REAL SPEAK":** It took me two hours ta get home b'cause 'ev the **bumper-da-bumper traffic**.

burn rubber (to) *exp.* to accelerate so quickly that a skid mark is left.

> **EXAMPLE:** Bob thinks it's cool to **burn rubber** every time he accelerates. He's going to ruin his tires.

> **TRANSLATION:** Bob thinks it's cool to **leave a skid mark** every time he accelerates. He's going to ruin his tires.

> **"REAL SPEAK":** Bob thinks it's cool da **burn rubber** ev'ry time 'e accelerates. He's gonna ruin 'is tires.

clunker *n.* an old car in poor condition.

> **EXAMPLE:** I finally sold my old **clunker** and bought a new Mercedes Benz!
>
> **TRANSLATION:** I finally sold my old **worn out car** and bought a new Mercedes Benz!
>
> **"REAL SPEAK":** I fin'lly sold my old **clunker** 'n bod a new Mercedes Benz!

conk out (to) *exp.* • **1.** to cease to function • **2.** to fall asleep.

> **EXAMPLE 1:** My car suddenly **conked out** for no apparent reason. So, I took a taxi here.
>
> **TRANSLATION:** My car suddenly **ceased to function** for no apparent reason. So, I took a taxi here.
>
> **"REAL SPEAK":** My car suddenly **conked out** fer no apparent reason. So, I took a taxi here.
>
> **EXAMPLE 2:** I was so tired after working all night that I went home and **conked out** for twelve hours
>
> **TRANSLATION:** I was so tired after working all night that I went home and **fell asleep** for twelve hours.
>
> **"REAL SPEAK":** I w'z so tired after working all night th'd I went home 'n **conked out** fer twelve hours.

cop *n.* (*extremely popular*) police officer.

> **EXAMPLE:** My car was stolen! Call a **cop**!
>
> **TRANSLATION:** My car was stolen! Call a **police officer**!
>
> **"REAL SPEAK":** My car w'z stolen! Call a **cop**!

Note: In old gangster movies, you may hear the term "*copper*" which is the original form of "*cop*." It's interesting to note that the term "*copper*" comes from the large copper buttons that were worn on the original police uniforms.

dash *n.* a common abbreviation of *dashboard* which is "a panel under the windshield of an automobile containing indicator dials and compartments."

> **EXAMPLE:** I put my coffee cup on the **dash** and when I stopped suddenly, the coffee spilled everywhere!
>
> **TRANSLATION:** I put my coffee cup on the **dashboard** and when I stopped suddenly, the coffee spilled everywhere!
>
> **"REAL SPEAK":** I put my coffee cup on the **dash** an' when I stopped suddenly, the coffee spilled ev'rywhere!

fender bender *exp.* a little car accident causing minor damage.

> **EXAMPLE:** I'm okay. It was just a little **fender bender**.
>
> **TRANSLATION:** I'm okay. It was just a little car **accident causing minor damage**.
>
> **"REAL SPEAK":** I'm okay. It w'z just a liddle **fender bender**.

flat *n.* a common, shortened version of "flat tire" meaning "ruptured tire."

> **EXAMPLE:** I hope my boss believes me when I tell him that I had a **flat** this morning. That's why I'm thirty minutes late.

TRANSLATION: I hope my boss believes me when I tell him that I had a **ruptured tire** this morning. That's why I'm thirty minutes late.

"REAL SPEAK": I hope my boss believes me when I tell 'im th'd I had a **flat** this morning. That's why I'm thirdy minutes late.

floor it (to) *exp.* to push the accelerator all the way down to the floor of the car.

EXAMPLE: We have only two minutes to get to the train station. **Floor it**!

TRANSLATION: We have only two minutes to get to the train station. **Push the accelerator all the way down to the floor**!

"REAL SPEAK": We have only two minutes ta get ta the train station. **Floor it**!

four-wheeler *n.* any size vehicle with four-wheel drive (meaning that "all four wheels have power, not just the back two").

EXAMPLE: My mother drives a **four-wheeler** because she loves going to the mountains where she needs the extra power.

TRANSLATION: My mother drives a **car with power in all four wheels** because she loves going to the mountains where she needs the extra power.

"REAL SPEAK": My mother drives a **four-wheeler** b'cause she loves going ta the mountains where she needs the extra power.

fully loaded *exp.* said of a car which is sold with lots of extra features such as air conditioning, power windows, CD player, etc.

EXAMPLE: You'll love this new car. It's **fully loaded**!

TRANSLATION: You'll love this new car. It **comes with lots of extra features**!

"REAL SPEAK": [no change]

fuzz-buster *n.* a device which is attached inside the car and used to detect a police officer's radar • (lit.): police officer catcher.

EXAMPLE: I was able to slow down before the cop checked my speed with his radar thanks to my **fuzz-buster**.

TRANSLATION: I was able to slow down before the cop checked my speed with his radar thanks to my **radar-detecting device**.

"REAL SPEAK": I w'z able da slow down b'fore the cop checked my speed with 'is radar thanks ta my **fuzz-buster**.

Note: The slang term *fuzz*, meaning "police officer," was extremely popular in the sixties and is now outdated. However, it's interesting to note that the term *fuzz-buster* is still common.

hauled in (to get) *exp.* to get taken to the police station, to get arrested.

EXAMPLE: Did you hear the news? Jim **got hauled in** for drunk driving!

TRANSLATION: Did you hear the news? Jim **got arrested** for drunk driving!

"REAL SPEAK": Did'ja hear the news? Jim **got hauled in** fer drunk driving!

head-on collision *exp.* a crash involving two cars where the fronts of both cars collide.

EXAMPLE: That guy was driving on the wrong side of the road and almost **had a head-on collision with me**.

TRANSLATION: That guy was driving on the wrong side of the road and almost **crashed the front of his car into the front of mine**.

"REAL SPEAK": That guy w'z driving on the wrong side 'a the road 'n almost **had a head-on collision with me**.

Also: **hit head-on (to)** *exp.* to hit the front of a car with another.

hop in (to) *v.* to get in.

EXAMPLE: I'd be happy to drive you to the grocery store this morning. **Hop in**!

TRANSLATION: I'd be happy to drive you to the grocery store this morning. **Get in**!

"REAL SPEAK": I'd be happy da drive ya da the groc'ry store this morning. **Hop in**!

jalopy *n.* an old broken-down car.

> **EXAMPLE:** I'm tired of driving this **jalopy** everywhere. I need to buy a new car.
>
> **TRANSLATION:** I'm tired of driving this **old broken-down car** everywhere. I need to buy a new car.
>
> **"REAL SPEAK":** I'm tired 'ev driving this **jalopy** ev'rywhere. I need ta buy a new car.

jam on the brakes (to) *exp.* to apply the brakes quickly.

> **EXAMPLE:** I **jammed on the brakes** when I saw the dog run across the road. Fortunately, I missed him.
>
> **TRANSLATION:** I **quickly applied the brakes** when I saw the dog run across the road. Fortunately, I missed him.
>
> **"REAL SPEAK":** I **jammed on the brakes** when I saw the dog run across the road. Forchunately, I missed 'im.

jaywalk (to) *v.* to cross the street not using a designated crosswalk.

> **EXAMPLE:** I got a ticket for **jaywalking**. The officer said that I forced cars to stop suddenly.
>
> **TRANSLATION:** I got a ticket for **crossing the street not using a designated crosswalk**. The officer said that I forced cars to stop suddenly.
>
> **"REAL SPEAK":** I god a ticket fer **jaywalking**. The officer said th'd I forced cars ta stop suddenly.

> *Also:* **jaywalker** *n.* one who crosses the street not using a designated crosswalk.

jump-start (to) *v.* to revive one's car battery by attaching a cable to someone else's battery.

> **EXAMPLE:** My car battery is dead. Can you help me **jump-start** it?
>
> **TRANSLATION:** My car battery is dead. Can you help me **revive it by attaching a cable from your battery to mine**?
>
> **"REAL SPEAK":** My car battery's dead. C'n ya help me **jump-stard** it?

> *Variation:* **one's car jumped (to get)** *exp.*

> *Also:* **jump-started (to get)** *exp.* to get oneself started • *A cup of coffee helps me to get jump-started in the morning; A cup of coffee helps me to get started in the morning.*

leave someone in the dust (to) *exp.* to leave someone behind.

> **EXAMPLE:** I haven't seen Tim in a long time. **I left him in the dust** a while ago.
>
> **TRANSLATION:** I haven't seen Tim in a long time. **I drove past him** a while ago.
>
> **"REAL SPEAK":** I haven't seen Tim 'n a long time. **I left 'im in the dust** a while ago.

lemon *n.* a worthless product.

> **EXAMPLE:** I just bought my car and it died! I think I bought a **lemon**.
>
> **TRANSLATION:** I just bought my car and it died! I think I bought a **worthless product**.
>
> **"REAL SPEAK":** I jus' bought my car 'n it died! I think I bod a **lemon**.

peel out (to) *exp.* to accelerate quickly.

> **EXAMPLE:** When Steve saw me coming, he **peeled out**! That was so rude!
>
> **TRANSLATION:** When Steve saw me coming, he **accelerated quickly**! That was so rude!
>
> **"REAL SPEAK":** When Steve saw me coming, he **peeled out**! That w'z so rude!

pileup *n.* an accident involving a number of cars piled up one on top of the other.

> **EXAMPLE:** There was a **pileup** on the highway this morning. That's why I was so late to work.
>
> **TRANSLATION:** There was an **accident involving a number of cars piled up one on top of the other** on the highway this morning. That's why I was so late to work.
>
> **"REAL SPEAK":** There w'z a **pileup** on the highway th's morning. That's why I w'z so late ta work.

pop the clutch (to) *exp.* to release the clutch too quickly causing the car to jump forward.

> **EXAMPLE:** I keep **popping the clutch** because I'm used to driving a car with automatic transmission.

TRANSLATION: I keep **releasing the clutch too quickly causing the car to jump forward** because I'm used to driving a car with automatic transmission.

"REAL SPEAK": I keep **popping the clutch** b'cause I'm usta driving a car with audamadic transmission.

pot hole *n.* a large hole in the street resembling the size and depth of a kitchen pot.

EXAMPLE: Unfortunately, the city doesn't have enough money to fix all the **pot holes**.

TRANSLATION: Unfortunately, the city doesn't have enough money to fix all the **holes in the street**.

"REAL SPEAK": Unforchunately, the cidy doesn't have anough money da fix all the **pot holes**.

punch it (to) *exp.* to accelerate quickly.

EXAMPLE: That car is about to hit us! **Punch it**!

TRANSLATION: That car is about to hit us! **Accelerate quickly**!

"REAL SPEAK": That car's about ta hid us! **Punch it**!

put it in high gear (to) *exp.* to hurry.

EXAMPLE: The play starts in twenty minutes. We'd better **put it in high gear** or we're going to be late

TRANSLATION: The play starts in twenty minutes. We'd better **hurry** or we're going to be late.

"REAL SPEAK": The play starts'n twen'y minutes. We'd bedder **pud id in high gear** 'r w'r gonna be late

Note: Most cars have four or five gears, the highest enabling the car to move fastest.

put the pedal to the metal (to) *exp.* to press the accelerator all the way down to the floor of the car.

EXAMPLE: The contractions are coming every five minutes! We need to get to the hospital fast. **Put the pedal to the metal**!

TRANSLATION: The contractions are coming every five minutes! We need to get to the hospital fast. **Hurry**!

"REAL SPEAK": The c'ntractions'er coming ev'ry five minutes! We need ta get ta the hospid'l fast. **Put the ped'l ta the med'l**!

rear-ender *n. (short for "rear-end collision")* an accident involving one car hitting another car from behind.

EXAMPLE: I was in a **rear-ender** on the way to work. I was the one who got hit, but I'm okay.

TRANSLATION: I was in a **rear-end collision** on the way to work. I was the one who got hit, but I'm okay.

"REAL SPEAK": I w'z in a **rear-ender** on the way da work. I w'z the one who got hit, b'd I'm okay.

rev up (to) *exp.* to push the accelerator while the car is in neutral as a way to warm up the engine.

EXAMPLE: Your heater is blowing out cold air! You need to **rev up** your engine for a while.

TRANSLATION: Your heater is blowing out cold air! You need to **warm up** your engine for a while.

"REAL SPEAK": Yer heeder's blowing out cold air! Ya need ta **rev up** yer engine fer a while.

Note: This expression refers not only to cars, but to people as well • *I'm all revved up. Let's play tennis!;* I'm all warmed up. Let's play tennis!

run a light (to) *exp.* to go through a traffic signal during a red light.

> **EXAMPLE:** Did you see that?! That guy **ran the light** and almost hit us!
>
> **TRANSLATION:** Did you see that?! That guy **went through the traffic signal** during a red light and almost hit us!
>
> **"REAL SPEAK":** Did'ja see that?! That guy **ran the lide** 'n almost hid us!

rush hour *n.* the time when most drivers are on the road (usually at the opening or close of business).

> **EXAMPLE:** Let's meet for dinner tonight, but let's make it around seven o'clock. I don't want to drive during **rush hour**.
>
> **TRANSLATION:** Let's meet for dinner tonight, but let's make it around seven o'clock. I don't want to drive during **the time when most drivers are on the road**.
>
> **"REAL SPEAK":** Let's meet fer dinner tanight, b't let's make id aroun' seven a'clock. I don't wanna drive during **rush hour**.

set of wheels *exp.* car.

> **EXAMPLE:** What do you think of my new **set of wheels**?
>
> **TRANSLATION:** What do you think of my new **car**?
>
> **"REAL SPEAK":** Whady'ya think 'a my new **sed 'a wheels**?
>
> *Variation:* **wheels** *n.pl.* • *Nice wheels!;* Nice car!

sideswipe (to) *v.* to scrape the side of another car with the side of one's own car.

> **EXAMPLE:** I honked my horn to warn the driver next to me that he was moving into my lane, but he didn't hear me and **sideswiped** my car.
>
> **TRANSLATION:** I honked my horn to warn the driver next to me that he was moving into my lane, but he didn't hear me and **scraped the side of** my car.
>
> **"REAL SPEAK":** I honked my horn ta warn the driver nex' ta me th't he w'z moving inta my lane, bud 'e didn't hear me 'n h **sideswiped** my car.

spare tire *n.* the fat area around a person's stomach resembling a tire.

> **EXAMPLE:** Don's starting to get a **spare tire**. He'd better start to diet or it's going to get worse.
>
> **TRANSLATION:** Don's starting to **get fat around his waist**. He'd better start to diet or it's going to get worse.
>
> **"REAL SPEAK":** Don's starding ta ged a **spare tire**. He'd bedder start ta diet or it's gonna get worse.

spin (to take a) *exp.* to take a short drive with no particular destination.

> **EXAMPLE:** It's such a beautiful day! Why don't we **take a spin** in my new car?
>
> **TRANSLATION:** It's such a beautiful day! Why don't we **take a relaxing drive** in my new car?
>
> **"REAL SPEAK":** It's such a beaudif'l day! Why don't we **take a spin** 'n my new car?

spin one's wheels (to) *exp.* to work hard but get nowhere (referring to a car that is unable to move though its wheels keep spinning around).

> **EXAMPLE:** Larry will never get a raise in his company no matter how hard he works. He's just **spinning his wheels**.
>
> **TRANSLATION:** Larry will never get a raise in his company no matter how hard he works. He **works hard but he'll never get anywhere**.
>
> **"REAL SPEAK":** Larry'll never ged a raise 'n his company no madder how hard 'e works. He's jus' **spinning 'is wheels**.

stick *n.* short for "a car with manual transmission that uses a stick shift."

> **EXAMPLE:** I prefer driving a **stick** because I feel like I'm more in control of the car.
>
> **TRANSLATION:** I prefer driving a **car with manual transmission** because I feel like I'm more in control of the car.
>
> **"REAL SPEAK":** I prefer driving a **stick** b'cause I feel like I'm more 'n c'ntrol 'a the car.

stop on a dime (to) *exp.* to stop in an instant (suggesting that one could actually stop precisely on a dime).

> **EXAMPLE:** It's a good thing my car can **stop on a dime**. If not, I may have accidentally hit that dog.
>
> **TRANSLATION:** It's a good thing my car can **stop in an instant**. If not, I may have accidentally hit that dog.
>
> **"REAL SPEAK":** It's a good thing my car c'n **stop on a dime**. If not, I may'ev accidentally hit that dog.

strip a car (to) *exp.* to steal parts of a car (that are then sold illegally).

> **EXAMPLE:** While I was eating at the restaurant, my car was **stripped**!
>
> **TRANSLATION:** While I was eating at the restaurant, my car was **disassembled and parts were taken**.
>
> **"REAL SPEAK":** While I w'z eading 'it the rest'rant, my car w'z **stripped**!
>
> *Also:* **a stripped car** *exp.* a car that has no extra features such as air conditioning, power windows, CD player etc. • *The car sells for $42,000 and that's stripped!;* The car sells for $42,000 and that's without any extra features!

tailgate (to) *v.* to follow at a dangerously close distance (almost touching the tailgate of the car in front).

> **EXAMPLE:** The car behind me is **tailgating** me. That's so dangerous!
>
> **TRANSLATION:** The car behind me is **driving too close to me**. That's so dangerous!

> **"REAL SPEAK":** The car b'hin' me's **tailgading** me. That's so dangerous!

total a car (to) *exp.* to completely destroy a car in an accident.

> **EXAMPLE:** Did you hear the news? Pat **totaled** his car in an accident last night! Luckily, no one was hurt

> **TRANSLATION:** Did you hear the news? Pat **destroyed** his car in an accident last night! Luckily, no one was hurt.
>
> **"REAL SPEAK":** Did'ja hear the news? Pat **todaled** 'is car in 'n accident las' night! Luckily, no one w'z hurt.

wheel *n.* short for "steering wheel."

> **EXAMPLE:** Take the **wheel**! I think I'm going to faint!
>
> **TRANSLATION:** Take the **steering wheel**! I think I'm going to faint!
>
> **"REAL SPEAK":** Take the **wheel**! I think I'm gonna faint!

wheelie (to pop a) *n.* an action where the driver pulls up on the handle bars of the bicycle or motorcycle making it roll forward on only the back wheel.

> **EXAMPLE:** When I was a little boy, I **popped a wheelie** in front of a girl I was trying to impress. Unfortunately, I lost control of the bicycle and fell!
>
> **TRANSLATION:** When I was a little boy, I **pulled back the handle bars of my bicycle and rode on only the back wheel** in front of a girl I was trying to impress. Unfortunately, I lost control of the bicycle and fell!
>
> **"REAL SPEAK":** When I w'z a liddle boy, I **popped a wheelie** 'n fron' 'ev a girl I w'z trying to impress. Unforchunately, I lost c'ntrol 'a the bicycle 'n fell!

LESSON 4 — AT THE PARK

"Wake up and smell the coffee!"

LET'S WARM UP!

MATCH THE PICTURES *(Answers on p. 220)*

As a fun way to get started, see if you can guess the meaning of the new slang words and expressions on the opposite page by using the pictures below and following the context of the sentences.

1. Someone stole my bicycle! I'm really *ticked off*!
   ❏ angry
   ❏ happy

2. Ernie is *crazy about* ice cream.
   ❏ passionate about
   ❏ angry at

3. Every time my cousin Sue visits, she kisses me. It *grosses me out*!
   ❏ excites me
   ❏ disgusts me

4. You're going to paint your entire house?! *Knock yourself out*!
   ❏ go ahead
   ❏ leave me alone

5. You didn't know our next door neighbor is crazy?! *Wake up and smell the coffee*!
   ❏ become aware of what's really happening
   ❏ have some coffee before work

6. *Don't got there*. Let's change the subject.
   ❏ let's talk about this in detail
   ❏ let's not talk about this subject

7. I've had the *nagging feeling* all day that I forgot to do something.
   ❏ persistently annoying thought
   ❏ calming thought

8. Todd got home *in the nick of time*!
   ❏ at just the right moment
   ❏ late

9. Jeff talks nonstop about chemistry. He's the most boring *geek* I've ever met!
   ❏ genius
   ❏ foolish and weak-looking person

10. Kirk went to the bar tonight to *pick up girls*.
    ❏ find girls for an intimate encounter
    ❏ lift up girls

11. Jim insulted Greg and got a *black eye* for it!
    ❏ bruised eye
    ❏ pair of reading glasses

12. After our discussion, Pat *is singing a different tune*.
    ❏ has changed his attitude
    ❏ has become a singer

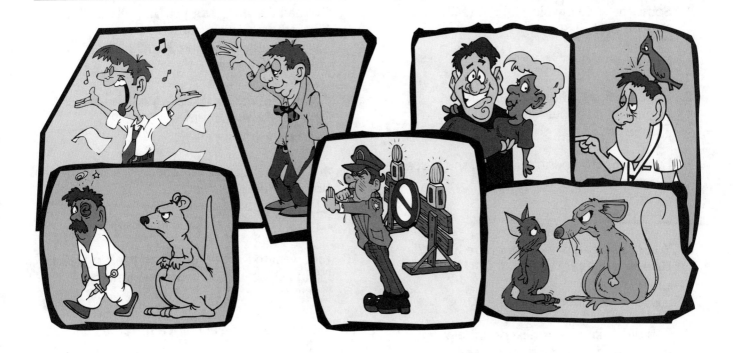

LET'S TALK!

A. DIALOGUE USING SLANG & IDIOMS

The words introduced on the first two pages are used in the dialogue below. See if you can understand the conversation. *Note:* The translation of the words in boldface is on the right-hand page.

CD-A: TRACK 16

Phyllis: You got here **just in the nick of time**. I have this **nagging feeling** that the **geek** over there is following me.

Carol: Maybe he's just taking a walk.

Phyllis: **Wake up and smell the coffee**. A lot of guys come to parks to **pick up** women. Guys like him really **tick me off**.

Carol: You know, I think you're right. He keeps looking over here.

Phyllis: Well, if he tries anything, I'm going to give him a **black eye**. That should make him **sing a different tune**. You know, he reminds me of that guy in math class who's **crazy about you**.

Carol: **Don't go there.** That guy really **grosses me out**! Besides, that's definitely not him. That guy over there is a lot taller.

Phyllis: Well, I've had it. I'm tired of him staring at me. I'm going to tell him to beat it!

Carol: I don't know why you don't just ignore him. But fine. If you really want to, **knock yourself out**.

B. DIALOGUE TRANSLATED INTO STANDARD ENGLISH

LET'S SEE HOW MUCH YOU REMEMBER!
Just for fun, bounce around in random order to the words
and expressions in boldface below. See if you can remember
their slang equivalents without looking at the left-hand page!

Phyllis: You got here **at just the right moment**. I have this **persistently annoying thought** that the **foolish and weak-looking person** over there is following me.

Carol: Maybe he's just taking a walk.

Phyllis: **Become aware of what's really happening**. A lot of guys come to parks to **look for an intimate encounter with** women. Guys like him really **make me angry**.

Carol: You know, I think you're right. He keeps looking over here.

Phyllis: Well, if he tries anything, I'm going to give him a **bruised eye**. That should make him **change his attitude**. You know, he reminds me of that guy in math class who's **infatuated with you**.

Carol: **Don't start that topic of conversation**. That guy really **makes me sick**! Besides, that's definitely not him. That guy over there is a lot taller.

Phyllis: Well, I've had it. I'm tired of him staring at me. I'm going to tell him to beat it!

Carol: I don't know why you don't just ignore him. But fine. If you really want to, **go ahead**.

C. DIALOGUE USING "REAL SPEAK"

The dialogue below demonstrates how the slang conversation on the previous page would *really* be spoken by native speakers!

Phyllis: Ya got here **just 'n the nick 'a time**. I have this **nagging feeling** that the **geek** over there's following me.

Carol: Maybe 'e's jus' taking a walk.

Phyllis: **Wake up 'n smell the coffee**. A lod 'a guys come ta parks ta **pick up** women. Guys like him really **tick me off**.

Carol: Ya know, I think y'r right. He keeps looking over here.

Phyllis: Well, if 'e tries anything, I'm gonna give 'im a **black eye**. That should make 'im **sing a differ'nt tune**. Ya know, he remin's me 'a that guy 'n math class oo's **crazy about 'chu**.

Carol: **Don't go there**. That guy **grosses me out**! Besides, that's definitely not him. That guy over there's a lot taller.

Phyllis: Well, I've had it. I'm tired of 'im staring at me. I'm gonna tell 'im da bead it!

Carol: I dunno why ya don't just ignore 'im. B't fine. If ya really wanna, **knock yerself out**.

LET'S LEARN!

CD-A: TRACK 17

VOCABULARY

The following words and expressions were used in the previous dialogues. Let's take a closer look at what they mean.

arrive [just] in the nick of time (to) *exp.* to arrive at the perfect moment (as a moment later would be too late).

EXAMPLE: Steve **arrived [just] in the nick of time**. A minute later would have been too late!

TRANSLATION: Steve **arrived at the perfect moment**. A minute later would have been too late!

"REAL SPEAK:" Steve **arrived [just] 'n the nick 'a time**. A minute lader would'a been too late!

Note: Other synonyms for the verb "arrive" could be used in this expression such as: **to make it**, **to show up**, **to turn up**, etc.

NOW YOU DO IT. COMPLETE THE PHRASE ALOUD:
I arrived [just] in the nick of time to...

black eye *n.* a bruise around the eye (due to a severe impact).

EXAMPLE:	Pat got mad and punched Eric in the face. You should see the **black eye** Pat gave him!
TRANSLATION:	Pat got mad and punched Eric in the face. You should see the **bruised eye** Pat gave him!
"REAL SPEAK:"	Pat got mad 'n punched Eric in the face. You should see the **black eye** Pat gave 'im!
Synonym:	**shiner** *n.*

NOW YOU DO IT. COMPLETE THE PHRASE ALOUD:
I got a black eye because...

crazy about someone or something (to be) *exp.* to be extremely fond of someone or something, to love with great intensity, to be deeply in love.

EXAMPLE:	My parents have been married for thirty years and they're still **crazy about** each other.
TRANSLATION:	My parents have been married for thirty years and they're still **deeply in love with** each other.
"REAL SPEAK:"	My parents've been married fer thirdy years 'n they're still **crazy aboud** each other.
Synonym:	**mad/nuts/wild about (to be)** *exp.*

NOW YOU DO IT. COMPLETE THE PHRASE ALOUD:
I'm crazy about...

"Don't go there" *exp. (extremely popular)* "Don't start that topic of conversation."

EXAMPLE:	– How is everything going with you and Shirley? – **Don't go there**. Let's change the subject.
TRANSLATION:	– How is everything going with you and Shirley? – **Don't start that topic of conversation**. Let's change the subject.
"REAL SPEAK:"	– How's ev'rything going with you 'n Shirley? – **Don't go there**. Let's change the subject.

NOW YOU DO IT:
Use "Don't go there" in a sentence.

geek *n.* a foolish and weak-looking person.

EXAMPLE:	Jim is a college athlete but his brother is a **geek**.
TRANSLATION:	Jim is a college athlete but his brother is a **foolish- and weak-looking person**.
"REAL SPEAK:"	Jim's a college athlete bud 'is brother's a **geek**.
Synonym 1:	**dweeb** *n.*
Synonym 2:	**nerd** *n.*

NOW YOU DO IT. COMPLETE THE PHRASE ALOUD:
...is the biggest geek I've ever met!

gross out someone (to) *exp.* to disgust someone.

> **EXAMPLE:** Did you taste that horrible appetizer Betty made for my party? It **grossed out** everyone!
>
> **TRANSLATION:** Did you taste that horrible appetizer Betty made for my party? It **disgusted** everyone!
>
> **"REAL SPEAK:"** Did'ja taste that horr'ble appetizer Beddy made fer my pardy? It **grossed oud** ev'ryone!
>
> *Synonym:* **"Gag me!"** *interj.* a humorous interjection signifying displeasure or disgust.

NOW YOU DO IT. COMPLETE THE PHRASE ALOUD:
...grosses me out!

"Knock yourself out" *exp.* "Go ahead" • (lit.): "Make yourself lose consciousness."

> **EXAMPLE:** You're cooking for fifty people?! That's too much work for me. But if you enjoy it, **knock yourself out**!
>
> **TRANSLATION:** You're cooking for fifty people?! That's too much work for me. But if you enjoy it, **go ahead**!
>
> **"REAL SPEAK:"** Y'r cooking fer fifdy people?! That's too much work fer me. Bud if you enjoy it, **knock yourself out**!
>
> *Also:* **knock oneself out (to)** *exp.* to exhaust oneself in order to do something • *I knocked myself out cleaning the house all day!;* I exhausted myself cleaning the house all day!

NOW YOU DO IT:
Use "Knock yourself out" in a sentence.

nagging feeling (to have a) *exp.* to have a persistently annoying thought.

> **EXAMPLE:** I have a **nagging feeling** that George forgot we had a meeting scheduled for this morning.
>
> **TRANSLATION:** I have a **persistently annoying feeling** that George forgot we had a meeting scheduled for this morning.
>
> **"REAL SPEAK:"** I have a **nagging feeling** th't George fergot we had a meeding scheduled fer this morning.
>
> *Synonym:* **sneaking suspicion (to have a)** *exp.*

NOW YOU DO IT. COMPLETE THE PHRASE ALOUD:
I have a nagging feeling that...

pick up someone (to) *exp.* to look for an intimate encounter with someone.

> **EXAMPLE:** The only reason Al came to my party was to **pick up** girls.
>
> **TRANSLATION:** The only reason Al came to my party was to **look for an intimate encounter with** girls.
>
> **"REAL SPEAK:"** The only reason Al came ta my pardy was ta **pick up** girls.
>
> *Synonym:* **cruise for (to) / cruising for (to go)** *exp.*

NOW YOU DO IT:
Use "pick up" in a sentence.

sing a different tune (to) *exp.* to have a change of attitude or behavior.

EXAMPLE: Mark was arrested for stealing?! Well, once he spends a few days in jail, he'll **sing a different tune**.

TRANSLATION: Mark was arrested for stealing?! Well, once he spends a few days in jail, he'll **change the way he behaves**.

"REAL SPEAK:" Mark w'z arrested fer stealing?! Well, once 'e spen's a few days 'n jail, he'll **sing a diff'rent tune**.

Synonym: **learn one's lesson (to)** *exp.*

NOW YOU DO IT:

Use "sing a different tune" in a sentence.

ticked [off] (to be) *exp.* to be angry.

EXAMPLE: I'm really **ticked [off]** because Tom forgot to pick me up at the airport.

TRANSLATION: I'm really **angry** because Tom forgot to pick me up at the airport.

"REAL SPEAK:" I'm really **ticked [off]** cuz Tom fergot ta pick me up 'it the airport.

Also: **tick someone off (to)** *exp.* to make someone angry.

Synonym 1: **ballistic (to go)** *exp.*

Synonym 2: **bent out of shape (to be)** *exp.*

Synonym 3: **blow one's top (to)** *exp.*

Synonym 4: **fly off the handle (to)** *exp.*

Synonym 5: **hit the ceiling (to)** *exp.*

Synonym 6: **tee'd off (to be)** *exp.*

NOW YOU DO IT:

Use "ticked [off]" in a sentence.

"Wake up and smell the coffee" *exp.* "Become aware of what's really happening."

EXAMPLE: You think Anne is your friend? She only likes you because you're rich! **Wake up and smell the coffee!**

TRANSLATION: You think Anne is your friend? She only likes you because you're rich! **Become aware of what's really happening!**

"REAL SPEAK:" Ya think Anne's yer friend? She only likes you b'cause y'r rich! **Wake up 'n smell the coffee!**

Synonym: **"Get a clue"** *exp.*

NOW YOU DO IT. COMPLETE THE PHRASE ALOUD:

You believed... when he told you...? Wake up and smell the coffee!

LET'S PRACTICE!

WRITING

CD-A: TRACK 18

A. CROSSWORD PUZZLE *(Answers on p. 221)*

Fill in the crossword puzzle by choosing the correct word
from the list below.

sing	black	feeling
knock	grosses	crazy
off	time	geek
pick	go	coffee

ACROSS

2. Bob actually drove his car after drinking two glasses of vodka?! He's crazy! Well, if he gets stopped by a cop, he'll ____ a different tune!

4. John likes to go to parties to ____ up girls. That's how he met his last girlfriend.

6. You actually believed what that slimy salesperson told you? Wake up and smell the ____! He was lying to get you to make a purchase!

8. Did you hear the news? Maggie punched John in the face and gave him a ____ eye!

10. The smell of eggs cooking really ____ out! It smells like sulfur!

DOWN

1. I don't know why you don't just take your car to a mechanic instead of trying to fix it yourself. But it's your decision. ____ yourself out!

3. The fire fighters arrived just in the nick of ____. One minute later the entire house would have been burned to the ground!

5. Don't ____ there! I told you I never want to talk about that again!

6. I'm ____ about ice cream. I could eat it for every meal!

7. I have a nagging ____ there was something I was supposed to do this morning. I wish I could remember what it was!

9. Did you see the new student in class today? He wears big glasses, his clothes are too big, and he's really thin. He looks like such a ____!

11. It really ticks me ____ when a driver parks in two spaces instead of one!

B. CHOOSE THE RIGHT WORD *(Answers on p. 221)*
Underline the appropriate word that best completes
the phrase.

CD-A: TRACK 19

1. – Would you like me to help you move these boxes?
   – Oh, thank you! You arrived just in the (**neck**, **nick**, **nerd**) of time! I was about to move all these boxes into the other room and they're too heavy for me.

2. – I'm going to paint my entire house all by myself.
   – I don't know why you don't get someone to help you. Well, if you really want to spend your weekend painting, knock yourself (**in**, **up**, **out**)!

3. – I just invited Henry to my party. He seems really nice.
   – Everyone knows he's really nasty! Wake (**down**, **up**, **out**) and smell the coffee!

4. – What's wrong? You seem upset about something.
   – I have this (**gagging**, **nagging**, **sagging**) feeling that something terrible is about to happen.

5. – What happened to you?!
   – I fell off my motorcycle and got a (**black**, **blue**, **gray**) eye. I'm lucky I didn't break anything!

6. – Did you taste the horrible cake Bernice made?
   – I sure did. The blue frosting really grossed me (**out**, **in**, **up**).

7. – How was your job interview?
   – Don't (**come**, **go**, **stay**) there. I'll just say that I didn't get the job. Now change the subject.

8. – You don't look very happy this morning!
   – Someone hit my car this morning and didn't even leave a note! That ticks me (**off**, **on**, **up**)!

9. – Look at the beautiful necklace Ted gave me!
   – Wow! He must really be (**smart**, **crazy**, **stupid**) about you!

10. – Sam cheated on his test again!
    – I'm going to report him to the teacher. That'll make him sing a different (**melody**, **song**, **tune**).

11. – Did you see the guy Jennifer is dating?
    – I sure did. He's so foolish and weak-looking. I've never seen such a (**leek**, **geek**, **week**) in my life!

12. – Why do you think Earl goes to bars every night?
    – He's probably trying to pick (**over**, **through**, **up**) women!

C. MATCH THE COLUMN *(Answers on p. 221)*

Match the words in boldface with the definition in the right column. Write the letter of the definition in the box.

CD-A: TRACK 20

1. I have a **nagging feeling** that I forgot to lock my car after I parked it.

2. You'd prefer to walk five miles to the market instead of having me drive you? Okay. **Knock yourself out**!

3. How could you trust him? Everyone knows he's a thief! **Wake up and smell the coffee**!

4. I couldn't eat the food in the school cafeteria today. The smell really **grossed me out**!

5. Bob insulted Tim so he punched Bob in the face and gave him a **black eye**!

6. I'm **crazy about** Paul! He's my best friend in the whole world!

7. As soon as Rob gets arrested for stealing, he'll **sing a different tune**.

8. You arrived **[just] in the nick of time**! One minute later would have been too late.

9. It really **ticks me off** when people lie!

10. **Don't go there**. I really don't want to talk about Steve again.

11. Jody goes to the bars every night hoping to **pick up** guys.

12. That's George? He used to be such a **geek**. Now he's absolutely gorgeous!

A. bruised eye

B. go ahead

C. extremely fond of

D. made me sick

E. don't bring up that topic of conversation

F. persistently annoying thought

G. have an intimate encounter with

H. foolish and weak-looking person

I. makes me angry

J. at just the right moment

K. change his attitude or behavior

L. become aware of what's really happening

THE SLANGMAN FILES

Clothing Used in Slang Expressions

As clothing certainly plays an important part of our everyday life, there was no way for it to escape being one of the targets for a variety of innovative slang expressions. There are many expressions containing clothing, and you certainly don't want to be **caught with your pants down** (*unprepared*). So, **hang onto your hat** (*get ready*) because this list is sure to **knock your socks off** (*amaze you*)!

BELT

belt *n.* swallow or gulp of an alcoholic drink.

> **EXAMPLE:** My boss is acting so strangely. I think he may have taken a couple of **belts** during lunch.

> **TRANSLATION:** My boss is acting so strangely. I think he may have taken a couple of **gulps** of alcohol during lunch.

> **"REAL SPEAK":** My boss is acting so strangely. I think 'e may'ev taken a couple 'a **belts** during lunch.

belt out a song (to) *exp.* to sing a song with energy.

> **EXAMPLE:** My sister really knows how to **belt out a song**!

> **TRANSLATION:** My sister really knows how to **sing a song with energy**!

> **"REAL SPEAK":** My sister really knows how da **belt oud a song**!

belt someone (to) *exp.* to hit or punch someone.

> **EXAMPLE:** When Bill insulted Hilary's mother, she hauled off and **belted him**.

> **TRANSLATION:** When Bill insulted Hilary's mother, she launched an attack and **punched him**.

> **"REAL SPEAK":** When Bill insulted Hilary's mother, she hauled off 'n **belted 'im**.

> *Note 1:* Although the term "belt" is used in this expression, it does not refer to hitting someone with a belt, rather the fist.

> *Note 2:* The expression "*to haul off*," meaning "to launch an attack," is extremely popular when used before describing an act of violence.

hit below the belt (to) *exp.* to commit a despicable or unfair act.

> **EXAMPLE:** Carl told his wife that if she files for divorce, he'll make sure he gets the children. That certainly was **hitting below the belt**.

> **TRANSLATION:** Carl told his wife that if she files for divorce, he'll make sure he gets the children. That certainly was **despicable**.

> **"REAL SPEAK":** Carl told 'is wife th'd if she files fer divorce, he'll make sher 'e gets the children. That certainly was **hidding below the belt**.

> *Note:* This expression originated from boxing where it is illegal to hit an opponent below the belt.

BOOT

boot camp n. military training for new recruits

> **EXAMPLE:** After spending a year in **boot camp**, Jamie became very disciplined.

> **TRANSLATION:** After spending a year in **military training**, Jamie became very disciplined.

> **"REAL SPEAK":** After spending a year 'n **boot camp**, Jamie b'came very disciplined.

boot someone (to) v. to eject someone.

> **EXAMPLE:** I got so mad at Larry that I **booted him** from my office.

> **TRANSLATION:** I got so mad at Larry that I **ejected him** from my office.

> **"REAL SPEAK":** I got so mad 'it Larry th'd I **booded 'im** fr'm my office.

boot up (to) exp. to start a computer.

> **EXAMPLE:** When I **booted up** my computer this morning, it gave me an error message.

> **TRANSLATION:** When I **started** my computer this morning, it gave me an error message.

> **"REAL SPEAK":** When I **booted up** my computer this morning, it gave me an error message.

> *Variation:* **boot (to)** v. a common shorted version of "to boot up" • *It takes such a long time for my computer to boot; It takes such a long time for my computer to start.*

> *Also:* **reboot (to)** v. to start the computer again • *My computer is doing strange things. I think I'd better reboot; My computer is doing strange things. I think I'd better start up my computer again.*

bootleg (to) • **1.** v. to sell products illegally • **2.** adj. bootlegged = illegally acquired.

> **EXAMPLE 1:** Andy was arrested for **bootlegging**.

> **TRANSLATION:** Andy was arrested for **selling products illegally**.

> **"REAL SPEAK":** Andy w'z arrested fer **bootlegging**.

> **EXAMPLE 2:** David bought a **bootlegged** computer program. That's why it was so inexpensive.

> **TRANSLATION:** David bought an **illegal** computer program. That's why it was so inexpensive.

> **"REAL SPEAK":** David bod a **bootlegged** c'mpuder program. That's why it w'z so inexpensive.

give someone the boot (to) exp. to fire someone from a job.

> **EXAMPLE:** The boss **gave** Smithers **the boot** for being late all the time.

> **TRANSLATION:** The boss **fired** Smithers for being late all the time.

> **"REAL SPEAK":** The boss **gave** Smithers **the boot** fer being lade all the time.

shake in one's boots (to) exp. to quiver with fear

> **EXAMPLE:** When I saw the bear running toward us, I started to **shake in my boots**.

> **TRANSLATION:** When I saw the bear running toward us, I started to **quiver with fear**.

> **"REAL SPEAK":** When I saw the bear running tord us, I starded ta **shake in my boots**.

COLLAR

blue-collar worker n. one who does manual work i.e. mechanic, chef, construction worker, etc.

> **EXAMPLE:** Dan is a mechanic. He's been a **blue-collar worker** all his life.

> **TRANSLATION:** Dan is a mechanic. He's been a **manual worker** all his life.

> **"REAL SPEAK":** Dan's a mechanic. He's been a **blue-collar worker** all 'is life.

hot under the collar (to be) exp. to be angry

> **EXAMPLE:** Why are you so **hot under the collar** this afternoon? This morning you seemed so cheerful!

> **TRANSLATION:** Why are you so **angry**? This morning you seemed so cheerful!

"REAL SPEAK": Why'er ya so **hod under the collar** this afternoon? Th's morning you seemed so cheerful!

white-collar worker *n.* one who does office work (as opposed to manual or physical labor) i.e. doctor, lawyer, teacher, etc.

EXAMPLE: My father used to be a manual laborer. Now he's an accountant. He prefers being a **white-collar worker**.

TRANSLATION: My father used to be a manual laborer. Now he's an accountant. He prefers being an **office worker**.

"REAL SPEAK": My father usta be a manual laborer. Now 'e's an accountant. He prefers being a **white-coller worker**.

CUFF

off the cuff *exp.* extemporaneously, unrehearsed.

EXAMPLE: Robin Williams is a brilliant comedian. He says the funniest things **off the cuff**.

TRANSLATION: Robin Williams is a brilliant comedian. He says the funniest things **extemporaneously**.

"REAL SPEAK": Robin Williams is a brilliant comedian. He says the funnies' things **off the cuff**.

cuff someone (to) *v.* to put handcuffs on someone.

EXAMPLE: That guy tried to rob the bank, but the security guard tackled him and then **cuffed him**.

TRANSLATION: That guy tried to rob the bank, but the security guard tackled him and then **put handcuffs on him**.

"REAL SPEAK": That guy tried ta rob the bank, b't the securidy guard tackled 'im 'n then **cuffed 'im**.

cuffs *n.pl.* a common abbreviation for "handcuffs."

EXAMPLE: The police officer took away the suspect in **cuffs**.

TRANSLATION: The police officer took away the suspect in **handcuffs**.

"REAL SPEAK": The police officer took away the suspect 'n **cuffs**.

GLOVE

fit like a glove *exp.* to fit perfectly.

EXAMPLE: That dress **fits you like a glove**! You should buy it!

TRANSLATION: That dress **fits you perfectly**! You should buy it!

"REAL SPEAK": That dress **fits ya like a glove**! You should buy it!

lay a glove on someone (not to) *exp.* not to touch someone.

EXAMPLE: Don't you **lay a glove on** my dog!

TRANSLATION: Don't you **touch** my dog!

"REAL SPEAK": Donchu **lay a glove on** my dog!

wear kid gloves (to) *exp.* to be very tactful in dealing with someone.

EXAMPLE: When you give Ernie a suggestion, you need to **wear kid gloves**. He's very sensitive and could get his feelings hurt.

TRANSLATION: When you give Ernie a suggestion, you need to **be very tactful**. He's very sensitive and could get his feelings hurt.

"REAL SPEAK": When ya give Ernie a suggestion, ya need ta **wear kid gloves**. He's very sensidive an' could ged 'is feelings hurt.

Variation: **handle someone with kid gloves (to)** *exp.*

white-glove inspection (to give the) *exp.* to make a careful and detailed inspection.

EXAMPLE: Every time my mother comes to visit, she gives my apartment **the white-glove inspection**.

TRANSLATION: Every time my mother comes to visit, she gives my apartment **a careful and detailed inspection**.

"REAL SPEAK": Ev'ry time my mother comes ta visit, she gives my apartment **the white-glove inspection**.

HAT

at the drop of a hat *exp.* without hesitation.

> **EXAMPLE:** My mother is always willing to go with me to the movies **at the drop of a hat**.

> **TRANSLATION:** My mother is always willing to go with me to the movies **without hesitation**.

> **"REAL SPEAK":** My mother's always willing ta go with me da the movies **at the drop of a hat**.

"Hang onto your hat!" *exp. (figurative)* •
1. "Prepare yourself for something so physical and vigorous, that your hat could come off!"
• **2.** "Prepare yourself for something shocking."

> **EXAMPLE 1:** I'll demonstrate how fast my car can move. Here we go. **Hang onto your hat!**

> **TRANSLATION:** I'll demonstrate how fast my car can move. Here we go. **Hold on tight!**

> **"REAL SPEAK":** A'll demonstrate how fast my car c'n move. Here we go. **Hang onta yer hat!**

> **EXAMPLE 2:** You won't believe what I just heard about Mitch and Carol. **Hang onto your hat!**

> **TRANSLATION:** You won't believe what I just heard about Mitch and Carol. **Prepare yourself!**

> **"REAL SPEAK":** Ya won't believe whad I just heard about Mitch 'n Carol. **Hang onta yer hat!**

> *Note 1:* Since this expression is figurative, it is used even when the people to whom you are speaking are not wearing hats.

> *Note 2:* When speaking to more than one person, the plural of "hat" is used: *"hats."*

> *Variation:* **"Hold onto your hat!"** *exp.*

hat off to someone (to have one's) *exp.* to admire someone.

> **EXAMPLE:** **My hat's off to her**. I could never work with mentally challenged children. I'd be too emotional.

> **TRANSLATION:** **I admire her**. I could never work with mentally challenged children. I'd be too emotional.

> **"REAL SPEAK":** **My hat's off ta her**. I could never work with men'ally challenged children. I'd be too emotional.

keep it under one's hat (to) *exp.* to keep it a secret.

> **EXAMPLE:** Jim just told me that he's breaking up with Donna. But **keep it under your hat**. I don't think he wants anyone to know yet.

> **TRANSLATION:** Jim just told me that he's breaking up with Donna. But **keep it a secret**. I don't think he wants anyone to know yet.

> **"REAL SPEAK":** Jim jus' told me thad 'e's breaking up with Donna. B't **keep id under yer hat**. I don' think 'e wants anyone ta know yet.

wear several hats (to) *exp.* to have several responsibilities or job positions.

> **EXAMPLE:** I'm not only a producer in the company, I'm also the creative director and art designer. As you can see, I **wear several hats** here.

> **TRANSLATION:** I'm not only a producer in the company, I'm also the creative director and art designer. As you can see, I **do several jobs** here.

> **"REAL SPEAK":** I'm nod only a praducer in the company, I'm also the creadive directer an' art designer. As ya can see, I **wear sev'ral hats** here.

HEEL

Achilles' heel *exp.* vulnerable area.

> **EXAMPLE:** Tell Bobby you won't let him watch television if he doesn't obey you. That's his **Achilles' heel**.

> **TRANSLATION:** Tell Bobby you won't let him watch television if he doesn't obey you. That's his **vulnerable area**.

> **"REAL SPEAK":** Tell Bobby ya won't led 'im watch TV if 'e doesn't obey you. That's 'is **Achilles' heel**.

cool one's heels (to) *exp.* to be forced to stay in one place.

> **EXAMPLE:** I've been **cooling my heels** here for the past hour waiting for you to arrive!

TRANSLATION:	I've been **forced to stay in one place** for the past hour waiting for you to arrive!
"REAL SPEAK":	I've been **cooling my heels** here fer the past hour waiding fer you do arrive!

dig one's heels in (to) *exp.* to refuse to change one's mind, to be stubborn.

EXAMPLE:	Tessa **dug her heels in** and told her mother that she wouldn't go to school.
TRANSLATION:	Tessa **got stubborn** and told her mother that she wouldn't go to school.
"REAL SPEAK":	Tessa **dug 'er heels in** 'n told 'er mother th't she wouldn't go da school.

drag one's heels (to) *exp.* to dawdle, to move slowly.

EXAMPLE:	Stop **dragging your heels**! We have only twenty minutes to get to the theater!
TRANSLATION:	Stop **dawdling**! We have only twenty minutes to get to the theater!
"REAL SPEAK":	Stop **dragging yer heels**! We have only twen'y minutes ta get ta the theater!

fall head over heels for someone (to) *exp.* to fall deeply in love with someone.

EXAMPLE:	George **fell head over heels for** Dana the moment he met her.
TRANSLATION:	George **fell deeply in love with** Dana the moment he met her.
"REAL SPEAK":	George **fell head over heels fer** Dana the moment 'e med her.

head over heels in debt (to be) *exp.* to be in extreme debt.

EXAMPLE:	I can't borrow any more money. I'm already **head over heels in** debt.
TRANSLATION:	I can't borrow any more money. I'm already **in extreme** debt.
"REAL SPEAK":	I can't borrow any more money. I'm already **head over heels 'n** debt.

"Heel!" *interj.* a common command given to a dog to walk next to its master.

EXAMPLE:	**Heel**! Good boy.
TRANSLATION:	**Walk next to me**! Good boy.
"REAL SPEAK":	[no change]

Also: **heel (to)** *v.* said of a dog who walks next to his master's heel • *I taught my dog to heel. He's so smart!*; I taught my dog to walk next to my heel. He's so smart!

heel (to feel like a) *exp.* to feel like a morally dishonorable person.

EXAMPLE:	I told William that he couldn't stay at my house any longer because he was so annoying as a houseguest. He almost started to cry. I felt like such a **heel**.
TRANSLATION:	I told William that he couldn't stay at my house any longer because he was so annoying as a houseguest. He almost started to cry. I felt like such a **morally dishonorable person**.
"REAL SPEAK":	I told William thad 'e couldn't stay 'it my house any longer b'cause 'e w'z so annoying as a houseguest. He almos' starded ta cry. I felt like such a **heel**.

PANTS

ants in one's pants (to have) *exp.* to be restless.

EXAMPLE:	Leon can never sit still. He **has ants in his pants**.
TRANSLATION:	Leon can never sit still. He's **so restless**.
"REAL SPEAK":	Leon c'n never sit still. He **has ants 'n 'is pants**.

Variation: **antsy** *adj.* restless.

beat the pants off someone (to) *exp.* to win completely in a competition.

EXAMPLE:	Louise **beat the pants off me** in our card game.
TRANSLATION:	Louise **beat me completely** in our card game.
"REAL SPEAK":	Louise **beat the pants off me** 'n 'ar card game.

by the seat of one's pants (to do something) *exp.* by luck and little skill.

EXAMPLE:	I graduated college **by the seat of my pants**.
TRANSLATION:	I graduated college by **luck and little skill**.
"REAL SPEAK":	I gradjuaded college **by the sead 'ev my pants**.

Variation: **fly by the seat of one's pants (to)** *exp.* to improvise • *I repaired my computer all by myself and I was just flying by the seat of my pants; I repaired my computer all by myself and I was just improvising.*

caught with one's pants down (to be) *exp.* to be caught unprepared.

EXAMPLE:	You've come here to discuss our new business plan? I wish you had given me some warning. I'm afraid you've **caught me with my pants down**. I haven't taken a look at it yet.
TRANSLATION:	You've come here to discuss our new business plan? I wish you had given me some warning. I'm afraid you've **caught me unprepared**. I haven't taken a look at it yet.
"REAL SPEAK":	You've come here da discuss 'ar new business plan? I wish you'd given me s'm warning. I'm afraid you've **caught me with my pants down**. I haven't taken a look ad it yet.

charm the pants off someone (to) *exp.* to enchant someone greatly.

EXAMPLE:	Your cousin really **charmed the pants off me**. What a wonderful guy!
TRANSLATION:	Your cousin **really enchanted me**. What a wonderful guy!
"REAL SPEAK":	Yer cousin really **charmed the pants off me**. Whad a wonderful guy!

scare the pants off someone (to) *exp.* to scare someone tremendously.

EXAMPLE:	My little niece ran into the street without even looking. She **scared the pants off me**!
TRANSLATION:	My little niece ran into the street without even looking. She **scared me tremendously**!
"REAL SPEAK":	My liddle niece ran inta the street withoud even looking. She **scared the pants off me**!

Note: This is the idiom shown on the cover of this book!

sue the pants off someone (to) *exp.* to take someone to court in hope of getting a lot of money.

EXAMPLE:	If you damage my car, I'll **sue the pants off you**!
TRANSLATION:	If you damage my car, I'll **take you to court and get a lot of money from you**!
"REAL SPEAK":	If ya damage my car, a'll **sue the pants off ya**!

wear the pants in the family (to) *exp.* to be the head of the family.

EXAMPLE:	It certainly is obvious who **wears the pants in that family**!
TRANSLATION:	It certainly is obvious who **is the head of that family**!
"REAL SPEAK":	It certainly is obvious who **wears the pants 'n that fam'ly**!

SHIRT

give the shirt off one's back (to) *exp.* to offer everything one can.

EXAMPLE:	Debbie is one of my closest friends. I'd give her **the shirt off my back**.
TRANSLATION:	Debbie is one of my closest friends. I'd give her **anything I could**.
"REAL SPEAK":	Debbie's one 'a my closest friends. I'd give 'er **the shird off my back**.

"Keep your shirt on!" *exp.* "Be patient!"

| EXAMPLE: | **Keep your shirt on**! I'll help you just as soon as I'm available. |

| TRANSLATION: | **Be patient!** I'll help you just as soon as I'm available. |
| "REAL SPEAK": | **Keep yer shird on**! A'll help ya just 'ez soon 'ez I'm available. |

lose one's shirt (to) *exp.* to lose everything one owns.

EXAMPLE:	I'll never gamble again. The last time I gambled, I **lost my shirt**.
TRANSLATION:	I'll never gamble again. The last time I gambled, I **lost everything I owned**.
"REAL SPEAK":	A'll never gamble again. The las' time I gambled, I **lost my shirt**.

stuffed shirt (to be a) *exp.* said of someone who is pompous and uptight.

EXAMPLE:	Our old boss was so fun and friendly, but the new one is a real **stuffed shirt**.
TRANSLATION:	Our old boss was so fun and friendly, but the new one is really **pompous and uptight**.
"REAL SPEAK":	'Ar old boss w'z so fun 'n friendly, b't the new one's a real **stuffed shirt**.

SHOES

fill someone's shoes (to) *exp.* to replace someone.

EXAMPLE:	She'll never be able to **fill his shoes**. He was the best teacher we ever had
TRANSLATION:	She'll never be able to **replace him**. He was the best teacher we ever had.
"REAL SPEAK":	She'll never be able da **fill 'is shoes**. He w'z the bes' teacher we ever had.

"If the shoe fits, wear it" *exp.* "The character trait we're talking about matches the person in question."

EXAMPLE:	– Are you calling me a liar?! – **If the shoe fits, wear it**!
TRANSLATION:	– Are you calling me a liar?! – **You match that characteristic**!
"REAL SPEAK":	– Are ya calling me a liar?! – **If the shoe fits, wear it**!

Variation: **"If the shoe fits!"** *exp.* (a common shortened version).

in one's shoes *exp.* in one's situation.

EXAMPLE:	If I were **in your shoes**, I'd quit and find another job.
TRANSLATION:	If I were **in your situation**, I'd quit and find another job.
"REAL SPEAK":	If I were **in yer shoes**, I'd quit 'n find another job.

put oneself in someone else's shoes (to) *exp.* to imagine what it would be like to be in the other person's situation.

EXAMPLE:	I know you're angry about his decision, but **put yourself in his shoes**. What would you have done instead?
TRANSLATION:	I know you're angry about his decision, but **imagine what it would be like to be in his situation**. What would you have done instead?
"REAL SPEAK":	I know y'r angry aboud 'is decision, b't **put cherself in his shoes**. What would'ju 'ev done instead?

shoe-in (to be a) *exp.* to be certain to get chosen for something.

EXAMPLE:	I know you'll get the job. You're a **shoe-in**!
TRANSLATION:	I know you'll get the job. You're **certain to get chosen**!
"REAL SPEAK":	I know you'll get the job. Y'r a **shoe-in**!

"The shoe is on the other foot" *exp.* "The reverse situation is happening."

EXAMPLE:	Bob used to be my boss, but he got demoted. Now I'm his boss. Suddenly **the shoe is on the other foot**!
TRANSLATION:	Bob used to be my boss, but he got demoted. Now I'm his boss. Suddenly **the situation is reversed**!
"REAL SPEAK":	Bob usta be my boss, bud 'e got demoded. Now I'm 'is boss. Suddenly **the shoe's on the other foot**!

wait for the other shoe to drop (to) *exp.* to anticipate something bad to happen.

EXAMPLE:	I've had the best week of my life. Now I'm **waiting for the other shoe to drop**.
TRANSLATION:	I've had the best week of my life. Now I'm **anticipating something bad**.
"REAL SPEAK":	I've had the best week 'a my life. Now I'm **waiding fer the other shoe da drop**.

SLEEVE

ace up one's sleeve (to have an) *exp.* to have an advantage held for future use.

EXAMPLE:	We thought we were going to have to close the company, but at the last moment my partner **had an ace up his sleeve**. He was able to get a large loan from the bank!
TRANSLATION:	We thought we were going to have to close the company, but at the last moment my partner **revealed an advantage he was holding for future use**. He was able to get a large loan from the bank!
"REAL SPEAK":	We thought we were gonna hafta close the company, bud 'it the last moment my partner **had 'n ace up 'is sleeve**. He w'az able da ged a large loan from the bank!

up one's sleeve (to have something) *exp.* to have a secret plan.

EXAMPLE:	I don't trust him. I think **he has something up his sleeve**.
TRANSLATION:	I don't trust him. I think **he's planning something dishonest**.
"REAL SPEAK":	I don't trust 'im. I think **'e has something up 'is sleeve**.

wear one's heart on one's sleeve (to) *exp.* to show one's feelings openly instead of keeping them hidden.

EXAMPLE:	You never have to guess what Dana is feeling. She **wears her heart on her sleeve**.
TRANSLATION:	You never have to guess what Dana is feeling. She **shows her emotions openly**.
"REAL SPEAK":	Ya never hafta guess what Dana's feeling. She **wears 'er hard on 'er sleeve**.

SOCKS

beat the socks off someone (to) *exp.* to win by a lot.

EXAMPLE:	Dan and I played tennis today and I **beat the socks off him**!
TRANSLATION:	Dan and I played tennis today and I **won by a lot**!
"REAL SPEAK":	Dan 'n I played tennis taday 'n I **beat the socks off 'im**!

knock one's socks off (to) *exp.* to surprise someone greatly.

EXAMPLE:	You won't believe the news I'm going to tell you. It'll **knock your socks off**!
TRANSLATION:	You won't believe the news I'm going to tell you. It'll **surprise you greatly**!
"REAL SPEAK":	Ya won't believe the news I'm gonna tell ya. Id'll **knock yer socks off**!

put a sock in it (to) *exp.* to shut one's mouth.

EXAMPLE:	When Gene started bragging again, I told him to **put a sock in it**.
TRANSLATION:	When Gene started bragging again, I told him to **shut his mouth**.
"REAL SPEAK":	When Gene starded bragging again, I told 'im da **pud a sock in it**.

LESSON 5 THE BIRTHDAY PARTY

"Don really bugs me!"

LET'S WARM UP!

MATCH THE PICTURES *(Answers on p. 221)*

As a fun way to get started, see if you can guess the meaning of the new slang words and expressions on the opposite page by using the pictures below and following the context of the sentences.

1. Let's leave the party. I'm bored **big time**!
   Definition: "slightly"

   ❑ True   ❑ False

2. Naomi shouldn't be allowed to drive. She's **as blind as a bat**.
   Definition: "unable to see"

   ❑ True   ❑ False

3. Kevin is having a **bad hair day**!
   Definition: "day where one's hair looks bad"

   ❑ True   ❑ False

4. Mimi's house is so **artsy-fartsy**. I prefer a home that's plain and simple
   Definition: "excessive"

   ❑ True   ❑ False

5. Roberta wasn't invited to my party so she's **crashed it**!
   Definition: "came without an invitation"

   ❑ True   ❑ False

6. Janet doesn't spend much money on her furniture. That's why it looks so **cheesy**.
   Definition: "expensive"

   ❑ True   ❑ False

7. My parents are **head over heels for** each other!
   Definition: "deeply in love"

   ❑ True   ❑ False

8. My brother and I **had it out** last night because he borrowed my new sweater and ruined it!
   Definition: "had a confrontation"

   ❑ True   ❑ False

9. Al is a millionaire?! I find that **hard to swallow**.
   Definition: "easy to believe"

   ❑ True   ❑ False

10. Trying to get Bob to agree with me on anything is **like pulling teeth**!
    Definition: "easy and painless"

    ❑ True   ❑ False

11. I **have a bone to pick with** you. Why did you lie to me about where you went last night?
    Definition: "have a personal complaint to discuss with you"

    ❑ True   ❑ False

12. I don't like Doug. He **bugs** me!
    Definition: "charms"

    ❑ True   ❑ False

LET'S TALK!

A. DIALOGUE USING SLANG & IDIOMS

The words introduced on the first two pages are used in the dialogue below. See if you can understand the conversation.
Note: The translation of the words in boldface is on the right-hand page.

CD-A: TRACK 21

Susie: Thank you so much for coming to my birthday party. Are you having a good time?

Judy: Oh, yes. **Big time!** *[Then as she walks away...]* Can you believe what she's done to her house? The green carpeting looks so **cheesy**. And why did she use so many different colors of paint on the walls? It's just too **artsy-fartsy** for me.

Linda: You're not kidding! Oh, no. Look who just walked in – Cynthia Harcourt. Talk about a **bad hair day**!

Judy: She must have **crashed the party**. I can't imagine Nancy would invite her. They finally **had it out** last month. Evidently Cynthia **fell head over heels for** Nancy's boyfriend and started calling him all the time!

Linda: If that happened to me, I'd have a **bone to pick with** her, too. She really **bugs** me. Every time she sees me, she tells me these exaggerated stories that I have a **hard time swallowing**.

Judy: I know. Talking to her is **like pulling teeth**. I hope she doesn't see us. Fortunately, she's **as blind as a bat**.

B. DIALOGUE TRANSLATED INTO STANDARD ENGLISH

LET'S SEE HOW MUCH YOU REMEMBER!
Just for fun, bounce around in random order to the words
and expressions in boldface below. See if you can remember
their slang equivalents without looking at the left-hand page!

Susie: Thank you so much for coming to my birthday party. Are you having a good time?

Judy: Oh, yes. **Enormously!** *[Then as she walks away...]* Can you believe what she's done to her house? The green carpeting looks so **cheap**. And why did she use so many different colors of paint on the walls? It's just too **pretentiously artistic** for me.

Linda: You're not kidding! Oh, no. Look who just walked in – Cynthia Harcourt. Talk about a **day when your hair looks terrible**!

Judy: She must have **come to the party without an invitation**. I can't imagine Nancy would invite her. They finally **had a confrontation** last month. Evidently Cynthia **fell in love with** Nancy's boyfriend and started calling him all the time!

Linda: If that happened to me, I'd have a **personal complaint to discuss with** her, too. She really **annoys** me. Every time she sees me, she tells me these exaggerated stories that I have a **hard time believing**.

Judy: I know. Talking to her is **difficult and painful**. I hope she doesn't see us. Fortunately, she's **unable to see at all**.

C. DIALOGUE USING "REAL SPEAK"

The dialogue below demonstrates how the slang conversation on the previous page would *really* be spoken by native speakers!

Susie: Thanks so much fer coming da my birthday pardy. Ya havin' a good time?

Judy: Oh, yeah. **Big time!** *[Then as she walks away...]* C'n you believe what she's done to 'er house? The green carpeding looks so **cheesy**. An' why'd she use so many diff'rent colors of paint on the walls? It's jus' too **artsy-fartsy** fer me.

Linda: Y'r not kidding! Oh, no. Look 'oo jus' walked in – Cynthia Harcourt. Talk aboud a **bad hair day**!

Judy: She must'a **crashed the pardy**. I can' imagine Nancy would 'nvite 'er. They fin'lly **had id out** las' month. Evidently Cynthia **fell head over heels fer** Nancy's boyfriend 'n starded calling 'im all the time!

Linda: If that happen' da me, I'd have a **bone da pick with** 'er, too. She really **bugs** me. Ev'ry time she sees me, she tells me these exaggeraded stories thad I have a **hard time swallowing**.

Judy: I know. Talking da her is **like pulling teeth**. I hope she doesn' see us. Fortunately, she's **'ez blind 'ez a bat**.

LET'S LEARN!

VOCABULARY

CD-A: TRACK 22

The following words and expressions were used in the previous dialogues. Let's take a closer look at what they mean.

artsy-fartsy (to be) *exp.* said of a person, place or thing that looks pretentiously artistic.

EXAMPLE:	Silvia likes to think she's part of the art world. That's why her house is so **artsy-fartsy**.
TRANSLATION:	Silvia likes to think she's part of the art world. That's why her house is so **pretentiously artistic**.
"REAL SPEAK:"	Silvia likes ta think she's pard 'a the art world. That's why 'er house is so **artsy-fartsy**.
Synonym:	**over the top (to be)** *exp.*

NOW YOU DO IT. COMPLETE THE PHRASE ALOUD:
...'s home is too artsy-fartsy for me!

bad hair day (to have a) *exp.* said of someone who's hair looks terrible.

EXAMPLE:	I can't go out in public. I'm **having a bad hair day**.
TRANSLATION:	I can't go out in public. I'm **having a day where my hair looks terrible**.
"REAL SPEAK:"	I can't go oud in public. I'm **having a bad hair day**.
Antonym:	**good hair day (to have a)** *exp.*

NOW YOU DO IT. COMPLETE THE PHRASE ALOUD:
... always seems to have a bad hair day.

big  **time** *exp. (used as a modifier) extremely, very much.*

EXAMPLE:	Gina is **big time** strange! She talks to her plants!
TRANSLATION:	Gina is **extremely** strange! She talks to her plants!
"REAL SPEAK:"	Gina's **big time** strange! She talks to 'er plants!

Synonym 1: **mucho** *adv. (from Spanish meaning "very").*

Synonym 2: **way** *adv. (popularized by teens).*

NOW YOU DO IT:
Use "big time" in a sentence.

blind as a bat (to be as) *exp.* to be unable to see at all.

EXAMPLE:	My mother is **as blind as a bat** without her glasses. Now she wears contact lenses during the day.
TRANSLATION:	My mother is **unable to see** without her glasses. Now she wears contact lenses during the day.
"REAL SPEAK:"	My mother's **as blind as a bat** withoud 'er glasses. Now she wears contact lenses during the day.

NOW YOU DO IT:
Use "as blind as a bat" in a sentence.

bone to pick with someone (to have a) *exp.* to have a personal complaint to discuss with someone.

EXAMPLE:	I have a **bone to pick** with you. You borrowed my bicycle two months ago and never returned it!
TRANSLATION:	I have a **personal complaint to discuss** with you. You borrowed my bicycle two months ago and never returned it!
"REAL SPEAK:"	I have a **bone da pick** with you. You borrowed my bicycle two munts ago 'n never returned it!

Synonym: **score to settle with someone (to have a)** *exp.*

NOW YOU DO IT:
Use "bone to pick with someone" in a sentence.

bug someone (to) *v.* to annoy someone.

EXAMPLE:	Every time I see Anthony, he talks nonstop about his problems. He really **bugs** me.
TRANSLATION:	Every time I see Anthony, he talks nonstop about his problems. He really **annoys** me.
"REAL SPEAK:"	Every time I see Anthony, he talks nonstop aboud 'is problems. He really **bugs** me.

Variation: **work someone's last good nerve (to)** *exp.*

NOW YOU DO IT. COMPLETE THE PHRASE ALOUD:
...really bugs me because...

cheesy *adj.* said of something cheap-looking and in poor taste.

EXAMPLE:	I can't believe Carol bought that couch just because it was on sale. It looks so **cheesy**!
TRANSLATION:	I can't believe Carol bought that couch just because it was on sale. It looks so **cheap**!
"REAL SPEAK:"	I can't believe Carol bought that couch jus' because it was on sale. It looks so **cheesy**!
Synonym:	**tacky** *adj.*

NOW YOU DO IT. COMPLETE THE PHRASE ALOUD:
...looked really cheesy!

crash a party (to) *exp.* to attend a party without an invitation.

EXAMPLE:	Isn't that Jamie Roach? I didn't invite her to my house! I can't believe she **crashed my party**!
TRANSLATION:	Isn't that Jamie Roach? I didn't invite her to my house! I can't believe she **came to my party without an invitation**!
"REAL SPEAK:"	Isn' that Jamie Roach? I didn' invide 'er da my house! I can't believe she **crashed my pardy**!

NOW YOU DO IT:
Use "crash a party" in a sentence.

fall head over heels for (to) exp. to fall in love with.

EXAMPLE:	When I met your father forty years ago, we **fell head over heels for** each other.
TRANSLATION:	When I met your father forty years ago, we **fell in love with** each other.
"REAL SPEAK:"	When I met cher father fordy years ago, we **fell head over heels fer** each other.
Synonyms:	**to flip for • to be crazy about • to be nuts about • to have it bad for • to be mad about • to be crazy about • to fall for.**

NOW YOU DO IT. COMPLETE THE PHRASE ALOUD:
The first person I fell head over heels for was...

hard time swallowing something (to have a) *exp.* to have difficulty believing something.

EXAMPLE:	Dan has twenty brothers and sisters? I **have a hard time swallowing that**.
TRANSLATION:	Dan has twenty brothers and sisters? I **have difficulty believing that**.
"REAL SPEAK:"	Dan has twen'y brothers 'n sisters? I **have a hard time swallowing that**.
Variation:	**find something hard to swallow (to)** *exp.*

NOW YOU DO IT. COMPLETE THE PHRASE ALOUD:
...? I have a hard time swallowing that.

have it out with someone (to) *exp.* to have a confrontation with someone.

EXAMPLE: Stewart took my car without asking my permission?! I'm going **to have it out with him** right now.

TRANSLATION: Stewart took my car without asking my permission?! I'm going **to have a confrontation with him** right now.

"REAL SPEAK:" Stewart took my car withoud asking my permission?! I'm gonna **have id out with 'im** right now.

Synonym: **hash it out with someone (to)** *exp.*

NOW YOU DO IT. COMPLETE THE PHRASE ALOUD:
I'm going to have it out with... because...

like pulling teeth (to be) *exp.* said of something extremely difficult to do.

EXAMPLE: Ed is so lazy that getting him to help me do a little work is **like pulling teeth**.

TRANSLATION: Ed is so lazy that getting him to help me do a little work is **extremely difficult**.

"REAL SPEAK:" Ed's so lazy th't gedding 'im da help me do a liddle work is **like pulling teeth**.

Synonym: **uphill battle (to be an)** *exp.*

NOW YOU DO IT. COMPLETE THE PHRASE ALOUD:
...is like pulling teeth!

LET'S PRACTICE!

A. YOU'RE THE AUTHOR *(Answers on p. 221)*
Complete the dialogue using the words below.

CD-A: TRACK 23

FARTSY	CRASH	OUT	BAT
DAY	HEELS	TEETH	BONE
CHEESY	SWALLOWING	TIME	BUGS

Jennifer: I finally had it _____ with Carol for telling me that my house is ugly and too fartsy-_____ . She really _____ me big _____! I've had a _____ to pick with her for a long time about her insults. Getting her to pay a compliment is like pulling _____ !

Louise: She told you that *you* have bad taste?! I have a hard time _____ that because she has the worst taste of anyone I've ever met. I mean, look at her! Her clothes are all old and _____ and she always looks like she's having a bad hair _____. And I have to tell you that I'm head over _____ with the way you've decorated your house. I think she's just blind as a _____ and can't see how pretty your house really is! You need to stop inviting her to your parties, although it won't matter. She'll probably just _____ them!

B. I KNOW THE ANSWER, BUT WHAT'S THE QUESTION?

(Answers on p. 221)
Read the answer and place a check next to the correct question.

CD-A: TRACK 24

1.

The answer is...

Yes, I've never seen anything so cheesy!

Questions:
☐ I hear that Nancy has a beautiful home!
☐ Did you see Nancy's new furniture?
☐ Did you meet Nancy parents yesterday?

2.

The answer is...

No, it was like pulling teeth!

Questions:
☐ Did you go to the party?
☐ Was the restaurant good last night?
☐ Was it easy getting Mike to drive you to the airport?

3.

The answer is...

Yes, we finally had it out! Now everything is better between us.

Questions:
☐ Did you and Steve ever become friends again?
☐ Did you see the new movie yet?
☐ Did you and Ted enjoy the play?

4.

The answer is...

No, she really bugs me!

Questions:
☐ How did your mother like her birthday present?
☐ Did you invite Louise to your party?
☐ Is that your baby sister?

5.

The answer is...

Big time!

Questions:
☐ Did you like the movie?
☐ How are your parents doing?
☐ What are you going to do on your vacation?

6.

The answer is...

No, she's as blind as a bat.

Questions:
☐ Was your mother ever able to get a driver's license?
☐ Did your mother ever get a new cat? I heard her old one ran away.
☐ Did your mother return from her trip yet? I heard she went to Africa!

C. FIND YOUR PERFECT MATCH *(Answers on p. 221)*

Write the number of the slang term or idiom from COLUMN A next to its matching picture in COLUMN B as well as next to the matching definition in COLUMN C.

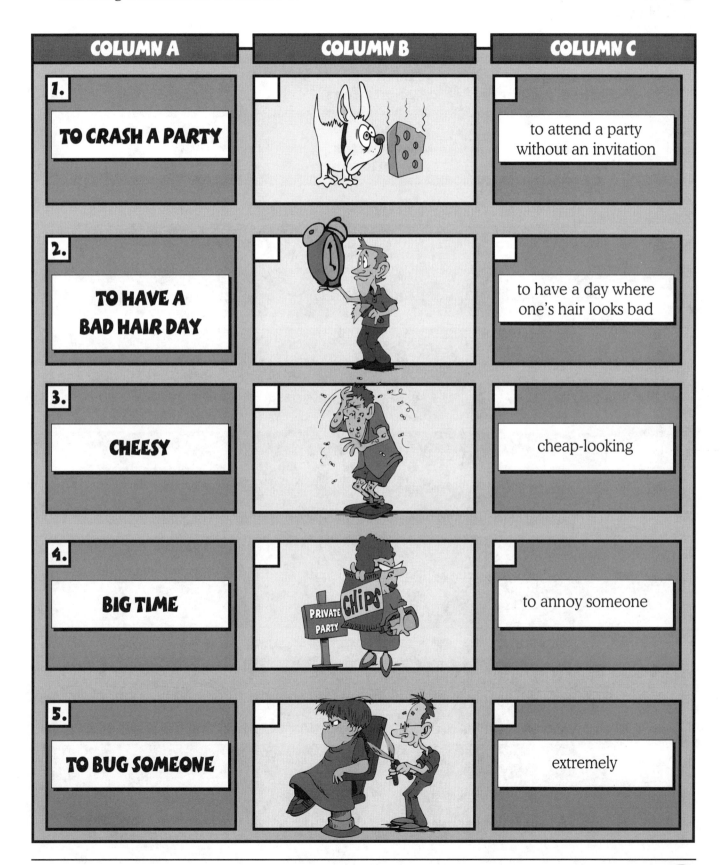

COLUMN A	COLUMN B	COLUMN C
1. TO CRASH A PARTY		to attend a party without an invitation
2. TO HAVE A BAD HAIR DAY		to have a day where one's hair looks bad
3. CHEESY		cheap-looking
4. BIG TIME		to annoy someone
5. TO BUG SOMEONE		extremely

D. IMAGINE THAT... *(Answers on p. 221)*

Someone has presented you with a situation as seen below. Respond to each situation aloud by making a complete sentence using one of the groups of words below. Use each group only once.

✔ big time ✔ crashed the party	✔ head over heels ✔ had it out	✔ blind as a bat ✔ artsy-fartsy
✔ big time ✔ had it out ✔ like pulling teeth	✔ bone to pick ✔ hard time swallowing	✔ bad hair day ✔ bug ✔ cheesy

IMAGINE THAT...

1. You and a friend are at a party together when someone you don't like arrives.

IMAGINE THAT...

2. Your best friend invites you the movies but you don't want to go because she already invited Marcy to come along.

IMAGINE THAT...

3. You're talking to your friend about the new neighbors.

IMAGINE THAT...

4. You're describing what happened in school today between you and another student.

IMAGINE THAT...

5. Your friend just asked you how your vacation was. Describe what happened at the hotel.

IMAGINE THAT...

6. You overheard an argument between two friends. Describe what they were arguing about.

Body Parts Used in Slang Expressions

Body parts are used in a variety of imaginative slang expressions in American slang.

Make no bones about it! *(Let's not be vague it!)* If you're **an old hand** *(a long-time expert)* at using slang, you know that there is quite a list of expressions using parts of the body:

ARM

cost an arm and a leg (to) *exp.* to be very expensive.

> **EXAMPLE:** My new computer **cost an arm and a leg**!
>
> **TRANSLATION:** My new computer **was very expensive**.
>
> **"REAL SPEAK":** My new c'mpuder **cost 'n arm 'n a leg**!

keep someone at arm's length (to) *exp.* to keep someone at a distance.

> **EXAMPLE:** I **keep John at arm's length** because I don't trust him.
>
> **TRANSLATION:** I **keep John at a distance** because I don't trust him.
>
> **"REAL SPEAK":** I **keep John 'it arm's length** b'cause I don't trust 'im.

twist someone's arm (to) *exp.* to force someone to do something.

> **EXAMPLE:** If you don't want to go to the movies with me, just say so. No one's **twisting your arm**!
>
> **TRANSLATION:** If you don't want to go to the movies with me, just say so. No one's **forcing you**!

> **"REAL SPEAK":** If ya don't wanna go da the movies with me, jus' say so. No one's **twisting yer arm**!

BACK

back-breaking (to be) *exp.* to be very physically difficult.

> **EXAMPLE:** I need to get a new job where the work isn't so **back-breaking**.
>
> **TRANSLATION:** I need to get a new job where the work isn't so **physically difficult**.
>
> **"REAL SPEAK":** I need ta ged a new job where the work isn't so **back-breaking**.

behind someone's back (to do something) *exp.* to do something without one's knowledge.

> **EXAMPLE:** I just found out that Stephanie has been **saying nasty things about me behind my back**!
>
> **TRANSLATION:** I just found out that Stephanie has been **saying nasty things about me without my knowledge**!
>
> **"REAL SPEAK":** I jus' found out th't Stephanie's been **saying nasty things about me behin' my back**!

get off someone's back (to) *exp.* to stop nagging someone.

> **EXAMPLE:** You always criticize the clothes I wear. I wish you'd **get off my back**!
>
> **TRANSLATION:** You always criticize the clothes I wear. I wish you'd **stop nagging me**!

"REAL SPEAK": Ya always criticize the clothes I wear. I wish ya'd **ged off my back**!

roll off one's back (to) *exp.* not to affect one.

EXAMPLE: If Sylvia says anything insulting to you, **let it roll off your back**.

TRANSLATION: If Sylvia says anything insulting to you, **don't let it affect you**.

"REAL SPEAK": If Sylvia says anything insulting ta you, **led it roll off yer back**.

"You scratch my back, I'll scratch yours" *exp.* "You do me a favor, I'll do you a favor."

EXAMPLE: I'll be glad to help you get your work done on time, but next week I'm going to need your help, too. **You scratch my back, I'll scratch yours**.

TRANSLATION: I'll be glad to help you get your work done on time, but next week I'm going to need your help, too. **You do me a favor, I'll do you a favor**.

"REAL SPEAK": A'll be glad da help ya get cher work done on time, b't next week I'm gonna need jer help, too. **You scratch my back, a'll scratch yours**.

BONE

bare bone essentials *exp.* the absolute necessities.

EXAMPLE: You need to evacuate your house immediately. The fire is getting closer. You only have time to take the **bare bone essentials** with you.

TRANSLATION: You need to evacuate your house immediately. The fire is getting closer. You only have time to take the **absolute necessities** with you.

"REAL SPEAK": Ya need ta evacuate cher house immediately. The fire's gedding closer. Ya only have time ta take the **bare bone essentials** with you.

bone to pick with someone (to have a) *exp.* to have a personal complaint to discuss with someone.

EXAMPLE: I **have a bone to pick with you**. I just found out that you lied to me.

TRANSLATION: I **have a personal complaint to discuss with you**. I just found out that you lied to me.

"REAL SPEAK": I **have a bone ta pick with you**. I jus' found out th't you lied ta me.

bone up (to) *exp.* to study or practice.

EXAMPLE: I need **to bone up** on my Italian before the test tomorrow.

TRANSLATION: I need **to study** my Italian before the test tomorrow.

"REAL SPEAK": I need **ta bone up** on my Italian b'fore the test tamorrow.

bony *adj.* extremely thin to the point where one's bones show.

EXAMPLE: Nancy needs to start eating more. She's so **bony**!

TRANSLATION: Nancy needs to start eating more. She's so **thin**!

"REAL SPEAK": Nancy needs ta start eading more. She's so **bony**!

feel something in one's bones (to) *exp.* to have a strong intuition about something.

EXAMPLE: Something terrible has happened to him. I **feel it in my bones**.

TRANSLATION: Something terrible has happened to him. I **have a strong intuition about it**.

"REAL SPEAK": Something terr'ble's happened to 'im. I **feel id in my bones**.

no bones about something (to make) *exp.* not to be vague.

EXAMPLE: John **made no bones about** telling Michelle that he had met another woman.

TRANSLATION: John **wasn't vague** about telling Michelle that he had met another woman.

"REAL SPEAK": John **made no bones about** telling Michelle thad 'e'd med another woman.

nothing but skin and bones (to be) *exp.* to be extremely thin.

EXAMPLE: You're **nothing but skin and bones**! Have you been sick?

TRANSLATION: You're **so thin I can see your bones**! Have you been sick?

"REAL SPEAK": Y'r **nothing b't skin 'n bones**! Have you been sick?

work one's fingers to the bone (to) *exp.* to work extremely hard.

EXAMPLE: With nine children, my parents **work their fingers to the bone** around the house to keep it clean.

TRANSLATION: With nine children, my parents **work extremely hard** around the house to keep it clean.

"REAL SPEAK": With nine children, my parents **work their fingers ta the bone** aroun' the house ta keep it clean.

BRAIN

brain (to be a) *n.* to be a genius.

EXAMPLE: My little brother is a **brain**. He already understands chemistry.

TRANSLATION: My little brother is a **genius**. He already understands chemistry.

"REAL SPEAK": My liddle brother's a **brain**. He already understands chemistry.

Variation: **brainy** *adj.* very intelligent.

pick someone's brain (to) *exp.* to question someone for advice or information.

EXAMPLE: I need to **pick your brain** about how to find a reasonable apartment in Los Angeles.

TRANSLATION: I need to **question you for advice** on how to find a reasonable apartment in Los Angeles.

"REAL SPEAK": I need ta **pick yer brain** about how da find a reasonable apartment in Los Angeles.

rack one's brain[s] (to) *exp.* to strain in order to remember something or arrive at a solution to a problem.

EXAMPLE: I've been **racking my brain[s]** for a half hour and I still can't think of that girl's name!

TRANSLATION: I've been **straining to remember** for a half hour and I still can't think of that girl's name!

"REAL SPEAK": I've been **racking my brain[s]** fer a half hour 'n I still can't think 'ev that girl's name!

scatterbrained *adj.* forgetful, incapable of connected thought.

EXAMPLE: I'm so **scatterbrained** today. I can't remember where I left my reading glasses.

TRANSLATION: I'm so **forgetful** today. I can't remember where I left my reading glasses.

"REAL SPEAK": I'm so **scadderbrained** taday. I can't remember where I left my reading glasses.

CHEEK

tongue in cheek *exp.* jokingly, insincerely.

EXAMPLE: Carla said that she thought my dress was unique, but she said it **tongue in cheek**.

TRANSLATION: Carla said that she thought my dress was unique, but she said it **jokingly**.

"REAL SPEAK": Carla said th't she thought my dress w'z unique, but she said it **tongue 'n cheek**.

turn the other cheek (to) *exp.* to ignore an offense.

EXAMPLE: Phil said something insulting to me, but I decided to **turn the other cheek** and remain friendly.

TRANSLATION: Phil said something insulting to me, but I decided to **ignore it and remain** friendly.

"REAL SPEAK": Phil said something insulting ta me, b'd I decided ta **turn the other cheek** 'n remain friendly.

CHEST

off one's chest (to get something) *exp.* to express something that is causing one to be upset.

> **EXAMPLE:** I have to **get something off my chest**. When you were an hour late picking me up at the airport, I was really angry.
>
> **TRANSLATION:** I have to **express why I'm so upset**. When you were an hour late picking me up at the airport, I was really angry.
>
> **"REAL SPEAK":** I hafta **get something off my chest**. When you were 'n hour late picking me up the airport, I w'z really angry.

EAR

all ears (to be) *exp.* to listen intently.

> **EXAMPLE:** What happened between Joan and Steve? I'm **all ears**.
>
> **TRANSLATION:** What happened between Joan and Steve? I'm **listening intently**.
>
> **"REAL SPEAK":** What happened b'tween Joan 'n Steve? I'm **all ears**.

ear for music (to have an) *exp.* to have an aptitude for music.

> **EXAMPLE:** Leon really **has an ear for music**. He started his cello lessons a month ago and he can already play entire pieces!
>
> **TRANSLATION:** Leon really **has an aptitude for music**. He started his cello lessons a month ago and he can already play entire pieces!
>
> **"REAL SPEAK":** Leon really **has 'n ear fer music**. He starded 'is cello lessons a month ago an' 'e c'n already play entire pieces!

go in one ear and out the other (to) *exp.* to be ignored, to go unheard.

> **EXAMPLE:** Everything you say to Connie **goes in one ear and out the other**.
>
> **TRANSLATION:** Everything you say to Connie **goes unheard**.
>
> **"REAL SPEAK":** Ev'rything ya say da Connie **goes in one ear 'n out the other**.

play by ear (to) *exp.* to improvise, to play a song on an instrument simply by having heard it previously.

> **EXAMPLE:** I love playing the piano but I don't know how to read music. I can only **play by ear**.
>
> **TRANSLATION:** I love playing the piano but I don't know how to read music. I can only **play a song that I've heard before**.
>
> **"REAL SPEAK":** I love playing the piano b'd I don't know how da read music. I c'n only **play by ear**.
>
> *Note:* This expression is also used outside the music world, carrying the definition "to improvise" or "not to make any specific plans." For example: *I'd love to go out to dinner with you, but I don't know what time I'm leaving work today. We'll just have to play it by ear; I'd love to go out to dinner with you, but I don't know what time I'm leaving work today. We'll just have to improvise.*

talk someone's ear off (to) *exp.* to talk endlessly to someone.

> **EXAMPLE:** Every time Darlene stops me in the street, she **talks my ear off**!
>
> **TRANSLATION:** Every time Darlene stops me in the street, she **talks to me endlessly**!
>
> **"REAL SPEAK":** Ev'ry time Darlene stops me 'n the street, she **talks my ear off**!

wet behind the ears (to be) *exp.* to be young and inexperienced.

> **EXAMPLE:** Tim is **wet behind the ears**, but in another few years I'm sure he'll be ready for a promotion.
>
> **TRANSLATION:** Tim is **young and inexperienced**, but in another few years I'm sure he'll be ready for a promotion.
>
> **"REAL SPEAK":** Tim's **wet behind the ears**, bud 'n another few years I'm sher 'e'll be ready fer a pruhmotion.

ELBOW

elbow grease *exp.* extra force applied to a physical job.

EXAMPLE: You'll never get that floor clean wiping so lightly. You need to **put some elbow grease into it**.

TRANSLATION: You'll never get that floor clean wiping so lightly. You need to **apply more force**.

"REAL SPEAK": You'll never get that floor clean wiping so lightly. Ya need ta **put s'm' elbow grease into it**.

elbow room (to give someone) *exp.* to give someone physical space.

EXAMPLE: I can't fix this computer with you standing so close. Give me some **elbow room**!

TRANSLATION: I can't fix this computer with you standing so close. Give me some **physical space**!

"REAL SPEAK": I can't fix this c'mpuder with you standing so close. Gimme s'm **elbow room**!

rub elbows with someone (to) *exp.* to socialize with someone.

EXAMPLE: Kim **rubs elbows with** movie stars and politicians.

TRANSLATION: Kim **socializes with** movie stars and politicians.

"REAL SPEAK": Kim **rubs elbows with** movie stars 'n politicians.

EYE

catch one's eye (to) *exp.* to attract someone's attention.

EXAMPLE: There's Shelly! Try to **catch her eye**!

TRANSLATION: There's Shelly! Try to **get her attention**!

"REAL SPEAK": There's Shelly! Try da **catch 'er eye**!

eye for something (to have an) *exp.* to show good taste, to be discerning.

EXAMPLE: Irene's house is so beautiful. She really **has an eye for** furniture.

TRANSLATION: Irene's house is so beautiful. She really **shows good taste in** furniture.

"REAL SPEAK": Irene's house is so beaudiful. She really **has 'n eye fer** furniture.

eyesore *n.* ugly thing or person (so much that it hurts the eye).

EXAMPLE: Did you see the statue Laura put in her living room? What an **eyesore**!

TRANSLATION: Did you see the statue Laura put in her living room? What an **ugly thing**!

"REAL SPEAK": Did'ja see the statue Laura pud in 'er living room? What 'n **eyesore**!

give someone a black eye (to) *exp.* to bruise someone's eye, usually through a punch.

EXAMPLE: When my girlfriend found out that I was seeing someone else, she gave me a **black eye**.

TRANSLATION: When my girlfriend found out that I was seeing someone else, she gave me a **bruised eye**.

"REAL SPEAK": When my girlfriend found out th'd I w'z seeing someone else, she gamme a **black eye**.

give someone the eye (to) *exp.* to look at someone with romantic interest.

EXAMPLE: That guy over there is **giving you the eye**. Go talk to him!

TRANSLATION: That guy over there is **looking at you with romantic interest**. Go talk to him!

"REAL SPEAK": That guy over there's **giving you the eye**. Go talk to 'im!

in the public eye *exp.* to have the attention of the public.

EXAMPLE: Politicians are constantly **in the public eye**.

TRANSLATION: Politicians constantly **have the attention of the public**.

"REAL SPEAK": Politicians'er constantly **in the public eye**.

keep an eye on someone (to) *exp.* to watch someone carefully.

EXAMPLE:	Keep an eye on Johnathan. I don't trust him.
TRANSLATION:	Watch Johnathan carefully. I don't trust him.
"REAL SPEAK":	Keep 'n eye on Johnathan. I don't trust 'im.

keep an eye out for someone (to) *exp.* to watch for someone's arrival.

EXAMPLE:	Keep an eye out for Greg. He should be here very soon.
TRANSLATION:	Watch for Greg's arrival. He should be here very soon.
"REAL SPEAK":	Keep 'n eye out fer Greg. He should be here very soon.

keep one's eyes peeled (to) *exp.* to watch carefully for someone or something.

EXAMPLE:	Keep your eyes peeled and let me know if you see my mom coming. I don't want her to see her birthday present before it's wrapped.
TRANSLATION:	Watch carefully and let me know if you see my mom coming. I don't want her to see her birthday present before it's wrapped.
"REAL SPEAK":	Keep yer eyes peeled 'n lemme know if ya see my mom coming. I don't wan' 'er da see 'er birthday present b'fore it's wrapped.

pull the wool over someone's eyes (to) *exp.* to deceive someone.

EXAMPLE:	I hired Sandy because her resume shows that she's had years of experience. She really pulled the wool over my eyes.
TRANSLATION:	I hired Sandy because her resume shows that she's had years of experience. She really deceived me.
"REAL SPEAK":	I hired Sandy b'cause 'er resume shows th't she's had years 'ev experience. She really pulled the wool over my eyes.

"There's more here than meets the eye" *exp.* "There's something happening here that's not yet obvious."

EXAMPLE:	Why is Ann being so nice to me? There's more here than meets the eye.

TRANSLATION:	Why is Ann being so nice to me? There's something happening here that's not yet obvious.
"REAL SPEAK":	Why's Ann being so nice ta me? There's more here th'n meets the eye.

FINGER

finger-pointing *exp.* placing of blame.

EXAMPLE:	When I asked everyone who was responsible for the project being late, there was a lot of finger-pointing.
TRANSLATION:	When I asked everyone who was responsible for the project being late, there was a lot of placing of blame.
"REAL SPEAK":	When I ast ev'ryone who w'z responsible fer the project being late, there w'z a lod 'ev finger-poin'ing.

keep one's fingers crossed (to) *exp.* to keep hoping for something.

EXAMPLE:	I'll keep my fingers crossed that you get the job!
TRANSLATION:	I'll keep hoping that you get the job!
"REAL SPEAK":	I'll keep my fingers crossed th't chu get the job!
Note:	When a person uses this expression, he/she may actually hold up two crossed fingers briefly as a show of support.

lift a finger (not to) *exp.* not to do any work.

EXAMPLE:	I spent five hours cleaning the house today and Earl didn't lift a finger!

TRANSLATION:	I spent five hours cleaning the house today and Earl **didn't do anything**!
"REAL SPEAK":	I spent five hours cleaning the house taday 'n Earl **didn' lift a finger**!

one's finger on something (to put) *exp.* to arrive at a correct conclusion.

EXAMPLE:	You just **put your finger on it**! Bob is acting strangely because he's planning a surprise party for my birthday!
TRANSLATION:	You just **arrived at a correct conclusion**! Bob is acting strangely because he's planning a surprise party for my birthday!
"REAL SPEAK":	Ya jus' **put cher finger on it**! Bob's acting strangely b'cause 'e's planning a serprise pardy fer my birthday!

FOOT

back on one's feet (to be/get) *exp.* • **1.** to recover from an illness • **2.** to reestablish oneself after a failure.

EXAMPLE 1:	I was sick for two weeks. I'm glad to be **back on my feet again**.
TRANSLATION:	I was sick for two weeks. I'm glad to be **recovered**.
"REAL SPEAK":	I w'z sick fer two weeks. I'm glad ta be **back on my feed again**.
EXAMPLE 2:	Having to declare bankruptcy was very difficult and emotional for me. But I'll be **back on my feet** soon.
TRANSLATION:	Having to declare bankruptcy was very difficult and emotional for me. But I'll **reestablish myself** soon.
"REAL SPEAK":	Having ta declare bankruptcy w'z very difficult 'n emotional fer me. B'd a'll be **back on my feet** soon.

cold feet (to get) *exp.* to lose one's courage.

EXAMPLE:	Go into the boss's office right now and ask him for a raise before you **get cold feet**!
TRANSLATION:	Go into the boss's office right now and ask him for a raise before you **lose your courage**!
"REAL SPEAK":	Go inta the boss's office right now 'n ask 'im fer a raise b'fore ya **get cold feet**!

get a foot in the door (to) *exp.* to take the first step in attaining one's goal.

EXAMPLE:	I finally **got my foot in the door** at the movie studio. I'm starting as a receptionist and hope to work my way up to producer.
TRANSLATION:	I finally **achieved my first step in working** at the movie studio. I'm starting as a receptionist and hope to work my way up to producer.
"REAL SPEAK":	I fin'lly **got my foot 'n the door** 'it the movie studio. I'm starding as a receptionist 'n hope ta work my way up ta pruhducer.

get off on the wrong foot (to) *exp.* to begin negatively.

EXAMPLE:	The professor and I **got off on the wrong foot**. On the first day of class, we got into a big argument.
TRANSLATION:	The professor and I **began our relationship negatively**. On the first day of class, we got into a big argument.
"REAL SPEAK":	The pruhfessor 'n I **god off on the wrong foot**. On the firs' day 'ev class, we god into a big argument.

lead foot (to have a) *exp.* said of a driver who has a tendency to drive fast (as if his/her foot were made of lead, causing the accelerator to be pressed all the way down).

EXAMPLE:	You drove from Los Angeles to San Francisco in only five hours? You must really **have a lead foot**!
TRANSLATION:	You drove from Los Angeles to San Francisco in only five hours? You must really **have a tendency to drive fast**!
"REAL SPEAK":	You drove fr'm L.A. da San Francisco 'n only five hours? You must really **have a lead foot**!

one foot in the grave (to have) *exp.* to be close to death.

> **EXAMPLE:** You'd better go visit Bill while you can. **He has one foot in the grave.**
>
> **TRANSLATION:** You'd better go visit Bill while you can. **He's close to death.**
>
> **"REAL SPEAK":** Ya'd better go visit Bill while ya can. **He has one food in the grave.**

put one's foot down (to) *exp.* to become firm and uncompromising about something.

> **EXAMPLE:** You broke my favorite vase?! I'm **putting my foot down.** You're not allowed to play in the house anymore!
>
> **TRANSLATION:** You broke my favorite vast?! I'm **going to be firm and uncompromising.** You're not allowed to play in the house anymore!
>
> **"REAL SPEAK":** You broke my fav'rite vase?! I'm **puddng my foot down.** Y'r nod allowed ta play 'n the house anymore!

put one's foot in one's mouth (to) *exp.* to say something unintentionally embarrassing.

> **EXAMPLE:** I told Carrie that she had the most beautiful teeth. Then she told me that they're actually dentures! I have a habit of **putting my foot in my mouth.**
>
> **TRANSLATION:** I told Carrie that she had the most beautiful teeth. Then she told me that they're actually dentures! I have a habit of **saying things that are unintentionally embarrassing.**
>
> **"REAL SPEAK":** I told Carrie th't she had the most beaudiful teeth. Then she told me that they're akshully dentures! I have a habid 'ev **pudding my food in my mouth.**
>
> *Variation:* **foot-in-mouth disease (to have)** *exp.* to have a habit of saying things that are unintentionally embarrassing.

stand on one's own two feet (to) *exp.* to support oneself financially, to be self-reliant.

> **EXAMPLE:** After relying on his parents for twenty years, Dan can finally **stand on his own two feet.**
>
> **TRANSLATION:** After relying on his parents for twenty years, Dan can finally **support himself.**
>
> **"REAL SPEAK":** After relying on 'is parents fer twen'y years, Dan c'n fin'lly **stand on 'is own two feet.**

swept off one's feet (to be) *exp.* to be overwhelmed romantically.

> **EXAMPLE:** When I met your father, **he swept me off my feet!**
>
> **TRANSLATION:** When I met your father, **I was overwhelmed romantically!**
>
> **"REAL SPEAK":** When I met cher father, **he swept me off my feet!**

"The shoe is on the other foot" *exp.* "The reverse situation is happening."

> **EXAMPLE:** Bob used to be my boss, but he got demoted. Now I'm his boss. Suddenly **the shoe is on the other foot!**
>
> **TRANSLATION:** Bob used to be my boss, but he got demoted. Now I'm his boss. Suddenly **the situation is reversed!**
>
> **"REAL SPEAK":** Bob usta be my boss, bud 'e got demoded. Now I'm 'is boss. Suddenly **the shoe's on the other foot!**

GUTS

gut (to get a) *exp.* to get a fat stomach.

> **EXAMPLE:** I can't believe how much cake you just ate. If you're not careful, you're going to **get a gut.**
>
> **TRANSLATION:** I can't believe how much cake you just ate. If you're not careful, you're going to **get a fat stomach.**
>
> **"REAL SPEAK":** I can't b'lieve how much cake you just ate. If y'r not careful, y'r gonna **ged a gut.**

gut reaction *exp.* instinctive and initial response.

> **EXAMPLE:** When I first met David, my **gut reaction** was that he is one of the nicest and most intelligent people I've ever met.

TRANSLATION: When I first met David, my **first response** was that he is one of the nicest and most intelligent people I've ever met.

"REAL SPEAK": When I first met David, my **gut reaction** w'z thad 'e's one 'a the nicest 'n most intelligent people I've ever met.

guts to do something (not to have the) *exp.* not to have the courage.

EXAMPLE: I **don't have the guts** to tell Ed that he's fired. Why don't you do it for me?

TRANSLATION: I **don't have the courage** to tell Ed that he's fired. Why don't you do it for me?

"REAL SPEAK": I **don't have the guts** ta tell Ed th'd 'e's fired. Why doncha do it for me?

Variation: **gutsy (to be)** *adj.* to be fearless, bold.

hate someone's guts (to) *exp.* to hate someone intensely.

EXAMPLE: I **hate Robert's guts** for cheating me!

TRANSLATION: I **hate Robert intensely** for cheating me!

"REAL SPEAK": I **hate Robert's guts** fer cheading me!

HAIR

hairy *adj.* scarey.

EXAMPLE: That car almost hit us! That was really **hairy**!

TRANSLATION: That car almost hit us! That was really **scarey**!

"REAL SPEAK": That car almost hid us! That w'z really **hairy**!

let one's hair down (to) *exp.* to let go of one's inhibitions.

EXAMPLE: At work, Jennifer is very serious. But at the office party, she was hilarious and danced all night! She really knows how to **let her hair down**.

TRANSLATION: At work, Jennifer is very serious. But at the office party, she was hilarious and danced all night! She really knows how to **let go of her inhibitions**.

"REAL SPEAK": At work, Jennifer's very serious. B'd 'it the office pardy, she w'z hilarious 'n danced all night! She really knows how da **led 'er hair down**.

make someone's hair stand on end (to) *exp.* to horrify someone.

EXAMPLE: When I heard about Becky's ordeal with the burglar, it **made my hair stand on end**.

TRANSLATION: When I heard about Becky's ordeal with the burglar, it **horrified me**.

"REAL SPEAK": [no change]

split hairs (to) *exp.* to argue about trivial details.

EXAMPLE: We could have signed the contract hours ago but the other side started **splitting hairs**.

TRANSLATION: We could have signed the contract hours ago but the other side started **arguing about trivial details**.

"REAL SPEAK": We could'ev signed the contract hours ago b't the other side starded **splidding hairs**.

HAND

catch someone red-handed (to) *exp.* to catch someone in the act of doing something unacceptable.

EXAMPLE: I **caught Frank red-handed** stealing pens from my desk.

TRANSLATION: I **caught Frank in the act of** stealing pens from my desk.

"REAL SPEAK": I **caught Frank red-handed** stealing pens fr'm my desk.

give someone a hand (to) *exp.* • **1.** to help someone • **2.** to give someone applause.

EXAMPLE 1: Can you **give me a hand** with this heavy box?

TRANSLATION:	Can you **help me** with this heavy box?
"REAL SPEAK":	C'n ya **gimme a hand** with this heavy box?
EXAMPLE 2:	Ladies and gentlemen, please welcome Jack Burke. Let's **give him a hand**!
TRANSLATION:	Ladies and gentlemen, please welcome Jack Burke. Let's **give him some applause**!
"REAL SPEAK":	Ladies 'n gen'lemen, please welcome Jack Burke. Let's **give 'im a hand**!

hand (to) *v.* to give.

EXAMPLE:	Could you **hand** me that hammer, please?
TRANSLATION:	Could you **give** me that hammer, please?
"REAL SPEAK":	Could'ja **han'** me that hammer, please?

Variation: **hand over something (to)** *exp.* • to surrender something • *Hand it over!; Give it to me!*

hand it to someone (to) *exp.* to give someone credit.

EXAMPLE:	I have to **hand it to you**. The presentation you gave this morning was fantastic.
TRANSLATION:	I have to **give you credit**. The presentation you gave this morning was fantastic.
"REAL SPEAK":	I hafta **hand it ta you**. The presentation ya gave this morning w'z fantastic.

hand-me-down *exp.* something pre-owned that is given or "handed down" to someone.

EXAMPLE:	Debbie wears nothing but **hand-me-downs** because she can't afford to buy new clothing.
TRANSLATION:	Debbie wears nothing but **pre-owned clothes** because she can't afford to buy new clothing.
"REAL SPEAK":	Debbie wears nothing b't **han'-me-downs** b'cause she can' afford ta buy new clothing.

hands down *exp.* • **1.** unquestionably • **2.** effortlessly.

EXAMPLE 1:	This is **hands down** the best restaurant I've ever been to.

TRANSLATION:	This is **unquestionably** the best restaurant I've ever been to.
"REAL SPEAK":	This 'ez **han's down** the best resterant I've ever been to.
EXAMPLE 2:	Paul won the election **hands down**.
TRANSLATION:	Paul won the election **effortlessly**.
"REAL SPEAK":	Paul won the election **han's down**.

have one's hands full (to) *exp.* to be very busy.

EXAMPLE:	**I have my hands full** raising a family. I don't have any time to do anything else.
TRANSLATION:	**I'm very busy** raising a family. I don't have any time to do anything else.
"REAL SPEAK":	**I have my han's full** raising a fam'ly. I don't have any time ta do anything else.

have the upper hand (to) *exp.* to be in a superior position.

EXAMPLE:	Bob always used to order me around. But now that I've been promoted to manager, **I finally have the upper hand**.
TRANSLATION:	Bob always used to order me around. But now that I've been promoted to manager, **I'm finally in a superior position**.
"REAL SPEAK":	Bob always usta order me around. B't now th'd I've been pruhmoded ta manager, **I fin'ly have the upper hand**.

in good hands (to be) *exp.* to be well taken care of by someone.

EXAMPLE:	**You're in good hands with** Mr. Johnson. He's our best car salesperson.
TRANSLATION:	**You'll be well taken care of by** Mr. Johnson. He's our best car salesperson.
"REAL SPEAK":	**Y'r 'n good han's with** Mr. Johnson. He's 'ar best car salesperson.

know something like the back of one's hand (to) *exp.* to know something exceptionally well.

EXAMPLE:	We're not lost. I **know this city like the back of my hand**.
TRANSLATION:	We're not lost. I **know this city exceptionally well**.
"REAL SPEAK":	W'r not lost. I **know this cidy like the back 'a my hand**.

on hand (to be) *exp.* to be in one's possession, available.

EXAMPLE:	We need to send two hundred books to Japan right away. How many books do we have **on hand**?
TRANSLATION:	We need to send two hundred books to Japan right away. How many books do we have **in our possession**?
"REAL SPEAK":	We need ta sen' two hundred books ta Japan ride away. How many books do we have **on hand**?

on [the] one hand... on the other hand... *exp.* a comparison of two options or points of view.

EXAMPLE:	**On [the] one hand**, George is a very nice guy. **On the other hand**, he's not a very good worker
TRANSLATION:	**One consideration is that** George is a very nice guy. **The other is that** he's not a very good worker.
"REAL SPEAK":	**On [the] one hand**, George 'ez a very nice guy. **On the other hand**, he's nod a very good worker

out of hand (to be) *exp.* to be out of control.

EXAMPLE:	The crowds were already **out of hand** by the time the police arrived.
TRANSLATION:	The crowds were already **out of control** by the time the police arrived.
"REAL SPEAK":	The crowds were already **oud 'ev han'** by the time the police arrived.

pay someone a back-handed compliment (to) *exp.* to give someone a compliment that is insulting at the same time.

| EXAMPLE: | Larry **paid me a back-handed compliment**. He said that I look great since I've been on my diet and that I'm not nearly as fat as I used to be! |

| TRANSLATION: | Larry **paid me a compliment and insulted me at the same time**. He said that I look great since I've been on my diet and that I'm not nearly as fat as I used to be! |
| "REAL SPEAK": | Larry **paid me a back-handed compliment**. He said th'd I look great since I've been on my diet 'n thad I'm not nearly 'ez fat 'ez I usta be! |

second-hand *adj.* • **1.** previously owned, used • **2.** indirectly, from someone else.

EXAMPLE 1:	Phil can only afford **second-hand** clothing.
TRANSLATION:	Phil can only afford **used** clothing.
"REAL SPEAK":	Phil c'n only afford **secon-hand** clothing.
EXAMPLE 2:	I can't be sure about this, but I heard Jim is getting married! I heard it **second-hand**, so I could be wrong.
TRANSLATION:	I can't be sure about this, but I heard Jim is getting married! I heard it **from someone else**, so I could be wrong.
"REAL SPEAK":	I can't be sher about this, b'd I heard Jim's gedding married! I heard it **secon'-hand**, so I could be wrong.

short-handed *exp.* to be lacking an efficient number of workers or helpers.

EXAMPLE:	I'm not going to be able to take lunch today because we're **short-handed**. Half our employees called in sick!
TRANSLATION:	I'm not going to be able to take lunch today because we're **lacking personnel**. Half our employees called in sick!
"REAL SPEAK":	I'm not gonna be able da take lunch taday b'cause w'r **short-handed**. Half 'ar employees called in sick!

show of hands (a) *exp.* a counting of people who raise their hands.

| EXAMPLE: | Let's take a vote. How many people want to raise the dues for our club. I'd like **to see a show of hands**. |
| TRANSLATION: | Let's take a vote. How many people want to raise the dues for our club. I'd like **you to raise your hands so that I can count**. |

| "REAL SPEAK": | Let's take a vote. How many people wanna raise the dues fer 'ar club. I'd like **ta see a show 'ev hands**. |

"Talk to the hand!" *exp. (very popular among younger generations)* "I'm not listening to you."

EXAMPLE:	That's a lot of nonsense. **Talk to the hand!**
TRANSLATION:	That's a lot of nonsense. **I'm not listening to you!**
"REAL SPEAK":	That's a lod 'a nonsense. **Talk ta the hand!**
Note:	This is an abbreviation of the expression, *Talk to the hand because the ears aren't listening*. The person using this expression typically turns his/her head away from the person and holds up a hand with the palm facing the other person.

try one's hand at something (to) *exp.* to test one's ability at something.

EXAMPLE:	I've decided that I'm going to **try my hand at** being an author.
TRANSLATION:	I've decided that I'm going to **attempt** being an author.
"REAL SPEAK":	I've decided th'd I'm gonna **try my hand 'it** being 'n author.

underhand[ed] *exp.* dishonest.

EXAMPLE:	I don't trust that car salesman. I think he's **underhand[ed]**.
TRANSLATION:	I don't trust that car salesman. I think he's **dishonest**.
"REAL SPEAK":	I don' trust that car salesman. I think 'e's **underhand[ed]**.

HEAD

airhead *n.* irresponsible and forgetful person.

EXAMPLE:	Betty left the water in her bathtub running all day. She's such an **airhead!**
TRANSLATION:	Betty left the water in her bathtub running all day. She's such an **irrespnsible and forgetful person!**
"REAL SPEAK":	Beddy left the wader in 'er bathtub running all day. She's such 'n **airhead!**

beat one's head against the wall (to) *exp.* to waste one's time trying to accomplish the impossible.

EXAMPLE:	I just can't seem to train my dog. I'm **beating my head against the wall**.
TRANSLATION:	I just can't seem to train my dog. I'm **wasting my time trying to accomplish the impossible**.
"REAL SPEAK":	I just can't seem ta train my dog. I'm **beading my head against the wall**.

big head (to have a) *exp.* to be conceited.

EXAMPLE:	Ever since Doug was on television, he's **gotten a big head**.
TRANSLATION:	Ever since Doug was on television, he's **become conceited**.
"REAL SPEAK":	Ever since Doug w'z on TV, he's **gotten a big head**.

bite someone's head off (to) *exp.* to explode with anger toward someone.

EXAMPLE:	When I asked Gene about his vacation, he **bit my head off** and said it was none of my business! I wonder what's really bothering him.
TRANSLATION:	When I asked Gene about his vacation, he **answered me angrily** and said it was none of my business! I wonder what's really bothering him.
"REAL SPEAK":	When I ast Gene aboud 'is vacation, he **bit my head off** 'n said it w'z none 'a my business! I wonder what's really bothering him.

come to a head (to) *exp.* to reach a final climactic and emotional level.

EXAMPLE:	Don and Richard never liked each other. Well, this morning **it came to a head** and they started fighting!
TRANSLATION:	Don and Richard never liked each other. Well, this morning **it reached a climax** and they started fighting!
"REAL SPEAK":	Don 'n Richard never liked each other. Well, th's morning **it came to a head** 'n they starded fighting!

get one's head above water (to) *exp.* to get out of trouble.

EXAMPLE:	I was drowning with all the work I had to do. I'm finally **getting my head above water**.
TRANSLATION:	I was drowning with all the work I had to do. I'm finally **getting caught up and out of trouble**.
"REAL SPEAK":	I w'z drowning with all the work I had ta do. I'm fin'lly **gedding my head above water**.

get something through someone's head (to) *exp.* to understand something after many attempts.

EXAMPLE:	When are you finally going to **get it through your head** that Betty doesn't want to see you again?
TRANSLATION:	When are you finally going to **understand** that Betty doesn't want to see you again?
"REAL SPEAK":	When're ya fin'lly gonna **ged it through yer head** th't Betty doesn' wanna see you again?

go to someone's head (to) *exp.* to make someone conceited.

EXAMPLE:	All the attention and fame **went to Susan's head**. She won't even speak to her old friends any more.
TRANSLATION:	All the attention and fame **made Susan conceited**. She won't even speak to her old friends any more.
"REAL SPEAK":	All the attention 'n fame **went ta Susan's head**. She won' even speak to 'er old friends any more.

hang over one's head (to) *exp.* to remain unsettled or uncompleted.

EXAMPLE:	I have a lot of work that's been **hanging over my head**. I'll be so relieved when it's all finished.
TRANSLATION:	I have a lot of work that's been **uncompleted**. I'll be so relieved when it's all finished.
"REAL SPEAK":	I have a lod 'a work that's been **hanging over my head**. A'll be so relieved when it's all finished.

"Heads are going to roll!" *exp.* "A lot of people are going to be in big trouble!"

| EXAMPLE: | When the boss finds out that we had lunch with his competitor, **heads are going to roll**. |

TRANSLATION:	When the boss finds out that we had lunch with his competitor, **we're going to be in big trouble**.
"REAL SPEAK":	When the boss finds out th't we had lunch with 'is c'mpedider, **heads'er gonna roll**.
Note:	This comes from a time in history when those acting against authority would be executed by having their heads cut off.

head out (to) *exp.* to leave.

EXAMPLE:	In order to get to the airport by one o'clock, we should **head out of** here around noon.
TRANSLATION:	In order to get to the airport by one o'clock, we should **leave** here around noon.
"REAL SPEAK":	In order da get ta the airport by one a'clock, we should **head oud 'ev** here aroun' noon.

"Heads up!" *exp.* • **1.** a warning used when something is flying toward you that could cause injury • **2.** warning, notification.

EXAMPLE 1:	**Heads up**!
TRANSLATION:	**Look upward**! You're in danger of being hit by something!
"REAL SPEAK":	[no change]
EXAMPLE 2:	Make sure to give everyone **a heads up** about the boss coming in today.
TRANSLATION:	Make sure to give everyone **warning** about the boss coming in today.
"REAL SPEAK":	Make sher da give ev'ryone **a heads up** about the boss coming in taday.

hit the nail on the head (to) *exp.* to arrive at a correct conclusion.

| EXAMPLE: | When you said that the reason Barry is nasty to me is because he's jealous, you **hit the nail on the head**. |
| TRANSLATION: | When you said that the reason Barry is nasty to me is because he's jealous, you **arrived at a correct conclusion**. |

"REAL SPEAK": When ya said that the reason Barry's nasty ta me is b'cause 'e's jealous, ya **hit the nail on the head**.

lose one's head (to) *exp.* to lose one's calm or ability to think clearly.

EXAMPLE: I never should have hired Bob to help me. I **lost my head**.

TRANSLATION: I never should have hired Bob to help me. I **wasn't thinking clearly**.

"REAL SPEAK": I never should'ev hired Bob ta help me. I **lost my head**.

off the top of one's head *exp.* an unofficial estimate.

EXAMPLE: **Off the top of my head**, I'd say there are about three thousand people here today.

TRANSLATION: **To give you an unofficial estimate**, I'd say there are about three thousand people here today.

"REAL SPEAK": **Off the top 'a my head**, I'd say there'er about three thousan' people here daday.

over one's head (to go) *exp.* • **1.** to be beyond one's comprehension • **2.** to appeal to a higher authority.

EXAMPLE 1: I didn't understand what the professor was talking about today. Everything **went over my head**.

TRANSLATION: I didn't understand what the professor was talking about today. Everything **went beyond my comprehension**.

"REAL SPEAK": I didn' understand what the pruhfessor w'z talking about taday. Ev'rything **wen' over my head**.

EXAMPLE 2: The manager of the store wouldn't give me a refund, so I **went over his head** and spoke directly to the owner.

TRANSLATION: The manager of the store wouldn't give me a refund, so I **appealed to a higher authority** and spoke directly to the owner.

"REAL SPEAK": The manager 'a the store wouldn't gimme a refund, so I **wen' over 'is head** 'n spoke directly ta the owner.

play head games (to) *exp.* to try to achieve something through psychological manipulation.

EXAMPLE: Don't **play head games with me**. Just tell me what you want and I'll tell you if I can do it for you.

TRANSLATION: Don't **try to manipulate me psychologically**. Just tell me what you want and I'll tell you if I can do it for you.

"REAL SPEAK": Don't **play head games with me**. Jus' tell me what chu want 'n a'll tell ya if I c'n do it for ya.

run around like a chicken with its head cut off (to) *exp.* to try frantically to do more things at one time than one is able.

EXAMPLE: You're **running around like a chicken with its head cut off**. You need to stop, organize, and do one task at a time.

TRANSLATION: You're **trying to do more things at one time than you can**. You need to stop, organize, and do one task at a time.

"REAL SPEAK": Y'r **running around like a chicken with its head cud off**. Ya need ta stop, organize, an' do one task 'id a time.

Note: This expression refers to the fact that after cutting off a chicken's head, the body often continues to run around frantically.

HEART

break someone's heart (to) *exp.* to make someone extremely sad.

EXAMPLE: When Christine left Patrick, she **broke his heart**.

TRANSLATION: When Christine left Patrick, she **made him extremely sad**.

"REAL SPEAK": When Christine left Patrick, she **broke 'is heart**.

cross one's heart [and hope to die] (to)
exp. to make a promise.

> **EXAMPLE:** I'll give you back the money you loaned me next week. **Cross my heart [and hope to die]**!

> **TRANSLATION:** I'll give you back the money you loaned me next week. **I promise**!

> **"REAL SPEAK":** A'll give ya back the money ya loaned me next week. **Cross my heart ['n hope ta die]**!

> *Note:* In this expression, it is common to drop the personal pronoun "I" (*I cross my heart [and hope to die!]*).

eat one's heart out (to) *exp.* to be envious.

> **EXAMPLE:** Tim is going to **eat his heart out** when he sees my new car.

> **TRANSLATION:** Tim is going to **be very envious** when he sees my new car.

> **"REAL SPEAK":** Tim's gonna **ead 'is hard out** when 'e sees my new car.

find it in one's heart to do something (to) *exp.* to be compassionate and merciful.

> **EXAMPLE:** I hope you'll **find it in your heart** to forgive me.

> **TRANSLATION:** I hope you'll **find the compassion** to forgive me.

> **"REAL SPEAK":** I hope you'll **find id in yer heart** ta fergive me.

from the bottom of my heart *exp.* with complete sincerity.

> **EXAMPLE:** I love you very much. I mean that **from the bottom of my heart**.

> **TRANSLATION:** I love you very much. I mean that **with complete sincerity**.

> **"REAL SPEAK":** I love you very much. I mean that **fr'm the boddom 'ev my heart**.

half-hearted *adj.* with little or no enthusiasm.

> **EXAMPLE:** Grant was **half-hearted** when he agreed to do me a favor.

> **TRANSLATION:** Grant was **not very enthusiastic** when he agreed to do me a favor.

> **"REAL SPEAK":** Grant w'z **half-harded** when 'e agreed ta do me a faver.

have a change of heart (to) *exp.* to change one's mind.

> **EXAMPLE:** I used to like Bill very much, but I've **had a change of heart**. I don't think he's a very nice person.

> **TRANSLATION:** I used to like Bill very much, but I've **changed my mind**. I don't think he's a very nice person.

> **"REAL SPEAK":** I usta like Bill very much, b'd I've **had a change 'ev heart**. I don't think 'e's a very nice person.

have one's heart in the right place (to)
exp. to have good intentions.

> **EXAMPLE:** Mary wouldn't accept Henry's offer to give her a loan, but she appreciated that Henry's **heart was in the right place**.

> **TRANSLATION:** Mary wouldn't accept Henry's offer to give her a loan, but she appreciated that Henry **had good intentions**.

> **"REAL SPEAK":** Mary wouldn' accept Henry's offer da give 'er a loan, b't she appreciaded th't Henry's **heart w'z in the right place**.

have one's heart set on something (to)
exp. to hope for something intensely.

> **EXAMPLE:** Would you mind if we didn't go get hamburgers? **I had my heart set on** seafood tonight.

> **TRANSLATION:** Would you mind if we didn't go get hamburgers? **I've been hoping for** seafood tonight.

> **"REAL SPEAK":** Would'ja mind if we didn' go get burgers? **I had my heart sed on** seafood tanight.

heart go out to someone (to have one's)
exp. to feel deep compassion for someone.

> **EXAMPLE:** John's mother died last week. My **heart goes out to** him and his family.

> **TRANSLATION:** John's mother died last week. I **have deep compassion for** him and his family.

> **"REAL SPEAK":** John's mother died last week. My **heart goes out ta** him 'n 'is fam'ly.

heart to do something (not to have the)
exp. to lack the courage to do something because of one's sense of compassion.

> **EXAMPLE:** I don't **have the heart** to tell Steve that he's fired. You do it.

> **TRANSLATION:** I don't **have the courage** to tell Steve that he's fired because I have too much compassion. You do it.

> **"REAL SPEAK":** I don't **have the heart** ta tell Steve th'd 'e's fired. You do it.

heart-to-heart *n.* an open and sincere discussion.

> **EXAMPLE:** We need to have **a heart-to-heart**.

> **TRANSLATION:** We need to have **an open and sincere discussion**.

> **"REAL SPEAK":** We need ta have **a heart-ta-heart**.

heartless (to be) *adj.* to have no compassion or feeling.

> **EXAMPLE:** The owner of the apartment building evicted all the old people who have lived there for thirty years. They have nowhere to go. He's **heartless**!

> **TRANSLATION:** The owner of the apartment building evicted all the old people who have lived there for thirty years. They have nowhere to go. He **has no compassion**!

> **"REAL SPEAK":** The owner 'a the apartment building evicted all the old people who've lived there fer thirdy years. They have nowhere da go. He's **heartless**!

know something by heart (to) *exp.* to know something from memory.

> **EXAMPLE:** My brother plays the piano without using any music. He **knows all the songs by heart**.

> **TRANSLATION:** My brother plays the piano without using any music. He **knows all the songs from memory**.

> **"REAL SPEAK":** [no change]

pour one's heart out (to) *exp.* to reveal one's deepest emotions.

> **EXAMPLE:** I never knew why Tina was always so sad until she finally **poured her heart out** to me.

> **TRANSLATION:** I never knew why Tina was always so sad until she finally **revealed her deepest emotions** to me.

> **"REAL SPEAK":** I never knew why Tina w'z always so sad until she fin'lly **poured 'er hard out** ta me.

KNUCKLE

knuckle down (to) *exp.* to work extra hard.

> **EXAMPLE:** We need to **knuckle down** if we're going to get this project done by next week.

> **TRANSLATION:** We need to **work extra hard** if we're going to get this project done by next week.

> **"REAL SPEAK":** We need ta **knuckle down** if w'r gonna get this project done by next week.

knuckle under (to) *exp.* to give up, to yield.

> **EXAMPLE:** After two days of negotiations, the other side finally **knuckled under** and met our demands.

> **TRANSLATION:** After two days of negotiations, the other side finally **yielded** and met our demands.

> **"REAL SPEAK":** After two days 'ev negotiations, the other side fin'lly **knuckled under** 'n med 'ar deman'z.

LEG

"Break a leg!" *exp.* (entertainment industry slang) "Good luck!"

> **EXAMPLE:** I hear you have your first performance tonight. **Break a leg!**

> **TRANSLATION:** I hear you have your first performance tonight. **Good luck!**

> **"REAL SPEAK":** I hear ya have yer first performance tanight. **Break a leg!**

> *Note:* In the world of entertainment, there is a superstition that wishing a

performer good luck will actually bring bad luck. Since getting a broken leg just before going on stage would be tragic for a performer, this phrase is used to trick the spirits of superstition into giving the performer the best possible luck.

leg to stand on (not to have a) *exp.* not to have any justification or logical basis for doing something.

> **EXAMPLE:** Larry will never win his case in court. **He doesn't have a leg to stand on.**
>
> **TRANSLATION:** Larry will never win his case in court. **He doesn't have logical basis for his case.**
>
> **"REAL SPEAK":** Larry'll never win 'is case 'n court. **He doesn' have a leg ta stand on.**

leg *n.* section or part of a journey.

> **EXAMPLE:** The first **leg** of our trip was to Paris and the second leg was to Italy.
>
> **TRANSLATION:** The first **part** of our trip was to Paris and the second part was to Italy.
>
> **"REAL SPEAK":** The first **leg** 'ev 'ar trip w'z ta Paris an' the secon' leg w'z ta Idaly.

pull someone's leg (to) *exp.* to joke, to kid, to tease.

> **EXAMPLE:** Stephanie won a million dollars last night? You're **pulling my leg**!
>
> **TRANSLATION:** Stephanie won a million dollars last night? You're **kidding me**!
>
> **"REAL SPEAK":** Stephanie won a million dollers las' night? Y'r **pulling my leg**!

LIP

button one's lip (to) *exp.* to stop talking, to keep quiet.

> **EXAMPLE:** We're going to have a big surprise party for David tomorrow. There he is! **Button your lip!**
>
> **TRANSLATION:** We're going to have a big surprise party for David tomorrow. There he is! **Keep quiet!**

> **"REAL SPEAK":** W'r gonna have a big serprise pardy fer David tamorrow. There 'e is! **Button yer lip!**

keep a stiff upper lip (to) *exp.* to be brave during misfortune.

> **EXAMPLE:** I know this is a very difficult time for you, but try to **keep a stiff upper lip**.
>
> **TRANSLATION:** I know this is a very difficult time for you, but try to **be brave in this time of misfortune**.
>
> **"REAL SPEAK":** I know this is a very difficult time fer you, b't try da **keep a stiff upper lip**.

"Read my lips!" *exp.* an insulting response to someone who did not understand what was said, insinuating that the person is deaf.

> **EXAMPLE:** **Read my lips**! I said, 'no!'
>
> **TRANSLATION:** **Watch me speak carefully**! I said, 'no!'
>
> **"REAL SPEAK":** [no change]

MOUTH

bad-mouth someone (to) *exp.* to speak badly about someone.

> **EXAMPLE:** Carl **bad-mouthed me** to all my friends after we broke up
>
> **TRANSLATION:** Carl **spoke badly about me** to all my friends after we broke up.
>
> **"REAL SPEAK":** Carl **bad-mouthed me** da all my frien'z after we broke up.

big mouth (to have a) *exp.* to be a gossip.

> **EXAMPLE:** Why did you tell Karen your secret? Don't you know **she has a big mouth**?
>
> **TRANSLATION:** Why did you tell Karen your secret? Don't you know **she's a gossip**?
>
> **"REAL SPEAK":** Why'd ja tell Karen yer secret? Doncha know **she has a big mouth**?

blabbermouth *n.* a gossip, one who reports everything he/she hears to everyone.

> **EXAMPLE:** Why did you tell Howard about the surprise party for Helen? He's such a **blabbermouth**! Now he's going to ruin the surprise.

TRANSLATION: Why did you tell Howard about the surprise party for Helen? He's such a **gossip**! Now he's going to ruin the surprise.

"REAL SPEAK": Why'd ja tell Howard about the serprise pardy fer Helen? He's such a **blabbermouth**! Now 'e's gonna ruin the serprise.

by word of mouth *exp.* said of news that has been communicated orally from person to person.

EXAMPLE: Erica just won the lottery! **I heard it by word of mouth**.

TRANSLATION: Erica just won the lottery! **Someone told me about it**.

"REAL SPEAK": Erica just won the loddery! **I heard it by word 'a mouth**.

leave a bad taste in one's mouth (to) *exp.* to leave a bad impression with someone.

EXAMPLE: Jonathan's bad attitude **left a bad taste in my mouth**.

TRANSLATION: Jonathan's bad attitude **left a bad impression with me**.

"REAL SPEAK": Jonathan's bad attitude **left a bad taste 'n my mouth**.

make one's mouth water (to) *exp.* to make one salivate.

EXAMPLE: The smell of those warm cookies is **making my mouth water**.

TRANSLATION: The smell of those warm cookies is **making me salivate**.

"REAL SPEAK": The smell 'a those warm cookies is **making my mouth wader**.

mouth off (to) *exp.* to speak in a disrespectful and offensive manner.

EXAMPLE: Ed **mouthed off at the teacher**, so she threw him out of class!

TRANSLATION: Ed **spoke to the teacher in a disrespectful and offensive manner**, so she threw him out of class!

"REAL SPEAK": Ed **mouthed off 'it the teacher**, so she threw 'im oudda class!

put words in someone's mouth (to) *exp.* to speak for someone.

EXAMPLE: I never said I was smarter than Gene! Stop **putting words in my mouth**!

TRANSLATION: I never said I was smarter than Gene! Stop **speaking for me**!

"REAL SPEAK": I never said I w'z smarter th'n Gene! Stop **pudding words 'n my mouth**!

run off at the mouth (to) *exp.* to talk endlessly.

EXAMPLE: I was on the phone for two hours with Natalie. She really **runs off at the mouth**!

TRANSLATION: I was on the phone for two hours with Natalie. She really **talks endlessly**!

"REAL SPEAK": I w'z on the phone fer two hours with Natalie. She really **runs off 'it the mouth**!

shoot off one's mouth (to) *exp.* to speak without thinking.

EXAMPLE: Don't listen to Bob. He always **shoots off his mouth**.

TRANSLATION: Don't listen to Bob. He always **speaks without thinking**.

"REAL SPEAK": Don't listen ta Bob. He always **shoots off 'is mouth**.

take the words right out of one's mouth (to) *exp.* to say something that someone else was about to say.

EXAMPLE: You're right. Steve is dishonest. **You took the words right out of my mouth**.

TRANSLATION: You're right. Steve is dishonest. **I was just about to say that**.

"REAL SPEAK": Y'r right. Steve is dishonest. **Ya took the words ride oudda my mouth**.

NERVE

get on someone's nerves (to) *exp.* to annoy someone.

EXAMPLE: I'm not going to invite Homer and Marge to my party. They **get on my nerves**.

TRANSLATION: I'm not going to invite Homer and Marge to my party. They **annoy me**.

"REAL SPEAK": I'm not gonna invite Homer 'n Marge ta my pardy. They **ged on my nerves**.

nerve *n.* audacity.

EXAMPLE: Tina asked you how much money you make? She has **nerve**!

TRANSLATION: Tina asked you how much money you make? She has **audacity**!

"REAL SPEAK": Tina asked'ju how much money ya make? She has **nerve**!

nervy (to be) *adj.* • **1.** to be offensively bold • **2.** to be fearless.

EXAMPLE 1: Alicia walked right up to Ralph and asked him if he was wearing a hairpiece! She's so **nervy**!

TRANSLATION: Alicia walked right up to Ralph and asked him if he was wearing a hairpiece! She's so **offensively bold**!

"REAL SPEAK": Alicia walked ride up ta Ralph 'n ast 'im if 'e w'z wearing a hairpiece! She's so **nervy**!

EXAMPLE 2: Nancy's mother went skydiving today! She's really **nervy** for a woman her age.

TRANSLATION: Nancy's mother went skydiving today! She's really **fearless** for a woman her age.

"REAL SPEAK": Nancy's mother went skydiving taday! She's really **nervy** fer a woman her age.

strike a nerve (to) *exp.* to bring up a sensitive and personal topic.

EXAMPLE: When you told me that you need to raise money for orphans, you really **struck a nerve**. I was an orphan myself.

TRANSLATION: When you told me that you need to raise money for orphans, you really **brought up a sensitive topic**. I was an orphan myself.

"REAL SPEAK": When ya told me that cha need ta raise money fer orphans, ya really **struck a nerve**. I w'z 'n orphan myself.

NOSE

as plain as the nose on one's face (to be) *exp.* to be extremely obvious.

EXAMPLE: – Do you think Eric is seeing another woman? – It's **as plain as the nose on your face**. Of course he is. That's why he tells you he's working late every night.

TRANSLATION: – Do you think Eric is seeing another woman? – It's **extremely obvious**. Of course he is. That's why he tells you he's working late every night.

"REAL SPEAK": – Do ya think Eric's seeing another woman? – It's **'ez plain 'ez the nose on yer face**. Of course 'e is. That's why 'e tells you 'e's working lade ev'ry night.

cut off one's nose to spite one's face (to) *exp.* to punish oneself unintentionally through one's own spite for someone or something else.

EXAMPLE: If you see Sharon at the party, just ignore her. I know you both had a fight, but if you don't go, you'll just be **cutting off your nose to spite your face**.

TRANSLATION: If you see Sharon at the party, just ignore her. I know you both had a fight, but if you don't go, you'll just be **punishing yourself unintentionally**.

"REAL SPEAK": If ya see Sharon 'it the pardy, just ignore her. I know you both had a fight, b'd if ya don't go, you'll just be **cudding off yer nose ta spite cher face**.

keep one's nose to the grindstone (to) *exp.* to work diligently.

EXAMPLE: To be successful, you need to **keep your nose to the grindstone**.

TRANSLATION: To be successful, you need to **work diligently**.

"REAL SPEAK": Ta be successful, ya need ta **keep yer nose ta the grin'stone**.

nosey *adj.* inappropriately curious.

EXAMPLE: Shiela asked me all sorts of personal questions about my relationship with Alan. She's really **nosey**!

TRANSLATION: Shiela asked me all sorts of personal questions about my relationship with Alan. She's really **inappropriately curious**!

"REAL SPEAK": Shiela ast me all sorts 'a personal questions about my relationship with Alan. She's really **nosey**!

pay through the nose (to) *exp.* to pay an excessive amount of money.

EXAMPLE: That dress is so beautiful and elegant! You must have **paid through the nose for it**!

TRANSLATION: That dress is so beautiful and elegant! You must have **paid a fortune for it**!

"REAL SPEAK": That dress 'ez so beaudiful 'n elegant! Ya must'a **paid through the nose for it**!

poke one's nose into someone's business (to) *exp.* to interfere in someone's affairs.

EXAMPLE: Brian tried to question me about my fight with Steve. I told him he shouldn't **poke his nose into other people's affairs**.

TRANSLATION: Brian tried to question me about my fight with Steve. I told him he shouldn't **interfere in other people's affairs**.

"REAL SPEAK": Brian tried da question me about my fight with Steve. I told 'im 'e shouldn't **poke 'is nose inta other people's affairs**.

right under one's nose (to be) *exp.* to be in plain sight.

EXAMPLE: I looked everywhere for my car keys but they turned out to be **right under my nose**.

TRANSLATION: I looked everywhere for my car keys but they turned out to be **in plain sight**.

"REAL SPEAK": I looked ev'rywhere fer my car keys b't they turned out ta be **ride under my nose**.

PALM

eating out of the palm of one's hand (to have someone) *exp.* to have complete control over someone.

EXAMPLE: I'm sure the teacher is going to give me a good grade. I **have him eating out of the palm of my hand**.

TRANSLATION: I'm sure the teacher is going to give me a good grade. I **have complete control over him**.

"REAL SPEAK": I'm sher the teacher's gonna give me a good grade. I **have 'im eading oudda the palm 'a my hand**.

Variation: **in the palm of one's hand (to have someone)** *exp.*

palm off something (to) *exp.* to dispose of something by trickery or fraud.

EXAMPLE: Marvin **palmed off** his old car on me. He told me it was in good condition but it's always breaking down!

TRANSLATION: Marvin **tricked me into buying** his old car. He told me it was in good condition but it's always breaking down!

"REAL SPEAK": Marvin **palmed off** 'is old car on me. He told me it w'z in good c'ndition bud it's always breaking down!

SHOULDER

cold shoulder (to give someone the) *exp.* to refuse to acknowledge someone (usually due to anger or hurt feelings).

EXAMPLE: I saw Chuck at the movies last night but he **gave me the cold shoulder**. I asked him what was wrong, but he ignored me.

TRANSLATION: I saw Chuck at the movies last night but he **wouldn't speak to me**. I asked him what was wrong, but he ignored me.

"REAL SPEAK": I saw Chuck 'it the movies las' night bud 'e **gamme the cold shoulder**. I ast 'im what w'z wrong, bud 'e ignored me.

have a chip on one's shoulder (to) *exp.* to be always ready for an argument.

EXAMPLE: Randy always gets upset over anything I say. He **has a chip on his shoulder**.

TRANSLATION: Randy always gets upset over anything I say. He's **always ready for an argument**.

"REAL SPEAK": Randy always gets upsed over anything I say. He **has a chip on 'is shoulder**.

rest on one's shoulders (to) *exp.* to be one's responsibility.

EXAMPLE: Since everyone abandoned me, the success of this project **rests on my shoulders**.

TRANSLATION: Since everyone abandoned me, the success of this project **is my responsibility**.

"REAL SPEAK": Since ev'ryone abandoned me, the success 'ev this project **rests on my shoulders**.

SPINE

spineless (to be) *adj.* to be cowardly and weak.

EXAMPLE: Every time the boss is verbally abusive to Pat, he just takes it and doesn't fight back. Pat is **spineless**!

TRANSLATION: Every time the boss is verbally abusive to Pat, he just takes it and doesn't fight back. Pat is **cowardly**.

"REAL SPEAK": Ev'ry time the boss 'ez verbally abusive ta Pat, he jus' takes it 'n doesn't fight back. Pat's **spineless**!

STOMACH

unable to stomach someone or something (to be) *exp.* to be unable to tolerate someone or something.

EXAMPLE: You invited Earl to the party? But why? You know I can't **stomach him**!

TRANSLATION: You invited Earl to the party? But why? You know I can't **tolerate him**!

"REAL SPEAK": You invided Earl ta the pardy? B't why? Ya know I can't **stomach him**!

THROAT

jump down one's throat (to) *exp.* to attack someone verbally without warning.

EXAMPLE: I gave Nancy some constructive criticism about her performance and she **jumped down my throat**!

TRANSLATION: I gave Nancy some constructive criticism about her performance and she **attacked me verbally without warning**!

"REAL SPEAK": I gave Nancy s'm c'nstrucdive cridicism aboud 'er performance 'n she **jump' down my throat**!

THUMB

all thumbs (to be) *exp.* to be clumsy.

EXAMPLE: I just dropped a glass and broke it! I'm **all thumbs today**.

TRANSLATION: I just dropped a glass and broke it! I'm **clumsy today**.

"REAL SPEAK": I just dropped a glass 'n broke it! I'm **all thumbs taday**.

rule of thumb *exp.* an informal procedure, a general rule.

> **EXAMPLE:** It's a **rule of thumb** to check the pressure in your car's tires about once a week.

> **TRANSLATION:** It's a **general rule** to check the pressure in your car's tires about once a week.

> **"REAL SPEAK":** It's a **rule 'a thumb** ta check the pressure in yer car's tires about once a week.

thumb a ride (to) *exp.* to hitchhike.

> **EXAMPLE:** I can't believe we ran out of gas! I wonder if we can **thumb a ride** to a gas station.

> **TRANSLATION:** I can't believe we ran out of gas! I wonder if we can **hitchhike** to a gas station.

> **"REAL SPEAK":** I can't b'lieve we ran oudda gas! I wonder if we c'n **thumb a ride** to a gas station.

TOE

on one's toes (to be) *exp.* to be alert.

> **EXAMPLE:** Tell all the security guards in the museum to **be on their toes**. Last week one of our priceless paintings was stolen.

> **TRANSLATION:** Tell all the security guards in the museum to **be alert**. Last week one of our priceless paintings was stolen.

> **"REAL SPEAK":** Tell all the securidy guards 'n the museum ta **be on their toes**. Last week one 'ev 'ar priceless pain'ings w'z stolen.

step on someone's toes (to) *exp.* to cross into someone else's area of responsibility.

> **EXAMPLE:** I never would have ordered supplies for the office if I had known that was your responsibility. I didn't mean to **step on your toes**.

> **TRANSLATION:** I never would have ordered supplies for the office if I had known that was your responsibility. I didn't mean to **cross into your area of responsibility**.

> **"REAL SPEAK":** I never would'ev ordered supplies fer the office if I'd known thad w'z yer responsibilidy. I didn' mean ta **step on yer toes**.

tiptoe around someone (to) *exp.* to be tentative and cautious in dealing with someone due to their unpredictable nature.

> **EXAMPLE:** Sometimes you get mad and scream at people for no reason. I'm tired of **tiptoeing** around you!

> **TRANSLATION:** Sometimes you get mad and scream at people for no reason. I'm tired of **being tentative and cautious** around you!

> **"REAL SPEAK":** Sometimes you get mad 'n scream 'it people fer no reason. I'm tired 'ev **tiptoeing** around you!

toe-to-toe (to go) *exp.* to fight (either physically or verbally).

> **EXAMPLE:** Dan and Rick have been disagreeing with each other on how to run their company. Well, this morning they finally **went toe-to-toe**!

> **TRANSLATION:** Dan and Rick have been disagreeing with each other on how to run their company. Well, this morning they finally **had a huge fight**!

> **"REAL SPEAK":** Dan 'n Rick'ev been disagreeing with each other on how da run their company. Well, th's morning they fin'lly **went toe-da-toe**!

TONGUE

"The cat's got your tongue?" *exp. (used after a long pause when the other person does not respond).*

> **EXAMPLE:** I just heard you've been seeing my husband! What's wrong? **The cat's got your tongue**?

TRANSLATION: "I just heard you've been seeing my husband! What's wrong? **Are you having trouble speaking**?

"REAL SPEAK": I just heard you've been seeing my husband! What's wrong? **The cat's got cher tongue**?

tip of one's tongue (to be on the) *exp.* to be on the verge of remembering something.

EXAMPLE: I can't remember the name of my first professor. **It's on the tip of my tongue.**

TRANSLATION: I can't remember the name of my first professor. **I'm on the verge of remembering it.**

"REAL SPEAK": I can't remember the name 'a my first professor. **It's on the tip 'a my tongue**.

tongue-tied (to be) *exp.* to be unable to speak clearly due to shyness or embarrassment.

EXAMPLE: I was so nervous during my acceptance speech that I **got tongue-tied**.

TRANSLATION: I was so nervous during my acceptance speech that I **was unable to speak clearly**.

"REAL SPEAK": I w'z so nervous during my acceptance speech th'd I **got tongue-tied**.

TOOTH

by the skin of one's teeth *exp.* barely.

EXAMPLE: The man escaped from his burning car **by the skin of his teeth**. It exploded two seconds later!

TRANSLATION: The man **barely** escaped from his burning car. It exploded two seconds later!

"REAL SPEAK": The man escaped fr'm 'is burning car **by the skin 'ev his teeth**. It exploded two seconds later!

get/sink one's teeth into something (to) *exp.* to delve into something with great enthusiasm.

EXAMPLE: I'm so excited to work with you on this project. I can't wait to **get/sink my teeth into it**.

TRANSLATION: I'm so excited to work with you on this project. I can't wait to **delve into it**.

"REAL SPEAK": I'm so excided ta work with you on this project. I can't wait ta **get/sink my teeth into it**.

go through something with a fine-tooth comb (to) *exp.* to inspect something extremely carefully.

EXAMPLE: I can't find my diamond ring! We need to **go through this** entire house **with a fine-tooth comb**.

TRANSLATION: I can't find my diamond ring! We need to **inspect** this entire house **extremely carefully**.

"REAL SPEAK": I can't find my diamond ring! We need ta **go through this** entire house **with a fine-tooth comb**.

lie through one's teeth (to) *exp.* to lie grossly.

EXAMPLE: Todd **lied through his teeth** when he said he planned to pay me back next week.

TRANSLATION: Todd **grossly lied** when he said he planned to pay me back next week.

"REAL SPEAK": Todd **lied through 'is teeth** when 'e said 'e plan' ta pay me back next week.

sweet tooth (to have a) *exp.* to have a passion for sweets.

EXAMPLE: Cecily has the biggest **sweet tooth** of anyone I've ever known.

TRANSLATION: Cecily has the biggest **passion for sweets** of anyone I've ever known.

"REAL SPEAK": Cecily has the biggest **sweet tooth** 'ev anyone I've ever known.

LESSON 6 IN THE SUBWAY

"Tim's not playing with a full deck!"

LET'S WARM UP!

MATCH THE PICTURES *(Answers on p. 222)*

As a fun way to get started, see if you can guess the meaning of the new slang words and expressions on the opposite page by using the pictures below and following the context of the sentences.

115

1. Bill's **not playing with a full deck**! I think he needs to see a psychiatrist.
   ❑ crazy
   ❑ handsome

2. Lulu hates going to the doctor. She's **scared stiff** of injections.
   ❑ extremely scared
   ❑ extremely fond

3. **Hand that over**! It's mine!
   ❑ keep it
   ❑ give that to me

4. My lawnmower can't be repaired. I'm afraid it's **a goner**.
   ❑ destined to die
   ❑ old

5. If you wear that to the party, everyone's going to **make fun of you**! Your dress is just too small!
   ❑ admire you
   ❑ ridicule you

6. I had no idea I was going to get a promotion. It **came out of the clear blue**!
   ❑ was inevitable
   ❑ was completely unexpected

7. Hey! That **crook** stole my wallet!
   ❑ woman
   ❑ thief

8. The thief **held up** the bank and stole one millions dollars!
   ❑ robbed
   ❑ left

9. I didn't see him take my purse. He **swiped it right from under my nose**.
   ❑ stole it right in front of me
   ❑ stole it from my nose

10. Laura doesn't like to go out very often. She's a **homebody**.
    ❑ person who prefers to stay home
    ❑ person who likes to go out

11. I don't think we should sleep in tents tonight. We're **sitting ducks** if a bear walks by!
    ❑ invulnerable to attack
    ❑ vulnerable to attack

12. I think that guy just **made a pass at you**. He's cute! Go say hello to him!
    ❑ looked away from you
    ❑ flirted with you

LET'S TALK!

A. DIALOGUE USING SLANG & IDIOMS

The words introduced on the first two pages are used in the dialogue below. See if you can understand the conversation. *Note:* The translation of the words in boldface is on the right-hand page.

CD-B: TRACK 1

Linda: I hate riding the subway late at night. We're **sitting ducks** if a **crook** decides to get on the train.

Jane: I don't mean to **make fun of you** but you're crazy. I've been riding this train for years and I've never had a problem.

Linda: Oh, really? Well, last month I was riding this very train when some guy who was obviously **not playing with a full deck** got on board and started **making a pass at me**. When I moved away, another guy **came from out of the blue** and told me to **hand over** my money. I thought I was **a goner**!

Jane: You must have been **scared stiff**! I can't imagine being **held up**!

Linda: It got worse. After he ran away with my money, I reached down to pick up my bags and someone had **swiped them right from under my nose**!

Jane: Well, after hearing that story, I'm not too sure I feel like riding the subway again. I think I'm going to become a **homebody**.

B. DIALOGUE TRANSLATED INTO STANDARD ENGLISH

LET'S SEE HOW MUCH YOU REMEMBER!
Just for fun, bounce around in random order to the words
and expressions in boldface below. See if you can remember
their slang equivalents without looking at the left-hand page!

Linda: I hate riding the subway late at night. We're **vulnerable to attack** if a **criminal** decides to get on the train.

Jane: I don't mean to **ridicule you** but you're crazy. I've been riding this train for years and I've never had a problem.

Linda: Oh, really? Well, last month I was riding this very train when some guy who was obviously **crazy** got on board and started **flirting with me**. When I moved away, another guy **appeared unexpectedly** and told me to **surrender** my money. I thought I was **going to die**!

Jane: You must have been **extremely scared**! I can't imagine being **robbed**!

Linda: It got worse. After he ran away with my money, I reached down to pick up my bags and someone had **stolen them right in front of me**!

Jane: Well, after hearing that story, I'm not too sure I feel like riding the subway again. I think I'm going to become a **person who prefers staying home**.

C. DIALOGUE USING "REAL SPEAK"

The dialogue below demonstrates how the slang conversation on the previous page would *really* be spoken by native speakers!

Linda: I hate riding the subway lade 'it night. W'r **sidding ducks** if a **crook** decides ta ged on the train.

Jane: I don't mean da **make fun 'a ya** but ch'er crazy. I've been riding this train fer years 'n I've never had a problem.

Linda: Oh, really? Well, las' month I w'z riding this very train when some guy who w'z obviously **not playing with a full deck** god on board 'n starded **making a pass 'it me**. When I moved away, another guy **came fr'm oudda the blue** 'n told me da **hand over** my money. I thod I w'z **a goner**!

Jane: You must'a been **scared stiff**! I can' imagine being **held up**!

Linda: It got worse. After 'e ran away with my money, I reach' down da pick up my bags 'n someone 'ed **swiped 'em right fr'm under my nose**!

Jane: Well, after hearing that story, I'm not too sher I feel like riding the subway again. I think I'm gonna become a **homebody**.

LET'S LEARN!

CD-B: TRACK 2

VOCABULARY

The following words and expressions were used in the previous dialogues. Let's take a closer look at what they mean.

come from out of the blue (to) *exp.* said of something that happens unexpectedly.

EXAMPLE:	My boss fired me today! It **came from out of the blue**!
TRANSLATION:	My boss fired me today! It **happened unexpectedly**!
"REAL SPEAK:"	My boss fired me taday! It **came fr'm oudda the blue**!

Variation: **come out of the clear blue (to)** *exp.* said of something that happens completely unexpectedly.

Synonym: **come from out of nowhere (to)** *exp.*

NOW YOU DO IT:

(Create a sentence using "came from out of the blue")

crook *n. (from crooked which is slang for "dishonest")* thief, dishonest person.

EXAMPLE: You're going into business with Ron? Haven't you heard? He has a reputation for being a **crook**. He stole money from his last company!

TRANSLATION: You're going into business with Ron? Haven't you heard? He has a reputation for being a **thief**. He stole money from his last company!

"REAL SPEAK:" Y'r goin' inda business with Ron? Haven' chu heard? He has a reputation fer bein' a **crook**. He stole money from 'is las' company!

NOW YOU DO IT:

(Create a sentence using "crook")

goner (to be a) *n.* to be dead or on the verge of death (of a person) or permanent disrepair (of machinery).

EXAMPLE: When I saw the bear running toward me, I thought I was **a goner**!

TRANSLATION: When I saw the bear running toward me, I thought I was **going to die**!

"REAL SPEAK:" When I saw the bear running tord me, I thod I w'z **a goner**!

Note: This term can also be used figuratively to mean "in big trouble." For example: *If my boss sees me leaving work early, I'm a goner!*; If my boss sees me leaving work early, I'm in big trouble!

Synonym 1: **dead duck (to be a)** *exp.*

Synonym 2: **dead meat (to be)** exp.

Synonym 3: **done for (to be)** *exp.*

NOW YOU DO IT:

(Create a sentence using "goner")

hand over something to someone (to) *exp.* to surrender something to someone.

EXAMPLE: That's my pen you're using! I've been looking everywhere for it! **Hand it over**!

TRANSLATION: That's my pen you're using! I've been looking everywhere for it! **Give it to me**!

"REAL SPEAK:" That's my pen y'r using! I been looking ev'rywhere for it! **Hand id over**!

Variation: **hand something over to someone (to)** *exp.*

Synonym: **fork over something to someone (to)** *exp.*

NOW YOU DO IT:

(Create a sentence using "hand it over")

held up (to be) *exp.* • **1.** to be robbed • **2.** to be detained.

EXAMPLE -1:	I was **held up** this morning on my way to work! Luckily, the thief just took my money and ran away!
TRANSLATION:	I was **robbed** this morning on my way to work! Luckily, the thief just took my money and ran away!
"REAL SPEAK:"	I w'z **held up** this morning on my way da work! Luckily, the thief jus' took my money 'n ran away!
EXAMPLE -2:	I'm sorry I'm late. I was **held up** in traffic.
TRANSLATION:	I'm sorry I'm late. I was **detained** in traffic.
"REAL SPEAK:"	I'm sorry I'm late. I w'z **held up** 'n traffic.

Also: **holdup** *n.* robbery • *There was a holdup at the bank today!;* There was a robbery at the bank today!

Synonym: **stick-up** *n.* (from the phrase "Stick 'em up!" meaning "Raise your hands up in the air" – Note that "em" is a common reduction for "them").

NOW YOU DO IT:
(Create a sentence using "held up")

homebody *n.* one who prefers staying at home.

EXAMPLE:	Bill doesn't want to go with us to the party. As usual, he'd rather stay home and read. He's definitely a **homebody**.
TRANSLATION:	Bill doesn't want to go with us to the party. As usual, he'd rather stay home and read. He's definitely a **person who prefers staying at home**.
"REAL SPEAK:"	Bill doesn' wanna go with us ta the pardy. As usual, 'e'd rather stay home 'n read. He's definitely a **homebody**.

Synonym: **a stay-at-home kind of person** *exp.*

NOW YOU DO IT:
(Create a sentence using "homebody")

make a pass at someone (to) *exp.* to flirt aggressively with someone (either nonphysically or physically).

EXAMPLE:	My sister's boyfriend just **made a pass at me**. I think I should tell my sister.
TRANSLATION:	My sister's boyfriend just **flirted aggressively with me**. I think I should tell my sister.
"REAL SPEAK:"	My sister's boyfrien' just **made a pass 'it me**. I think I should tell my sister.

Synonym 1: **come on to someone (to)** *exp.*

Synonym 2: **hit on someone (to)** *exp.*

NOW YOU DO IT:
(Create a sentence using "make a pass")

make fun of someone (to) *exp.* to tease someone maliciously, to ridicule.

EXAMPLE: The other kids in school used to **make fun of** Ed because he was so small. I wish they could see him now that he's become a bodybuilder.

TRANSLATION: The other kids in school used to **tease** Ed because he was so small. I wish they could see him now that he's become a bodybuilder.

"REAL SPEAK:" The other kids 'n school usta **make fun of** Ed cuz 'e w'z so small. I wish they could see 'im now thad 'e's become a bodybuilder.

Synonym 1: **give someone a bad/hard time (to)** *exp.*

Synonym 2: **pick on someone (to)** *exp.*

Synonym 3: **poke fun at someone (to)** *exp.*

NOW YOU DO IT:

(Create a sentence using "make fun of")

playing with a full deck (not to be) *exp.* to be mentally ill, crazy.

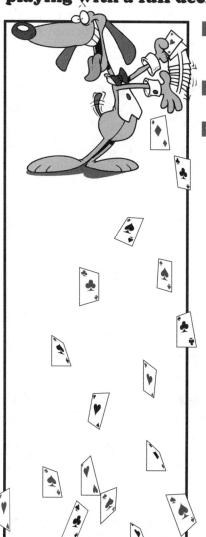

EXAMPLE: Our new teacher **isn't playing with a full deck**. She wears her purse on her head because she thinks it makes a nice hat!

TRANSLATION: Our new teacher **is mentally ill**. She wears her purse on her head because she thinks it makes a nice hat!

"REAL SPEAK:" 'Are new teacher **isn't playing with a full deck**. She wears 'er purse on 'er head because she thinks it makes a nice hat!

Note: In this expression, "*deck*" refers to a "deck of playing cards."

Synonym 1: **both oars in the water (not to have)** *exp.*

Synonym 2: **lost one's marbles (to have)** *exp.*

Synonym 3: **off one's rocker (to be)** *exp.*

Synonym 4: **out to lunch (to be)** *exp.*

Synonym 5: **the lights are on but nobody's home** *exp.*

Synonym 6: **tripping (to be)** *exp.*

Note: This expression – commonly pronounced: *to be trippin'* – is extremely popular in teen slang of the new millennium. It's very interesting to note that this comes from a slang expression of the 1960's, "*to be on a trip*" meaning "to be hallucinating on illegal drugs."

NOW YOU DO IT:

(Create a sentence using "not playing with a full deck")

scared stiff (to be) *exp.* to be extremely scared.

> **EXAMPLE:** We were all **scared stiff** during the tornado. Luckily, it passed over us without doing any damage to the house.
>
> **TRANSLATION:** We were all **extremely scared** during the tornado. Luckily, it passed over us without doing any damage to the house.
>
> **"REAL SPEAK:"** We were all **scared stiff** during the tornado. Luckily, it passed over us without doing any damage ta the house.

Synonym 1: **scared out of one's wits (to be)** *exp.*

Synonym 2: **scare the bejesus out of someone (to)** *exp.*

Synonym 3: **scare someone to death (to)** *exp.*

Synonym 4: **scare the living daylights out of someone (to)** *exp.*

Synonym 5: **scare the pants off someone (to)** *exp.*

> **NOW YOU DO IT:**
>
> *(Create a sentence using "scared stiff")*

sitting duck (to be a) *exp.* to be vulnerable to an attack.

> **EXAMPLE:** I can't believe Wanda went to Central Park tonight when it's known that there are a lot of robbers there. She's a **sitting duck**!
>
> **TRANSLATION:** I can't believe Wanda went to Central Park tonight when it's known that there are a lot of robbers there. She's **vulnerable to an attack**!
>
> **"REAL SPEAK:"** I can't believe Wanda went ta Central Park tanight when it's known th't there'er a lod 'a robbers there. She's a **sidding duck**!

> **NOW YOU DO IT:**
>
> *(Create a sentence using "sitting duck")*

swipe something right from under someone's nose (to) *exp.* to steal something right in front of the victim.

> **EXAMPLE:** Hey! Where's my bag? That guy who was sitting next to me **swiped it right from under my nose**!
>
> **TRANSLATION:** Hey! Where's my bag? That guy who was sitting next to me **stole it right in front of me**!
>
> **"REAL SPEAK:"** Hey! Where's my bag? That guy who w'z sidding nex' ta me **swiped it fr'm ride under my nose**!
>
> *Note:* The verb "swipe" is a slang synonym for "steal." In this expression, any synonym for "steal" could be used, such as: **rip off • snatch • score.**

> **NOW YOU DO IT:**
>
> *(Create a sentence using "swiped it right from under my nose")*

LET'S PRACTICE!

A. THE UNFINISHED CONVERSATION *(Answers on p. 222)*
Read the conversations then fill in the last line with your own words in response to what you've just read. Make sure to use the suggested words in your response. Your response can be in the form of a question or statement.

1

Jodi: I just met the new boss this morning.

Angela: So, tell me! What did you think of him. I hear he's a little strange.

Jodi:

use: *not playing with a full deck*

2

Mark: I went to Steve's party last night.

Al: How was it? What did everyone think of your new haircut?

Mark:

use: *made fun of me*

3

Kim: Today I caught David using my favorite pen and he didn't even ask my permission.

Doug: What did you do?

Kim:

use: *hand it over*

4

Tessa: I met Tom's cousin today at school.

Nick: What did you think of him? Is he a nice guy?

Tessa:

use: *made a pass at me*

5

Carl: I had the worst day of my life today.

Mitch: Why? What happened?

Carl:

use: *held up*

B. CHOOSE THE RIGHT WORD *(Answers on p. 222)*
Underline the appropriate word that best completes
the phrase.

CD-B: TRACK 3

1. I was scared (**straight**, **soft**, **stiff**) when the neighbor's dog ran toward me and started growling. Luckily he was only playing!

2. If we don't get to our house by the time the lightening storm strikes, we're sitting (**cows**, **ducks**, **ostriches**)!

3. You won't believe what happened to me today. I was walking home from the market when I was stopped by a robber and held (**over**, **down**, **up**)!

4. Janet never goes out much. Every time I ask her to go with me to the movies or to dinner, she says that she wants to stay home. I guess she's a real (**home**, **house**, **apartment**)body.

5. Don and I used to own a company together, but I found out that he was stealing money. I guess he's nothing but a (**cook**, **crook**, **rookie**).

6. When I walked into the subway, I had two bags with me. When I got up to leave, they were gone! Someone must have swiped them right from under my (**chin**, **toes**, **nose**)!

7. That man is talking to that streetlight over there. I don't think he's playing with a full (**desk**, **deck**, **door**).

8. I bought the most beautiful dress yesterday, but when I wore it to work, everyone made (**fun**, **amusement**, **entertainment**) of me because they said it was too short.

9. When I was alone with the boss, he tried to make a (**pass**, **gas**, **sitting duck**) at me! He even invited me to his house for dinner tonight!

10. When my house collapsed during the earthquake, I thought I was a (**goner**, **crook**, **homebody**). Somehow I managed to get out alive!

11. Last week, a baseball hit me right on the nose and broke it. I didn't even see it coming. It came from out of the (**green**, **pink**, **blue**)!

12. That's my jacket you're wearing! I've been looking all over the house for that. (**Foot**, **Hand**, **Ankle**) it over right now!

C. COMPLETE THE STORY _(Answers on p. 222)_

Use the illustrations to help you fill in the blanks with the correct slang term or expression from the list below.

CD-B: TRACK 4

homebody	make a pass	crook
sitting duck	held up	make fun of me
playing with a full deck	hand over	goner
came from out of the blue	scared stiff	

You're probably going to _____ for being so stupid, but

I walked home late last night and was _____ by a _____.

I should have known I'd be a _____ in that neighborhood. At first I just

thought it was some guy trying to _____ at me; then I realized he

wasn't _____. He _____

and told me to _____ my money. I was _____!

I really thought I was a _____. After an experience like

that, I think I'm going to become more of a _____.

D. *CREATE YOUR OWN SENTENCE* (Answers on p. 222)
Read Person A's questions aloud using the suggested words to create your answer for Person B.

PERSON A		PERSON B
1.	What's wrong? You're shaking!	[use: **held up**]
2.	Where's your purse?	[use: **swiped it right from under my nose**]
3.	I heard you got hit by a baseball. Is that true?	[use: **came from out of the blue**]
4.	What was it like to be in the earthquake?	[use: **scared stiff**]
5.	Did a bear really run after you in the mountains?	[use: **goner**]
6.	Did you meet the new employee?	[use: **made a pass at me**]
7.	What a bad lightening storm! Should we go inside?	[use: **sitting ducks**]
8.	Why did Pete laugh when I walked in the room?	[use: **making fun of**]
9.	Do you think Jim is rational?	[use: **playing with a full deck**]
10.	Did Steve really steal money from the company?	[use: **crook**]

THE SLANGMAN FILES

Proper Names Used in Slang

In the previous lessons, we saw how animals make up a significant part of American slang and idioms. But wait! Have we humans been unfairly neglected? There is only one answer to that question: **No way, José**! *(Absolutely not)*!

Proper names have given birth to many other imaginative expressions in American slang, as demonstrated by the following list.

Note: Although the expressions below are based on proper names, many of them are not capitalized.

BETSY

"Heavens to Betsy!" *interj.* an interjection denoting surprise.

> **EXAMPLE:**
> – I just heard that Mr. Anderson's house was destroyed in a fire!
> – **Heavens to Betsy**! When did that happen?

> **TRANSLATION:**
> – I just heard that Mr. Anderson's house was destroyed in a fire!
> – **How terrible**! When did that happen?

> **"REAL SPEAK":**
> – I just heard th't Mr. Anderson's house w'z destroyed 'n a fire!
> – **Heavens ta Betsy**! When did that happen?

> *Note:* This expression is somewhat outdated. However, it is still occasionally used by older generations or in jest.

ADAM

know someone from Adam (not to) *exp.* to be totally unfamiliar with someone.

> **EXAMPLE:** That guy said that I owe him money? **I don't know him from Adam**!

> **TRANSLATION:** That guy said that I owe him money? **I don't know him at all**!

> **"REAL SPEAK":** That guy said th'd I owe 'im money? **I don't know 'im fr'm Adam**!

CHARLEY

charley horse *exp.* a painful muscle cramp.

> **EXAMPLE:** I wonder why that runner is limping. I guess he got a **charley horse** in his leg.

> **TRANSLATION:** I wonder why that runner is limping. I guess he got a **painful muscle cramp** in his leg.

> **"REAL SPEAK":** I wonder why that runner's limping. I guess 'e god a **charley horse** 'n 'is leg.

DICK

dick *n.* • **1.** penis • **2.** jerk.

> **EXAMPLE 1:** I get the feeling that George thinks more with his **dick** than his brain!

> **TRANSLATION:** I get the feeling that George thinks more with his **penis** than his brain!

> **"REAL SPEAK":** I get the feeling th't George thinks more with 'is **dick** than 'is brain!

EXAMPLE 2: I told Bob a secret and he told everyone! What a **dick**!

TRANSLATION: I told Bob a secret and he told everyone! What a **jerk**!

"REAL SPEAK": I told Bob a secret an' 'e told ev'ryone! Whad a **dick**!

Note: As one might suspect, since *dick* is a person's first name as well as a slang term for "penis," a lot of joking and teasing often arises around this. During my first day at college, our French school principal greeted the new students but was unaware that *dick* was slang for "penis." She began her greeting by saying, *"My son, Dick, went to this very university when he was your age. How many "Dicks" do we have here in the auditorium?"* After a moment, every male in the entire auditorium raised his hand and laughed. Moral: If you don't know your American slang, you could get into trouble!

dick head *exp.* fool, jerk • (lit.): penis head.

EXAMPLE: This is the third time my brother accidentally put salt in his coffee thinking it was sugar! He can be such a **dick head** sometimes!

TRANSLATION: This is the third time my brother accidentally put salt in his coffee thinking it was sugar! He can be such a **fool** sometimes!

"REAL SPEAK": This 'ez the third time my brother accident'lly put salt in 'is coffee thinking it w'ez sugar! He c'n be such a **dick head** sometimes!

house dick *exp.* detective hired by an establishment such as a nightclub, hotel, etc. for an investigation.

EXAMPLE: One of the guests in our hotel was robbed last night. We'd better have the **house dick** investigate this.

TRANSLATION: One of the guests in our hotel was robbed last night. We'd better have the **house detective** investigate this.

"REAL SPEAK": One 'a the guess' 'n 'ar hotel w'z robbed las' night. We'd bedder have the **house dick** investigate this.

private dick *exp.* private detective.

EXAMPLE: Larry is one of the best **private dicks** in this city. He never leaves a crime unsolved.

TRANSLATION: Larry is one of the best **private detectives** in this city. He never leaves a crime unsolved.

"REAL SPEAK": Larry's one 'a the best **private dicks** 'n this cidy. He never leaves a crime unsolved.

FANNY

fanny *prn.* buttocks, rear end.

EXAMPLE: My mother gave me a loving slap on my **fanny** as I walked out the door.

TRANSLATION: My mother gave me a loving slap on my **rear end** as I walked out the door.

"REAL SPEAK": My mother gamme a loving slap on my **fanny** 'ez I walked out the door.

Note: It is extremely important to note that although the term *fanny* is acceptable in American slang as a synonym for "buttocks," in British slang it is a crude synonym for "vagina."

FRITZ

on the fritz (to be) *exp.* to be inoperative.

EXAMPLE: I need to call a computer technician. My computer is **on the fritz again**!

TRANSLATION: I need to call a computer technician. My computer is **broken again**!

"REAL SPEAK": I need ta call a c'mpuder technician. My computer's **on the fritz again**!

fritz out (to) *exp.* to cease to function.

EXAMPLE: The television just **fritzed out**. I think it's time to buy a new one.

TRANSLATION: The television just **stopped working**. I think it's time to buy a new one.

"REAL SPEAK": The TV just **fritzed out**. I think it's time ta buy a new one.

GEORGE

"By George" *interj.* (British slang) an interjection indicating surprise or excitement.

EXAMPLE: **By George**! Those two girls must be twins!

TRANSLATION: **Wow**! Those two girls must be twins!

"REAL SPEAK": [no change]

Note: Although this expression is from British slang, it is occasionally used in jest in the U.S.

JACK

"Hit the road, Jack!" *interj.* "Leave!" "Get out!"

EXAMPLE: I never want to see you again. **Hit the road, Jack**!

TRANSLATION: I never want to see you again. **Get out**!

"REAL SPEAK": I never wanna see you again. **Hit the road, Jack**!

Variation: **"Hit the road!"** *interj.*

Note: **hit the road (to)** *exp.* to leave • *It's getting late. I need to hit the road; It's getting late. I need to leave.*

jack *exp.* nothing at all.

EXAMPLE: John **doesn't know jack** about computers.

TRANSLATION: John **doesn't know anything at all** about computers.

"REAL SPEAK": John **doesn' know jack** about c'mpuders.

Note: This is a euphemism for the popular yet vulgar expression, *jack shit* • *I don't know jack shit about mechanics; I don't know anything at all about mechanics.*

Jack-of-all-trades *exp.* a person who has skill in many areas.

EXAMPLE: David fixed my computer, then repaired my television. He's a **Jack-of-all-trades**.

TRANSLATION: David fixed my computer, then repaired my television. He **has skill in many areas**.

"REAL SPEAK": David fixed my c'mpuder, then repaired my TV. He's a **Jack-'ev-all-trades**.

Note: A common expression is *Jack-of-all-trades, master of none* meaning "a person who has a little expertise in many areas but is not an expert in any one area."

jack someone around (to) *exp.* to mislead someone.

EXAMPLE: I thought the car salesman was being honest with me. Then after an hour, I realized that I was just being **jacked around**.

TRANSLATION: I thought the car salesman was being honest with me. Then after an hour, I realized that I was just being **misled**.

"REAL SPEAK": I thought the car salesm'n w'z being honest with me. Then after 'n hour, I realized th'd I w'z just being **jacked around**.

jack something up (to) *exp.* to raise something.

EXAMPLE: The market just **jacked up** all its prices.

TRANSLATION: The market just **raised** all its prices.

"REAL SPEAK": The market jus' **jacked up** all its prices.

JANE

Jane Doe *exp.* a name given to a woman who has no identity.

EXAMPLE: The detective is trying to determine who the victim is. For now, she's just **Jane Doe**.

TRANSLATION: The detective is trying to determine who the victim is. For now, she's just **a woman with no identity**.

"REAL SPEAK": The detective's trying ta determine who the victim is. Fer now, she's just **Jane Doe**.

plain Jane *exp.* an ordinary-looking woman or girl.

> **EXAMPLE:** When Tina was a little girl, she was **a plain Jane**. Now she's a beautiful woman.

> **TRANSLATION:** When Tina was a little girl, she was **ordinary-looking**. Now she's a beautiful woman.

> **"REAL SPEAK":** When Tina w'z a liddle girl, she w'z **a plain Jane**. Now she's a beaudif'l woman.

JOE

Joe [*fill in category*] *exp.* the prototype.

> **EXAMPLE:** You're definitely ready for your first day in college. You look like **Joe college** with all your books!

> **TRANSLATION:** You're definitely ready for your first day in college. You look like **the prototype of a college student** with all your books!

> **"REAL SPEAK":** Y'r definitely ready fer yer firs' day 'n college. You look like **Joe college** with all yer books!

Joe Blow *exp.* person in general.

> **EXAMPLE:** Every **Joe Blow** in Hollywood thinks he's going to be a movie star.

> **TRANSLATION:** Every **person** in Hollywood thinks he's going to be a movie star.

> **"REAL SPEAK":** Ev'ry **Joe Blow** 'n Hollywood thinks 'e's gonna be a movie star.

Joe Schmoe *exp.* person in general.

> **EXAMPLE:** Every **Joe Schmoe** wants to become a millionaire.

> **TRANSLATION:** Every **person** wants to become a millionaire.

> **"REAL SPEAK":** Ev'ry **Joe Schmoe** wants ta become a millionaire.

JOHN

john *n.* • **1.** lavatory, toilet • **2.** a prostitute's customer.

> **EXAMPLE 1:** With all the water I drank, I think I should go to the **john** before we leave.

> **TRANSLATION:** With all the water I drank, I think I should go to the **lavatory** before we leave.

> **"REAL SPEAK":** With all the wader I drank, I think I should go da the **john** b'fore we leave.

> **EXAMPLE 2:** That prostitute is so ugly, I wonder how she ever gets any **johns**.

> **TRANSLATION:** That prostitute is so ugly, I wonder how she ever gets any **customers**.

> **"REAL SPEAK":** That prostitute's so ugly, I wonder how she ever gets any **johns**.

John Doe *exp.* a name given to a man who has no identity.

> **EXAMPLE:** We have a **John Doe** in the morgue that we can't seem to identify.

> **TRANSLATION:** We have an **unknown man** in the morgue that we can't seem to identify.

> **"REAL SPEAK":** We have a **John Doe** 'n the morgue th't we can't seem to identify.

John Hancock *exp.* a signature.

> **EXAMPLE:** I need you to put your **John Hancock** at the bottom of this contract.

> **TRANSLATION:** I need you to put your **signature** at the bottom of this contract.

> **"REAL SPEAK":** I need'ja da put cher **John Hancock** 'it the boddom 'a this contract.

> *Note:* John Hancock was one of the signers of the Declaration of Independence and known for his prominent signature.

JOSÉ

"No way, José!" *exp.* "There's no possibility of that happening!"

> **EXAMPLE:** You want me to lend you some money? **No way, José**! You still owe me money from last time!

> **TRANSLATION:** You want me to lend you some money? **There's no possibility of that happening**! You still owe me money from last time!

"REAL SPEAK": Ya want me da len'ja s'm money? **No way, José!** Ya still owe me money fr'm last time!

JUAN

Don Juan *exp.* a handsome and romantic man.

EXAMPLE: You should see Rachel's new boyfriend. He's a **Don Juan**!

TRANSLATION: You should see Rachel's new boyfriend. He's a **very handsome and romantic man**.

"REAL SPEAK": [no change]

Note: This expression comes from the fictional character Don Juan who was known for being exceptionally romantic.

LOUISE

"Geez, Louise!" *interj.* an interjection signifying surprise or disbelief.

EXAMPLE: **Geez, Louise!** Why did you let Tom drive your new car? He ruined his last one!

TRANSLATION: **I can't believe it!** Why did you let Tom drive your new car? He ruined his last one!

"REAL SPEAK": **Geez, Louise!** Why'd ja let Tom drive yer new car? He ruined 'is last one!

MICKY

slip someone a Micky (to) *exp.* to sneak a drug into someone's drink.

EXAMPLE: The detective said that the woman poisoned her husband by **slipping him a Micky**.

TRANSLATION: The detective said that the woman poisoned her husband by **sneaking a drug into his drink**.

"REAL SPEAK": The detective said that the woman poisoned 'er husband by **slipping 'im a Micky**.

NICK

Saint Nick *(proper name)* • an affectionate nickname for "Saint Nicholas" popularly known as "Santa Claus."

EXAMPLE: You'd better be good because **Saint Nick** will be here tomorrow.

TRANSLATION: You'd better be good because **Santa Claus** will be here tomorrow.

"REAL SPEAK": Ya'd bedder be good b'cause **Saint Nick**'ll be here damorrow.

PAT

have something down pat (to) *exp.* to understand something thoroughly.

EXAMPLE: I **have this computer program down pat**.

TRANSLATION: I **understand this computer program thoroughly**.

"REAL SPEAK": I **have this c'mpuder program down pat**.

PAUL

rob Peter to pay Paul (to) *exp.* to create a debt by borrowing money in order to pay another debt.

EXAMPLE: Tiffany used her credit card to pay off the debt to her mother. All she did was **rob Peter to pay Paul**!

TRANSLATION: Tiffany used her credit card to pay off the debt to her mother. All she did was **to create a debt by borrowing money in order to pay another debt**.

"REAL SPEAK": Tiffany used 'er credit card ta pay off the debt to 'er mother. All she did w'z **rob Peder ta pay Paul**!

PETE / PETER

"For Pete's sake!" *interj.* an interjection indicating surprise or annoyance.

EXAMPLE: **For Pete's sake!** Someone scratched my car!

TRANSLATION:	**I don't believe this**! Someone scratched my car!
"REAL SPEAK":	**Fer Pete's sake**! Someone scratched my car!

peter out (to) *exp.* to diminish into nothing.

EXAMPLE:	Ted and I started a new company, but it just sort of **petered out**.
TRANSLATION:	Ted and I started a new company, but it just sort of **diminished into nothing**.
"REAL SPEAK":	Ted 'n I starded a new company, bud it jus' sort 'a **pedered out**.

RANDY

randy *adj. (borrowed from British slang)* sexually excited.

EXAMPLE:	George thinks about sex constantly. I've never met anyone so **randy**!
TRANSLATION:	George thinks about sex constantly. I've never met anyone so **sexually excited**!
"REAL SPEAK":	George thinks about sex constantly. I've never med anyone so **randy**!

ROGER

"Roger" *exp. (originally walkie-talkie/radio jargon)* "Communication received and understood."

EXAMPLE:	– David, I want you to land the plane as soon as you can. – **Roger**. I'll do that as soon as it's safe.
TRANSLATION:	– David, I want you to land the plane as soon as you can. – **Communication received and understood**. I'll do that as soon as it's safe.
"REAL SPEAK":	– David, I wan'chu da land the plane 'ez soon 'ez ya can. – **Roger**. I'll do thad 'ez soon 'ez it's safe.
Also:	**"Roger and out"** *exp.* "Communication received, understood, and now terminated."
Note:	This expression was originally used in the Air Force to signal completion of a conversation between pilot and ground control.

SAM

Uncle Sam *exp.* the United States government.

EXAMPLE:	It's shocking how much money **Uncle Sam** takes out of my paycheck each week!
TRANSLATION:	It's shocking how much money **the United States government** takes out of my paycheck each week!
"REAL SPEAK":	It's shocking how much money **Uncle Sam** takes oudda my paycheck each week!

SCROOGE

Scrooge *prn.* • **1.** a miser • **2.** a person who doesn't like Christmas.

EXAMPLE 1:	Mike never gives donations to charities. He's such a **Scrooge**
TRANSLATION:	Mike never gives donations to charities. He's such a **miser**.
"REAL SPEAK":	Mike never gives donations ta charidies. He's such a **Scrooge**
EXAMPLE 2:	Jon hates the Christmas season. He's such a **Scrooge**!
TRANSLATION:	Jon hates the Christmas season. He's **like the character from Charles Dickens novel, "A Christmas Carol."**
"REAL SPEAK":	Jon hates the Chris'mas season. He's such a **Scrooge**!
Note:	Scrooge, an old businessman known for being a miser and hating Christmas, is a character from the Charles Dicken's novel, *"A Christmas Carol."*

SUSAN

Lazy Susan *exp.* a revolving tray used for serving food or condiments.

EXAMPLE:	The waiter put a **Lazy Susan** on the table so that we could all reach the condiments easily.
TRANSLATION:	The waiter put a **revolving tray** on the table so that we could all reach the condiments easily.

"REAL SPEAK":	The waider pud a **Lazy Susan** on the table so th't we could all reach the condim'nts easily.

TOM / THOMAS

Peeping Tom *exp.* a man who spies in windows.

EXAMPLE:	My sister called the police because she saw a **Peeping Tom** outside her window!
TRANSLATION:	My sister called the police because she saw a **man spying** outside her window!
"REAL SPEAK":	My sister called the police b'cause she saw a **Peeping Tom** outside 'er window!

WILLY

willies (to give one the) *exp.* to make one nervous and uneasy.

EXAMPLE:	This house **gives me the willies**. Let's get out of here!
TRANSLATION:	This house **makes me nervous and uneasy**. Let's get out of here!
"REAL SPEAK":	This house **gives me the willies**. Let's ged oudda here!
Variation:	**give one the willies (to)** *exp.* to make one nervous and uneasy.

willy *n. (borrowed from British slang)* penis.

EXAMPLE:	It was so embarrassing. My little brother started playing with his **willy** in front of my friends!
TRANSLATION:	It was so embarrassing. My little brother started playing with his **penis** in front of my friends!
"REAL SPEAK":	It w'z so embarrassing. My liddle brother starded playing with 'is **willy** in fronna my friends!
Note:	It was during the beginning of the 1990's that Americans were introduced to the British slang term "willy" when American film makers exported the movie "Free Willy" to England. Not having a knowledge of British slang, the Americans were quite unaware that they had just exported a movie interpreted by the British as "Free the Penis." This amusing cultural mistake got so much publicity that the term "willy" has become known throughout the U.S. as "penis."

willy-nilly *exp.* • **1.** haphazardly • **2.** without having a choice.

EXAMPLE 1:	Don't just throw the files in the cabinet **willy-nilly**. You need to arrange them in alphabetical order.
TRANSLATION:	Don't just throw the files in the cabinet **haphazardly**. You need to arrange them in alphabetical order.
"REAL SPEAK":	Don't jus' throw the files in the cabinet **willy-nilly**. Ya need ta arrange 'em 'n alphabedic'l order.
EXAMPLE 2:	You have to go to school **willy-nilly**.
TRANSLATION:	You have to go to school **whether you want to or not**.
"REAL SPEAK":	Ya hafta go da school **willy-nilly**.

LESSON 7 — ACHES & PAINS

"I'm not myself today"

LET'S WARM UP!

MATCH THE PICTURES (Answers on p. 222)

As a fun way to get started, see if you can guess the meaning of the new slang words and expressions on the opposite page by using the pictures below and following the context of the sentences.

☐ 1. I'm **not myself** today. Maybe I'm getting sick.

☐ 2. Ernie is such a **wimp**. He needs to gain some muscle!

☐ 3. David works out all the time. That's why he's so **buff**.

☐ 4. Bob's dreams **went up in smoke** since he lost his money.

☐ 5. You want me to lift that for you? **No sweat**! It's easy!

☐ 6. I **tweaked** my back trying to lift too much weight.

☐ 7. You need to work less. You're really **overdoing it**.

☐ 8. I'd never go see that doctor. I think he's **a quack**.

☐ 9. **Hang in there**. I'm sure you'll feel better soon.

☐ 10. **Don't let it get you down**. You'll do better next time.

☐ 11. Bill has to **go under the knife** to get his tonsils removed.

☐ 12. After being sick for a week, I'm finally **up and at 'em (them)**!

☐ 13. At age 77, my mother is in **tip-top shape**.

☐ 14. Earl does nothing but watch the **tube** all day.

A. television

B. strained

C. weak and unforceful person

D. not feeling well

E. excellent physical condition

F. it's not a problem

G. an incompetent doctor

H. don't let it make you depressed

I. be patient

J. were destroyed

K. undergo surgery

L. active and busy

M. being excessive

N. muscular

LET'S TALK!

A. DIALOGUE USING SLANG & IDIOMS

The words introduced on the first two pages are used in the dialogue below. See if you can understand the conversation. *Note:* The translation of the words in boldface is on the right-hand page.

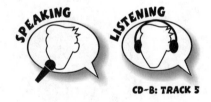

SPEAKING   LISTENING

CD-B: TRACK 5

Tom: What's wrong?

Pat: I'm **not myself** today. I was tired of looking like a **wimp** and decided to work out extra hard at the gym to get **buff**. I lifted a hundred pounds over my head thinking that it would be **no sweat**, which is when I **tweaked** my back. I guess I **overdid it**. My vacation plans **went up in smoke**.

Tom: That's a shame! Did you see a doctor?

Pat: Yeah. I saw some **quack** who said I might have to **go under the knife,** but I told him to forget it! I've always been in **tip-top shape** and wasn't going to let a little back pain **get me down**.

Tom: Well, just **hang in there**. I'm sure you'll be **up and at them** soon.

Pat: I hope so. I'm getting tired of watching the **tube** all day!

B. DIALOGUE TRANSLATED INTO STANDARD ENGLISH

LET'S SEE HOW MUCH YOU REMEMBER!
Just for fun, bounce around in random order to the words
and expressions in boldface below. See if you can remember
their slang equivalents without looking at the left-hand page!

Tom: What's wrong?

Pat: I'm **not feeling well** today. I was tired of looking like a **weak and unforceful person** and decided to work out extra hard at the gym to get **muscular**. I lifted a hundred pounds over my head thinking that it would be **no problem**, which is when I **strained** my back. I guess I **went beyond my ability**. My vacation plans **were destroyed**.

Tom: That's a shame! Did you see a doctor?

Pat: Yeah. I saw some **incompetent doctor** who said I might have to **undergo surgery**, but I told him to forget it! I've always been in **excellent physical condition** and wasn't going to let a little back pain **make me depressed**.

Tom: Well, just **be patient**. I'm sure you'll be **active and busy** soon.

Pat: I hope so. I'm getting tired of watching **television** all day!

C. DIALOGUE USING "REAL SPEAK"

The dialogue below demonstrates how the slang conversation on the previous page would *really* be spoken by native speakers!

Tom: What's wrong?

Pat: I'm **not myself** taday. I w'z tired 'a looking like a **wimp** 'n decided da work oud extra hard 'it the gym ta get **buff**. I lifted a hundred poun's over my head thinking thad it'd be **no sweat**, which is when I **tweaked** my back. I guess I **overdid it**. My vacation plans **wen' up 'n smoke**.

Tom: That's a shame! Did'ja see a docter?

Pat: Yeah. I saw some **quack** who said I might hafta **go under the knife,** bud I told 'im da ferget it! I've always been in **tip-top shape** 'n wasn't gonna led a liddle back pain **get me down**.

Tom: Well, just **hang in there**. I'm sher you'll be **up 'n ad 'em** soon.

Pat: I hope so. I'm gedding tired of watching the **tube** all day!

LET'S LEARN!

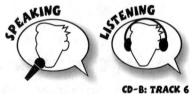

CD-B: TRACK 6

VOCABULARY

The following words and expressions were used in the previous dialogues. Let's take a closer look at what they mean.

buff *adj.* muscular.

EXAMPLE:	It really shows that you've been working out a lot at the gym. You're really **buff**!
TRANSLATION:	It really shows that you've been working out a lot at the gym. You're really **muscular**!
"REAL SPEAK:"	It really shows that chu've been working oud a lot 'it the gym. Y'r really **buff**!

Variation: **buffed out** *adj.*

Also: **buff** *n.* enthusiast • **movie buff** = movie enthusiast; **music buff** = music enthusiast; etc.

Synonym: **hunky** *adj.* muscular / **hunk** *n.* muscular man.

NOW YOU DO IT. COMPLETE THE PHRASE ALOUD:
...has really gotten buff!

get one down (to) *exp.* • to get one depressed.

> **EXAMPLE:** I don't like to watch sad movies. They **get me down**.
>
> **TRANSLATION:** I don't like to watch sad movies. They **depress me**.
>
> **"REAL SPEAK:"** I don't like ta watch sad movies. They **get me down**.
>
> *Synonym:* **bum one out (to)** *exp.* • *Don't let it bum you out; Don't let it depress you.*
>
> *Also:* **"Get down!"** *exp.* "Let yourself lose control!"
>
> **NOW YOU DO IT. COMPLETE THE PHRASE ALOUD:**
> *...gets me down.*

go up in smoke (to) *exp.* to be destroyed.

> **EXAMPLE:** My dream of competing in the Olympics as an ice skater **went up in smoke** when I broke my leg.
>
> **TRANSLATION:** My dream of competing in the Olympics as an ice skater **was destroyed** when I broke my leg.
>
> **"REAL SPEAK:"** My dream 'ev c'mpeding in the Olympics as 'n ice skader **wen' up 'n smoke** when I broke my leg.
>
> *Synonym:* **down the tubes (to go)** *exp.*
>
> **NOW YOU DO IT. COMPLETE THE PHRASE ALOUD:**
> *My plans to... went up in smoke.*

hang in there (to) *exp.* to be patient.

> **EXAMPLE:** I know it's hard to find a new job, but **hang in there**. I'm sure you'll find one if you keep looking.
>
> **TRANSLATION:** I know it's hard to find a new job, but **be patient**. I'm sure you'll find one if you keep looking.
>
> **"REAL SPEAK:"** I know it's hard da find a new job, b't **hang in there**. I'm sher you'll find one if ya keep looking.
>
> *Synonym:* **hang tough (to)** *exp.*
>
> **NOW YOU DO IT. COMPLETE THE PHRASE ALOUD:**
> *I know it's hard to... but hang in there!*

no sweat *exp.* no problem (said of something so easy to do, that it won't cause one to sweat).

> **EXAMPLE:** **No sweat**! It would be my pleasure to drive you to the airport. What time is your flight?
>
> **TRANSLATION:** **No problem**! It would be my pleasure to drive you to the airport. What time is your flight?
>
> **"REAL SPEAK:"** **No sweat**! It'd be my pleasure da drive ya da the airport. What time's yer flight?
>
> *Synonym:* **no biggy** *exp.* short for "it's not a big deal."
>
> **NOW YOU DO IT. COMPLETE THE PHRASE ALOUD:**
> *No sweat! I'd be happy to...*

not to be oneself *exp.* not to feel as well as usual.

EXAMPLE:	I'm **not myself** today. Yesterday I played with my little niece and she had a cold. I hope I didn't catch it!
TRANSLATION:	I'm **not feeling as well as usual** today. Yesterday I played with my little niece and she had a cold. I hope I didn't catch it!
"REAL SPEAK:"	I'm **not myself** taday. Yesderday I played with my little niece 'n she had a cold. I hope I didn't catch it!
Synonym 1:	**feel blah (to)** *exp.* / **have the blahs (to)** *exp.*
Synonym 2:	**out of it (to be)** *exp.*

NOW YOU DO IT. COMPLETE THE PHRASE ALOUD:
I'm not myself today because...

overdo something (to) *exp.* to be excessive.

EXAMPLE:	I made enough food for a hundred people and I've only invited eight for dinner. I think I **overdid it**.
TRANSLATION:	I made enough food for a hundred people and I've only invited eight for dinner. I think I **was excessive**.
"REAL SPEAK:"	I made anuf food fer a hundred people 'n I've only invided eight fer dinner. I think I **overdid it**.
Synonym:	**overboard (to go)** *adj.* (lit.) to fall off a boat or ship.

NOW YOU DO IT. COMPLETE THE PHRASE ALOUD:
I think I really overdid it when I...

quack *n.* incompetent doctor.

EXAMPLE:	Dr. Payne is **a quack**! He told me I had an ulcer but I was actually pregnant!
TRANSLATION:	Dr. Payne is **an incompetent doctor**! He told me I had an ulcer but I was actually pregnant!
"REAL SPEAK:"	Dr. Payne's a **quack**! He told me I had 'n ulcer b'd I w'z akshelly pregnant!
Synonym:	**phoney** *n.* said of anyone who makes people think he/she has more experience and ability than he/she really does.

NOW YOU DO IT. COMPLETE THE PHRASE ALOUD:
I think that doctor is a quack because...

tip-top shape (to be in) *exp.* to be in excellent physical condition.

EXAMPLE:	Jordan's grandparents are both in **tip-top shape**. They go jogging every morning!
TRANSLATION:	Jordan's grandparents are both in **excellent physical condition**. They go jogging every morning!
"REAL SPEAK:"	Jordan's gran'parents 'er 'n **tip-top shape**. They go jogging every morning!
Synonym:	**in topnotch shape (to be)** *exp.*

NOW YOU DO IT. COMPLETE THE PHRASE ALOUD:
...will keep you in tip top shape.

tweak something (to) *exp.* • **1.** to strain something • **2.** to adjust slightly.

EXAMPLE -1:	I **tweaked** my back trying to pick up a heavy box.
TRANSLATION:	I **strained** my back trying to pick up a heavy box.
"REAL SPEAK:"	I **tweaked** my back trying da pick up a heavy box.
EXAMPLE -2:	My stereo sounds strange. I think it needs to be **tweaked**.
TRANSLATION:	My stereo sounds strange. I think it needs to be **adjusted**.
"REAL SPEAK:"	My stereo sounds strange. I think it needs ta be **tweaked**.

NOW YOU DO IT. COMPLETE THE PHRASE ALOUD:
I tweaked my... when I tried to...

tube *n.* television (short for "television tube").

EXAMPLE:	My uncle spends hours watching the **tube** at night.
TRANSLATION:	My uncle spends hours watching **television** at night.
"REAL SPEAK:"	My uncle spends hours watching the **tube** 'it night.
Variation:	**boob tube** *exp.* from *boob* which is slang for "idiot" – since some people feel that too much television can make you into an idiot – and *tube* which refers to the "television tube."
Synonym:	**idiot box** *exp.*

NOW YOU DO IT. COMPLETE THE PHRASE ALOUD:
The last show I saw on the tube was...

under the knife (to go) *exp.* to undergo surgery.

EXAMPLE:	Tomorrow Cynthia is **going under the knife** to make her nose smaller!
TRANSLATION:	Tomorrow Cynthia is **undergoing surgery** to make her nose smaller!
"REAL SPEAK:"	Tomorrow Cynthia's **going under the knife** ta make 'er nose smaller!

NOW YOU DO IT. COMPLETE THE PHRASE ALOUD:
The last time I went under the knife was...

up and at them (to be) *exp.* to get active and busy.

EXAMPLE:	It's time to wake up. You don't want to be late for work. **Up and at them**!
TRANSLATION:	It's time to wake up. You don't want to be late for work. **Get active and busy**!
"REAL SPEAK:"	It's time ta wake up. Ya don't wanna be late fer work. **Up 'n ad 'em**!
Note:	This expression is always reduced to: *up 'n ad 'em*. In fact, it would actually sound unnatural to a native speaker to hear this expression in its unreduced form!
Synonym:	**rise and shine (to)** *exp.*

NOW YOU DO IT. COMPLETE THE PHRASE ALOUD:
I'm finally up and at them after being sick for...

wimp *n.* • **1.** a weak and unforceful person • **2.** coward.

EXAMPLE -1:	Dan used to be so big and strong. Now he's such a **wimp**!
TRANSLATION:	Dan used to be so big and strong. Now he's such a **weak and unforceful person**!
"REAL SPEAK:"	Dan usta be so big 'n strong. Now 'e's such a **wimp**!
EXAMPLE -2:	You're afraid to go parachuting with me? Don't be such a **wimp**! It will be so much fun!
TRANSLATION:	You're afraid to go parachuting with me? Don't be such a **coward**! It will be so much fun!
"REAL SPEAK:"	Y'r afraid da go parachuding with me? Don't be such a **wimp**! It'll be so much fun!

Synonym: **wieney** *n.* (applies to both definitions **1.** and **2.**)

NOW YOU DO IT. COMPLETE THE PHRASE ALOUD:
..has become such a wimp!

LET'S PRACTICE!

CD-B: TRACK 7

A. YOU'RE THE AUTHOR *(Answers on p. 222)*

Complete the dialogue using the words below.

myself	smoke	sweat	top	them
overdid	buff	knife	down	tube
wimp	quack	tweaked	hang	

Joe: I'm not _____ today. I _____ my back yesterday lifting some heavy boxes. I've been wanting to clean the basement for months and I needed to move some big boxes upstairs. So, I thought, "No _____!" I'm in tip- _____ shape. But I guess I _____ it. I used to be so _____ when I worked out every day. Now I'm such a _____ . It really gets me _____ . My plans for cleaning the basement this month just went up in _____ .

Doug: The most important thing is that you rest. Once when I hurt my back, I went to a back specialist who wanted me to go under the _____ right away! What a _____ ! I knew if I could just _____ in there for a couple of weeks, I'd be up and at _____ soon. Besides, it was actually fun watching the _____ all day!

B. CROSSWORD PUZZLE (*Answers on p. 223*)

Fill in the crossword puzzle using the words from the list.

CD-B: TRACK 8

down	smoke	buff	tube	tweaked
up	wimp	overdid	quack	hang
top	myself	sweat	knife	

ACROSS

2. No ____! I'd be happy to help you.

4. Get lots of rest and you'll be ____ and at them soon.

5. I'm never sick. I'm always in tip- ____ shape.

6. I'm not ____ today. I hope I'm not sick.

8. Tomorrow I'm going under the ____ to get my tonsils out.

10. I think I ____ it. I bought too much food for my party.

12. What a ____! He shouldn't be practicing medicine!

13. Jon is such a ____! He really needs to start working out at the gym.

DOWN

1. Eric has a great body. He's so ____!

3. I can't move! I ____ my back!

5. I'm tired of watching the ____. Let's go out.

7. After my car accident, my vacation plans went up in ____.

9. ____ in there. You're almost finished.

11. I'm sorry you failed your test but don't let it get you ____. You'll do better next time.

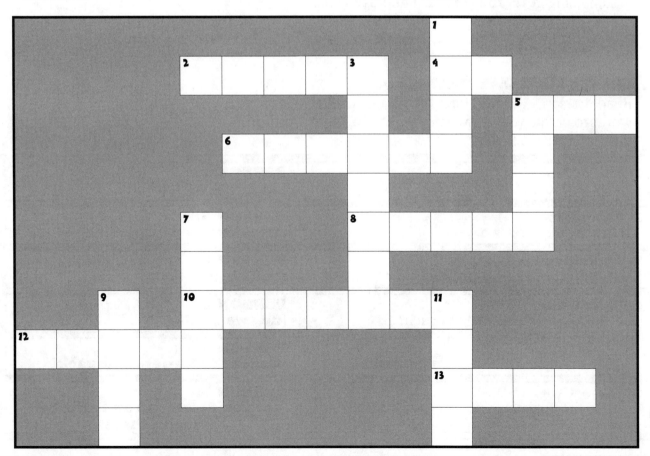

C. *TRUE OR FALSE* (Answers on p. 223)
Decide if the sentence is true or false.

READING

CD–B: TRACK 9

1. A **wimp** is a muscular individual.
   ❏ True ❏ False

2. A **quack** is a very competent and qualified doctor.
   ❏ True ❏ False

3. If someone tells you to **hang in there**, you are being told to "give up."
   ❏ True ❏ False

4. If you go **under the knife**, you are a chef.
   ❏ True ❏ False

5. If you **tweak** your neck, you sprained it.
   ❏ True ❏ False

6. **No sweat**! means "No problem!"
   ❏ True ❏ False

7. If you are **buff**, you are muscular.
   ❏ True ❏ False

8. If you are in **tip-top shape**, you're sick and weak.
   ❏ True ❏ False

9. If your plans **go up in smoke**, they're no longer possible.
   ❏ True ❏ False

10. If something **gets you down**, it depresses you.
    ❏ True ❏ False

D. *CREATE YOUR OWN SENTENCE* (Answers on p. 223)
Read Person A's questions aloud using the suggested words to create your answer for Person B. The words from this lesson are in boldface.

SPEAKING

1. **PERSON A:** What are your plans tonight?	**PERSON B:** [home] [movie] [**tube**]
2. **PERSON A:** I haven't seen you in a week!	**PERSON B:** [**tweaked**] [back] [bed]
3. **PERSON A:** Have you been exercising lately?	**PERSON B:** [**buff**] [gym] [**wimp**]
4. **PERSON A:** Can you help me move this couch?	**PERSON B:** [**no sweat**] [glad] [help]
5. **PERSON A:** Are you going to the hospital tomorrow?	**PERSON B:** [**under the knife**] [leg] [**quack**]
6. **PERSON A:** I'm so tired of being sick!	**PERSON B:** [**get you down**] [**up and at them**] [**hang in there**]

Initials Used in Slang Expressions

At first, the following initials may seem like a confusing code that's reserved only for native speakers. This doesn't have to be the case! These initials are used by virtually *everyone* and are extremely popular in everyday conversation. So **F.Y.I.** *(for your information)*, you'd better learn them **A.S.A.P.** *(as soon as possible)*, **O.K.** *(okay)*?

-A-

A.A. • Alcoholics Anonymous – a popular organization whose goal is to help alcoholics with their recovery.

> **EXAMPLE:** Ever since John started going to **A.A.**, he hasn't had a drink in six years!
>
> **TRANSLATION:** Ever since John started going to **Alcoholics Anonymous**, he hasn't had a drink in six years!
>
> **"REAL SPEAK":** Ever since John starded going ta **A.A.**, he hasn' had a drink 'n six years!

A.A.A. • *(prounounced: "Triple A")* Automobile Association of America – a well-known membership organization helps drivers with a variety of motor vehicle issues such as problems that arise on the road and travel information.

> **EXAMPLE:** You'd better call **Triple A**. I think your car is really dead this time.
>
> **TRANSLATION:** You'd better call the **Automobile** Association of America. I think your car is really dead this time.
>
> **"REAL SPEAK":** Ya'd bedder call **Triple A**. I think ye car's really dead this time.

A.B.C. • American Broadcasting Corporation – one of the three most popular television networks in the United States.

> **EXAMPLE:** I got a job acting on a TV show for **ABC**!
>
> **TRANSLATION:** I got a job acting on a TV show for the **American Broadcasting System**!

> **"REAL SPEAK":** I god a job acting on a TV show fer **ABC**!

A.C. • air conditioning

> **EXAMPLE:** It's so hot in here! I think we need to turn on the **A.C.**
>
> **TRANSLATION:** It's so hot in here! I think we need to turn on the **air conditioning**.
>
> **"REAL SPEAK":** It's so hod in here! I think we need ta turn on the **A.C.**

A.C./D.C. • alternating current/direct current – commonly used in slang to mean "bisexual."

> **EXAMPLE:** Do you think Gary is **A.C./D.C**?
>
> **TRANSLATION:** Do you think Gary is **bisexual**?
>
> **"REAL SPEAK":** Ya think Gary's **A.C./D.C**?

A.I.D.S. • *(pronounced: "aids")* Acquired Immune Deficiency Syndrome.

> **EXAMPLE:** Cases of **A.I.D.S.** increased this year from last year. I hope there's a cure soon!
>
> **TRANSLATION:** Cases of **Acquired Immune Deficiency Syndrome** increased this year from last year. I hope there's a cure soon!
>
> **"REAL SPEAK":** Cases 'ev **A.I.D.S.** increased this year fr'm last year. I hope there's a cure soon!

A.M. • **1.** ante meridiem (meaning "morning")
• **2.** amplitude modulation (referring to one of the two bands on most radios).

> **EXAMPLE 1:** I have to wake up at seven o'clock **A.M.**
>
> **TRANSLATION:** I have to wake up at seven o'clock **in the morning**.

"REAL SPEAK":	I hafta wake up 'it seven a'clock **A.M.**
EXAMPLE 2:	I always listen to my favorite news station every morning, KFWB 98.0 on the **A.M.** band.
TRANSLATION:	I always listen to my favorite news station every morning, KFWB 98.0 on the **amplitude modulation** band.
"REAL SPEAK":	I always listen ta my favorite news station ev'ry morning, KFWB 98.0 on the **A.M.** band.

A.O.K. • fine – a variation of the popular "O.K."

EXAMPLE:	– How are you doing? – **A.O.K.**
TRANSLATION:	– How are you doing? – Fine.
"REAL SPEAK":	– How'er ya doing? – **A.O.K.**

A.P.B. • *(police jargon)* all points bulletin (where all the police officers are notified throughout a particular city).

EXAMPLE:	The police put out an **A.P.B.** in order to catch the criminal.
TRANSLATION:	The police put out an **all points bulletin** in order to catch the criminal.
"REAL SPEAK":	The police pud oud 'n **A.P.B.** in order da catch the criminal.

A.S.A.P. • *(pronounced either: "A-S-A-P" or "ay-sap")* as soon as possible.

EXAMPLE:	You'd better leave **A.S.A.P.** or you're going to miss your flight!
TRANSLATION:	You'd better leave **as soon as possible** or you're going to miss your flight!
"REAL SPEAK":	Ya'd bedder leave **A.S.A.P.** 'r y'r gonna miss yer flight!
Note:	This is another peculiarity in American slang. To the native ear, the phrase "as soon as possible" implies a mild urgency. However, in its abbreviated form, **A.S.A.P.**, the connotation is extreme urgency. Therefore, the phrase *"Mail this letter for me as soon as possible"* feels less urgent than *"Mail this letter for me A.S.A.P."*

A.W.O.L. • *(army jargon – pronounced either "A.W.O.L" or "ay wol")* absent without leave (meaning "absent without permission to leave").

EXAMPLE:	Sir, three of our soldiers are **A.W.O.L.**
TRANSLATION:	Sir, three of our soldiers are **absent without leave**.
"REAL SPEAK":	Sir, three 'ev 'ar sol'jers 'er **A.W.O.L.**

–B–

B.A. • Bachelor of Arts degree.

EXAMPLE:	Kim just got her **B.A.** in theater!
TRANSLATION:	Kim just got her **Bachelor of Arts degree** in theater!
"REAL SPEAK":	Kim jus' god 'er **B.A.** in theater!

B.L.T. • a popular sandwich containing bacon, lettuce, and tomato.

EXAMPLE:	Waitress, I'd like a **B.L.T.**, please.
TRANSLATION:	Waitress I'd like a **bacon, lettuce, and tomato sandwich**, please.
"REAL SPEAK":	[no change]

B.O. • body odor.

EXAMPLE:	That guy smells terrible! He has the worst **B.O**!
TRANSLATION:	That guy smells terrible! He has the worst **body odor**!
"REAL SPEAK":	That guy smells terr'ble! He has the worst **B.O**!

B.S. • **1.** *interj.* This is a common euphemism for the interjection *"Bullshit!"* meaning "Nonsense!" • **2.** *v.* to deceive someone by speaking nonsense and lies • **3.** *n.* Bachelor of Science degree.

EXAMPLE 1:	Bob said his family is royalty. What a bunch of **B.S**!
TRANSLATION:	Bob said his family is royalty. What a bunch of **nonsense**!
"REAL SPEAK":	Bob said 'is fam'ly's royalty. Whad a bunch 'a **B.S**!
EXAMPLE 2:	I think Karen was **B.S.ing** you when she said she spoke eight languages.
TRANSLATION:	I think Karen was **deceiving** you when she said she spoke eight languages.
"REAL SPEAK":	I think Karen w'z **B.S.ing** you when she said she spoke eight languages.

EXAMPLE 3: Noah got his **B.S.** degree in psychology.

TRANSLATION: Noah got his **Bachelor of Science** degree in psychology.

"REAL SPEAK": Noah god 'is **B.S.** degree 'n psychology.

B.Y.O.B. • bring your own bottle – a common expression applied to a party at which each person brings his/her own alcoholic beverage.

EXAMPLE: Tonight, Tom is having a **B.Y.O.B.** Do you want to come with us?

TRANSLATION: Tonight, Tom is having a **party where each person brings his own alcohol**. Do you want to come with us?

"REAL SPEAK": Tanight, Tom's having a **B.Y.O.B.** Ya wanna come with us?

-C-

C.B.S. • Columbia Broadcasting System – one of the three most popular television networks in the United States.

EXAMPLE: I heard you're starring in a new show for **C.B.S**! Congratulations!

TRANSLATION: I heard you're starring in a new show for the **Columbia Broadcasting System**! Congratulations!

"REAL SPEAK": I heard y'r starring in a new show fer **C.B.S**! Congradjalations!

C.D. • 1. compact disc •
2. Certificate of Deposit.

EXAMPLE 1: I just bought a new **C.D.** made by my favorite musical group.

TRANSLATION: I just bought a new **compact disc** made by my favorite musical group.

"REAL SPEAK": I jus' bod a new **C.D.** made by my fav'rite musical group.

EXAMPLE 2: I have over two thousand dollars in my **C.D.**

TRANSLATION: I have over two thousand dollars in my **Certificate of Deposit**.

"REAL SPEAK": I have over two thousan' dollers in my **C.D.**

C.E.O. • Chief Executive Officer.

EXAMPLE: Jason is our new **C.E.O.** He's made some great changes in our company!

TRANSLATION: Jason is our new **Chief Executive Officer**. He's made some great changes in our company!

"REAL SPEAK": Jason's 'ar new **C.E.O.** He's made s'm great changes 'n 'ar company!

C.N.N. • Cable News Network – a popular television cable network which broadcasts the news 24 hours a day.

EXAMPLE: **C.N.N.** is known for excellence in reporting the news.

TRANSLATION: The **Cable News Network** is known for excellence in reporting the news.

"REAL SPEAK": **C.N.N.**'s known fer excellence 'n reporting the news.

C.P.A. • Certified Public Accountant.

EXAMPLE: As a **C.P.A.**, my father gets really busy around tax time!

TRANSLATION: As a **Certified Public Accountant**, my father gets really busy around tax time!

"REAL SPEAK": As a **C.P.A.**, my father gets really busy aroun' tax time!

C.P.R. • cardiopulmonary resuscitation.

EXAMPLE: That man stopped breathing! Quick! Does anyone here know **C.P.R.**?

TRANSLATION: That man stopped breathing! Quick! Does anyone here know **cardiopulmonary resuscitation**?

"REAL SPEAK": [no change]

-D-

3-D • three-dimensional.

EXAMPLE: With my new graphics program, I can make objects look **3-D**.

TRANSLATION: With my new graphics program, I can make objects look **three-dimensional**.

"REAL SPEAK": With my new graphics program, I c'n make objec's look **3-D**.

D.A. • District Attorney.

EXAMPLE: My father is a **D.A.** He's in court almost every day!

TRANSLATION: My father is a **District Attorney**. He's in court almost every day!

"REAL SPEAK": My father's a **D.A.** He's 'n cord almost ev'ry day!

D.C. • District of Columbia – This refers to Washington, D.C.

EXAMPLE: I've lived in **D.C.** most of my life.

TRANSLATION: I've lived in **Washington, D.C.** most of my life.

"REAL SPEAK": I've lived 'n **D.C.** most 'a my life.

D.J. • disk jockey.

EXAMPLE: I just called the local radio show and asked the **D.J.** to play my favorite song.

TRANSLATION: I just called the local radio show and asked the **disk jockey** to play my favorite song.

"REAL SPEAK": I jus' called the local radio show 'n ast the **D.J.** da play my fav'rite song.

D.N.A. • Deoxyribonucleic Acid – a nucleic acid associated with the transmission of genetic information.

EXAMPLE: The man was convicted of rape because the scientists found traces of his **DNA** on the victim's dress.

TRANSLATION: The man was convicted of rape because the scientists found traces of his **genetic information** on the victim's dress.

"REAL SPEAK": The man w'z c'nvicded 'ev rape b'cause the scientists found traces of 'is **DNA** on the victim's dress.

D.O.A. • dead on arrival.

EXAMPLE: I'm afraid the victim is **D.O.A.**

TRANSLATION: I'm afraid the victim is **dead on arrival**.

"REAL SPEAK": I'm afraid the victim's **D.O.A.**

D.U.I. • driving under the influence – a serious traffic violation citing a driver who is "driving under the influence" of alcohol or drugs.

EXAMPLE: Eric got a **D.U.I.** last night! He had to spend the night in jail!

TRANSLATION: Eric got a **traffic violation for driving under the influence** last night! He had to spend the night in jail!

"REAL SPEAK": Eric god a **D.U.I.** las' night! He had ta spend the night 'n jail!

Variation: **D.W.I.** • driving while intoxicated.

D.V.D. • digital video disk.

EXAMPLE: I just bought my first movie on **D.V.D.** The clarity is amazing!

TRANSLATION: I just bought my first movie on **digital video disk**. The clarity is amazing!

"REAL SPEAK": I jus' bought my first movie on **D.V.D.** The claridy's amazing!

-E-

E.R. • emergency room.

EXAMPLE: I had to go to the **E.R.** in the middle of the night because I tripped on my way to the bathroom and broke my arm!

TRANSLATION: I had to go to the **emergency room** in the middle of the night because I tripped on my way to the bathroom and broke my arm!

"REAL SPEAK": I had ta go da the **E.R.** in the middle the night b'cause I tripped on my way da the bathroom 'n broke my arm!

E.S.P. • extra sensory perception.

EXAMPLE: How did you know what I was thinking? You must have **E.S.P**!

TRANSLATION: How did you know what I was thinking? You must have **extra sensory perception**!

"REAL SPEAK": How'd ja know whad I w'z thinking? You must have **E.S.P**!

E.S.P.N. • Entertainment Sports Network – a popular television cable network which broadcasts sports and sports news 24 hours a day.

EXAMPLE: Did you see the basketball game on **E.S.P.N.** yesterday? It was great!

TRANSLATION: Did you see the basketball game on the **Entertainment Sports Network** yesterday? It was great!

"REAL SPEAK": Did'ja see the basketball game on **E.S.P.N.** yesderday? It w'z great!

-F-

F.B.I. • Federal Bureau of Investigation.

EXAMPLE: The **F.B.I.** is investigating the alleged illegal activity of our senator.

TRANSLATION: The **Federal Bureau of Investigation** is investigating the alleged illegal activity of our senator.

"REAL SPEAK": The **F.B.I.**'s invesdigading the alleged illegal actividy 'ev 'ar senader.

F.D.R. • Franklin Delano Roosevelt.

EXAMPLE: **F.D.R.** was the 32nd president of the United States of America.

TRANSLATION: **Franklin Delano Roosevelt** was the 32nd president of the United States of America.

"REAL SPEAK": **F.D.R.** w'z the 32nd president of the Unided States 'ev America.

FedEx (to) – [pronounced: Fed-Ex] to send a package using Federal Express – a popular overnight delivery service.

EXAMPLE: The only way I can get the report in time for our meeting is if you **FedEx** it to me right away.

TRANSLATION: The only way I can get the report in time for our meeting is if you **send it using Federal Express, the overnight delivery service** right away.

"REAL SPEAK": The only way I c'n get the repord in time fer 'ar meeding is if ya **FedEx** it ta me ride away.

F.M. • frequency modulation (referring to one of the two bands on most radios).

EXAMPLE: I only listen to **F.M.** because you get stereo sound, whereas on A.M. it's mono.

TRANSLATION: I only listen to **frequency modulation** because you get stereo sound, whereas on A.M. it's mono.

"REAL SPEAK": I only listen ta **F.M.** b'cause ya get stereo sound, whereas on A.M. it's mono.

F.Y.I. • for your information.

EXAMPLE: **F.Y.I.**, you're not allowed to park in the white zone. You'll need to move your car into an authorized parking lot.

TRANSLATION: **For your information**, you're not allowed to park in the white zone. You'll need to move your car into an authorized parking lot.

"REAL SPEAK": **F.Y.I.**, y'r nod allowed ta park 'n the white zone. You'll need ta move yer car into 'n authorized parking lot.

Note: This is another peculiarity in American slang. The phrase *"For your information..."* is typically used in anger when expressing opposition to someone's comment. For example:
– *I don't want you to park in front of my house!*
– *For your information, this is a free country and I'll park wherever I please!*
However, in its abbreviated form, F.Y.I., the connotation is quite friendly and even helpful:
– *F.Y.I. You shouldn't park there because the police will give you a ticket.*

~G~

G.Q. • Gentleman's Quarterly magazine (which is a popular magazine focusing on men's fashion) – This has become a popular adjective describing a man who is very handsome and stylish like the models in *G.Q.* magazine.

EXAMPLE: Chris looks very **G.Q.** with his new haircut.

TRANSLATION: Chris looks very **handsome and stylish** with his new haircut.

"REAL SPEAK": Chris looks very **G.Q.** with 'is new haircut.

~I~

I. • interstate highway.

EXAMPLE: Did you see the big accident on **I**-5 today?

TRANSLATION: Did you see the big accident on **interstate highway** 5 today?

"REAL SPEAK": Did'ja see the big accident on **I**-5 taday?

I.D. • identification.

EXAMPLE: Before I can sell you this alcohol, I'll need to see your **I.D.**

TRANSLATION: Before I can sell you this alcohol, I'll need to see your **identification**.

"REAL SPEAK": B'fore I c'n sell you this alcohol, a'll need ta see yer **I.D.**

I.O.U. • "I owe you" – an informal contract that one gives after borrowing money to insure reimbursement.

EXAMPLE: Can you lend me one hundred dollars? If you want, I'll give you an **I.O.U.**

TRANSLATION: Can you lend me one hundred dollars? If you want, I'll give you an **informal contract stating that I will reimburse you the entire amount.**

"REAL SPEAK": C'n ya len' me one hundred dollers? If ya want, a'll give ya 'n **I.O.U.**

I.Q. • intelligence quotient.

EXAMPLE: Tessa has an enormous **I.Q.** She may even be a genius!

TRANSLATION: Tessa has an enormous **intelligence quotient**. She may even be a genius!

"REAL SPEAK": Tessa has 'n enormous **I.Q.** She may even be a genius!

Note: Interestingly enough, the abbreviation *I.Q.* is actually more commonly known than what it stands for!

I.V. • intravenous (which is the bottle of nutritious liquid that is fed into a patient through a thin tube usually inserted into the back of the hand).

EXAMPLE: We need to put this patient on an **I.V.** immediately!

TRANSLATION: We need to put this patient on an **intravenous** immediately!

"REAL SPEAK": We need ta put this patient on 'n **I.V.** immediately!

-J-

J.F.K. • John F. Kennedy.

EXAMPLE: **J.F.K.** was the 35th president of the United States of America.

TRANSLATION: **John F. Kennedy** was the 35th president of the United States of America.

"REAL SPEAK": **J.F.K.** w'z the 35th president of the Unided States 'ev America.

-L-

L.A. • Los Angeles – an extremely popular abbreviation of "Los Angeles" and is used by virtually everyone.

EXAMPLE: **L.A.** is known as the entertainment capital of the world.

TRANSLATION: **Los Angeles** is known as the entertainment capital of the world.

"REAL SPEAK": **L.A.**'s known 'ez the entertainment capid'l 'a the world.

L.C.D. • liquid crystal display (as seen on many watch faces).

EXAMPLE: I used to wear a watch with hands to tell the time. But I prefer my new **L.C.D.** because I can read it in the dark as well!

TRANSLATION: I used to wear a watch with hands to tell the time. But I prefer my new **liquid crystal display** because I can read it in the dark as well!

"REAL SPEAK": I usta wear a watch with han'z ta tell the time. B'd I prefer my new **L.C.D.** b'cause I c'n read it in the dark 'ez well!

-M-

M.C. • Master of Ceremonies (which means "the host of a show").

EXAMPLE: I wonder who is going to be the **M.C.** of the Academy Awards next year!

TRANSLATION: I wonder who is going to be the **Master of Ceremonies** of the Academy Awards next year!

"REAL SPEAK": I wonder who's gonna be the **M.C.** of the Academy Awards next year!

M.D. • medical doctor.

EXAMPLE: My sister became an **M.D.** at the age of nineteen!

TRANSLATION: My sister became a **medical doctor** at the age of nineteen!

"REAL SPEAK": My sister became 'n **M.D.** 't the age 'ev nineteen!

M.I.A. • missing in action (said of a soldier).

EXAMPLE: Karen's son is **M.I.A.** She's still hoping he'll come home some day.

TRANSLATION:	Karen's son is **missing in action**. She's still hoping he'll come home some day.
"REAL SPEAK":	Karen's son's **M.I.A.** She's still hoping 'e'll come home some day.

~N~

N.F.L. • National Football League.

EXAMPLE:	Some day, I'm going to play for the **N.F.L**!
TRANSLATION:	Some day, I'm going to play for the **National Football League**!
"REAL SPEAK":	Some day, I'm gonna play fer the **N.F.L**!

N.H.L. • National Hockey League.

EXAMPLE:	Players for the **N.H.L.** make thousands of dollars a year.
TRANSLATION:	Players for the **National Hockey League** make thousands of dollars a year.
"REAL SPEAK":	Players fer the **N.H.L.** make thousan'z 'a dollars a year.

N.B.A. • National Basketball Association.

EXAMPLE:	The **N.B.A.** rejected me because I'm too short.
TRANSLATION:	The **National Basketball Association** rejected me because I'm too short.
"REAL SPEAK":	The **N.B.A.** rejected me b'cause I'm too short.

~O~

OB-GYN • obstetrician-gynecologist.

EXAMPLE:	My **OB-GYN** just gave me the news that I'm pregnant!
TRANSLATION:	My **obstetrician-gynecologist** just gave me the news that I'm pregnant!
"REAL SPEAK":	My **OB-GYN** jus' gamme the news th'd I'm pregnant!

O.D. • overdose.

EXAMPLE:	One of the kids in our school **O.D.**ed last night.
TRANSLATION:	One of the kids in our school **overdosed** last night.

"REAL SPEAK":	One 'a the kids 'n 'ar school **O.D.**ed las' night.

Note: "O.D." can be used in reference to products other than drugs as well: *I couldn't eat another bite of that cake. I've totally O.D.ed on chocolate.*

O.J. • orange juice.

EXAMPLE:	Would you like a glass of **O.J.** with your breakfast?
TRANSLATION:	Would you like a glass of **orange juice** with your breakfast?
"REAL SPEAK":	Would'ja like a glass 'ev **O.J.** with yerr breakfast?

O.K. • all right (used as an affirmation; also "okay").

EXAMPLE:	– Do you want to go to the movies tonight? – **Okay**. That sounds like fun.
TRANSLATION:	– Do you want to go to the movies tonight? – **All right**. That sounds like fun.
"REAL SPEAK":	– Wanna go da the movies tonight? – **Okay**. That soun'z like fun.

O.R. • operating room.

EXAMPLE:	I have to get to the **O.R.** immediately. I'm performing surgery in five minutes.
TRANSLATION:	I have to get to the **operating room** immediately. I'm performing surgery in five minutes.
"REAL SPEAK":	I hafta get ta the **O.R.** immediately. I'm performing surgery 'n five minutes.

O.T. • overtime.

EXAMPLE:	I put in three hours of **O.T.** last night.
TRANSLATION:	I put in three hours of **overtime** last night.
"REAL SPEAK":	I pud in three hours 'ev **O.T.** las' night.

~P~

P.B.&J. • (*pronounced: "Pee-Bee-'n-Jay"*) peanut butter and jelly sandwich – one of the most popular sandwiches among children in the United States.

EXAMPLE: My nephew eats at least one **P.B.&J.** a day. He never gets tired of them!

TRANSLATION: My nephew eats at least one **peanut butter and jelly sandwich** a day. He never gets tired of them!

"REAL SPEAK": My nephew eats 'it least one **P.B. 'n J.** a day. He never gets tired of 'em!

P.C. • 1. personal computer • 2. politically correct.

EXAMPLE 1: I just bought a new **P.C.** You wouldn't believe how fast it is!

TRANSLATION: I just bought a new **personal computer**. You wouldn't believe how fast it is!

"REAL SPEAK": I jus' bod a new **P.C.** You wouldn't b'lieve how fast id is!

EXAMPLE 2: It's not **P.C.** to use the term "policeman." Nowadays, you have to use "police officer" out of respect for the women on the police force.

TRANSLATION: It's not **politically correct** to use the term "policeman." Nowadays, you have to use "police officer" out of respect for the women on the police force.

"REAL SPEAK": It's not **P.C.** da use the term "policem'n." Nowadays, ya hafta use "police officer" oudda respect fer the women on the police force.

P.E. • physical education class.

EXAMPLE: I hate **P.E.** I'd rather sit somewhere and read.

TRANSLATION: I hate **physical education class**. I'd rather sit somewhere and read.

"REAL SPEAK": I hate **P.E.** I'd rather sit somewhere 'n read.

Variation: **Phys. Ed.**

P.J.s • pajamas.

EXAMPLE: It's time to go to bed. Put on your **P.J.s**.

TRANSLATION: It's time to go to bed. Put on your **pajamas**.

"REAL SPEAK": It's time ta go da bed. Pud on yer **P.J.s**.

P.M. • post meridiem (afternoon or evening).

EXAMPLE: My plane leaves at two o'clock **P.M.**

TRANSLATION: My plane leaves at two o'clock **in the afternoon**.

"REAL SPEAK": My plane leaves 'it two a'clock **P.M.**

P.M.S. • 1. *n.* premenstrual syndrome (usually resulting in mood changes) • 2. *v.* to have premenstrual syndrome.

EXAMPLE 1: My sister is in such a bad mood today. She has terrible **P.M.S.**

TRANSLATION: My sister is in such a bad mood today. She has terrible **premenstrual syndrome**.

"REAL SPEAK": My sister's in such a bad mood taday. She has terr'ble **P.M.S.**

EXAMPLE 2: Nancy's really in a bad mood today. She must be **P.M.S.**-ing.

TRANSLATION: Nancy's really in a bad mood today. She must be **having her premenstrual syndrome**.

"REAL SPEAK": Nancy's really in a bad mood taday. She must be **P.M.S.**-ing.

P.O. • post office.

EXAMPLE: If you have a package for me, please send it to my **P.O.** box.

TRANSLATION: If you have a package for me, please send it to my **post office** box.

"REAL SPEAK": If ya have a package fer me, please send it ta my **P.O.** box.

P.O.'d. • pissed off, which is American slang for "angry."

EXAMPLE: I'm really **P.O.ed** at my little brother. He ruined my new bicycle.

TRANSLATION: I'm really **pissed off** at my little brother. He ruined my new bicycle.

"REAL SPEAK": I'm really **P.O.ed** 'it my liddle brother. He ruined my new bicycle.

P.O.W. • prisoner of war.

EXAMPLE: My uncle was a **P.O.W.** in the last World War.

TRANSLATION: My uncle was a **prisoner of war** in the last World War.

"REAL SPEAK": My uncle w'z a **P.O.W.** 'n the last World War.

P.S. • postscript – This abbreviation is added to the end of a letter when the writer decides to add a closing remark. If an additional remark is to be added, the initials "P.P.S." are added. It can also be used in spoken language:

EXAMPLE:	John Smith is coming to my party tomorrow. **P.S.** Don't say anything about his new hairpiece!
TRANSLATION:	John Smith is coming to my party tomorrow. **One more thing:** Don't say anything about his new hairpiece!
"REAL SPEAK":	John Smith 'ez coming ta my pardy tamorrow. **P.S.** Don't say anything aboud 'is new hairpiece!

P.U. • This comes from "Pew!" which is an interjection used to signify an unpleasant smell. When "Pew!" is said slowly, it sounds like "P.U."

EXAMPLE:	**P.U**! What a horrible smell!
TRANSLATION:	**That stinks**! What's the horrible smell!
"REAL SPEAK":	**P.U**! Whad a horr'ble smell!

-R-

R.&B. • *(music)* rhythm and blues.

EXAMPLE:	Whitney Houston is a famous **R.&B.** singer.
TRANSLATION:	Whitney Houston is a famous **rhythm and blues** singer.
"REAL SPEAK":	Whitney Houston's a famous **R. 'n B.** singer.

R.&R. • 1. rest and recreation • 2. rock and roll.

EXAMPLE 1:	I need some **R. & R.** I've been working too hard.
TRANSLATION:	I need some **rest and recreation**. I've been working too hard.
"REAL SPEAK":	I need s'm **R. 'n R.** I've been working too hard.
EXAMPLE 2:	My favorite style of music is **R.&R.**
TRANSLATION:	My favorite style of music is **rock and roll**.
"REAL SPEAK":	My fav'rite style 'ev music is **R. 'n R.**

R.N. • registered nurse.

| EXAMPLE: | Right now I'm working as an **R.N.**, but I'm hoping to become a medical doctor in another few years. |
| TRANSLATION: | Right now I'm working as a **registered nurse**, but I'm hoping to become a medical doctor in another few years. |

| "REAL SPEAK": | Right now I'm working as 'n **R.N.**, b'd I'm hoping ta become a medical docter in another few years. |

R.S.V.P. • répondez s'il-vous-plaît (French for "reply please") – common initials at the end of an invitation requesting a response.

EXAMPLE:	"You are invited to attend the wedding between Nancy Burke and Dominic Holzhaus. **R.S.V.P.** by June 1st."
TRANSLATION:	"You are invited to attend the wedding between Nancy Burke and Dominic Holzhaus. **Please respond** by June 1st."
"REAL SPEAK":	"Y'r invited to attend the wedding b'tween Nancy Burke 'n Dominic Holzhaus. **R.S.V.P.** by June 1st."

R.V. • recreational vehicle.

EXAMPLE:	We drove my new **R.V.** to the mountains for the weekend.
TRANSLATION:	We drove my new **recreational vehicle** to the mountains for the weekend.
"REAL SPEAK":	We drove my new **R.V.** da the mountains fer the weekend.

-S-

S.O.B. • a popular euphemism for the expression "Son of a bitch."

EXAMPLE:	That **S.O.B.** stole my car!
TRANSLATION:	That **son of a bitch** stole my car!
"REAL SPEAK":	Thad **S.O.B.** stole my car!

S.O.S. • *(nautical term)* save our ship – a general distress call.

EXAMPLE:	Something's wrong with our boat. We'd better send out an **S.O.S.**
TRANSLATION:	Something's wrong with our boat. We'd better send out an **distress call**.
"REAL SPEAK":	Something's wrong with 'ar boat. We'd bedder send out 'n **S.O.S.**

S.T.D. • sexually transmitted disease.

| EXAMPLE: | Due to the rise in **S.T.D.**s, safe sex is now more important than ever. |
| TRANSLATION: | Due to the rise in **sexually transmitted diseases**, safe sex is now more important than ever. |

"REAL SPEAK": Due da the rise 'n **S.T.D.**s, safe sex is now more important th'n ever.

-T-

T.A. • teaching assistant.

EXAMPLE: Class, I'd like you to meet our new **T.A.** She's going to be helping me every afternoon.

TRANSLATION: Class, I'd like you to meet our new **teaching assistant**. She's going to be helping me every afternoon.

"REAL SPEAK": Class, I'd like you da meet 'ar new **T.A.** She's gonna be helping me ev'ry afternoon.

T.G.I.F. • "Thank God it's Friday."

EXAMPLE: The weekend starts in five minutes! **T.G.I.F!**

TRANSLATION: The weekend starts in five minutes! **Thank God, it's Friday**!

"REAL SPEAK": The weeken' starts 'n five minutes! **T.G.I.F**!

T.L.C. • tender loving care.

EXAMPLE: You look sad today. I think you need some **T.L.C.**

TRANSLATION: You look sad today. I think you need some **tender loving care**.

"REAL SPEAK": You look sad taday. I think you need s'm **T.L.C.**

T.N.T. • (high explosive) trinitrotoluene.

EXAMPLE: The demolition workers blew up the building with a few sticks of **T.N.T.**

TRANSLATION: The demolition workers blew up the building with a few sticks of **trinitrotoluene**.

"REAL SPEAK": The demolition workers blew up the building with a few sticks 'ev **T.N.T.**

Note: It's interesting to note that only the abbreviation is commonly known, not the actual word it represents.

T.P. • 1. n. toilet paper • 2. v. to spread toilet paper all over something.

EXAMPLE 1: We need to buy some **T.P.** at the market.

TRANSLATION: We need to buy some **toilet paper** at the market.

"REAL SPEAK": We need ta buy s'm **T.P.** 'it the market.

EXAMPLE 2: The students **T.P.ed** their professor's house as a joke.

TRANSLATION: The students **spread toilet paper all over** their professor's house as a joke.

"REAL SPEAK": The students **T.P.ed** their pruhfesser's house 'ez a joke.

T.V. • television.

EXAMPLE: There's a great new comedy on **T.V.** tonight. Do you want to come to my house and watch it with me?

TRANSLATION: There's a great new comedy on **television** tonight. Do you want to come to my house and watch it with me?

"REAL SPEAK": There's a great new comedy on **T.V.** danight. Wanna come ta my house 'n watch it with me?

-U-

U. • university.

EXAMPLE: My father graduated from Chicago **U**.

TRANSLATION: My father graduated from Chicago **University**.

"REAL SPEAK": My father gradjuaded fr'm Chicago **U**.

U.F.O. • unidentified flying object (such as a flying saucer).

EXAMPLE: Did you see that light streak across the sky? I think it was a **U.F.O**!

TRANSLATION: Did you see that light streak across the sky? I think it was an **unidentified flying object**!

"REAL SPEAK": Did'ju see that light streak across the sky? I think it w'ez a **U.F.O**!

U.K. • United Kingdom.

EXAMPLE: My mother was born in the **U.K.** but she has lived in the U.S. most of her life. She still sounds like she just arrived here!

TRANSLATION: My mother was born in the **United Kingdom** but she has lived in the U.S. most of her life. She still sounds like she just arrived here!

"REAL SPEAK": My mother w'z born 'n the **U.K.** b't she's lived in the U.S. most 'ev 'er life. She still soun'z like she just arrived here!

UPS • [pronounced: U-P-S] United Parcel Service – a popular overnight delivery service.

> **EXAMPLE:** I need you to send my files to me **UPS**. They have to be here tomorrow!
>
> **TRANSLATION:** I need you to send my files to me **United Parcel Service**. They have to be here tomorrow!
>
> **"REAL SPEAK":** I need 'ja da sen' my files ta me **UPS**. They hafta be here damorrow!
>
> *Note:* This can also be used as a verb: *I need you to UPS my files to me right away!; I need you to send my files to me using United Parcel Service right away!*

U.S. • United States.

> **EXAMPLE:** I was born in the **U.S.** but I've lived most of my life in France.
>
> **TRANSLATION:** I was born in the **United States** but I've lived most of my life in France.
>
> **"REAL SPEAK":** I w'z born 'n the **U.S.** b'd I've lived most 'a my life 'n France.
>
> *Variation 1:* **U.S.A.** • United States of America.
>
> *Variation 2:* **U.S. of A.** • United States of America.

-V-

V.C.R. • video cassette recorder.

> **EXAMPLE:** Since I'm not going to be home tonight, I need to set my **V.C.R.** There's a great TV show on at eight o'clock that I don't want to miss.
>
> **TRANSLATION:** Since I'm not going to be home tonight, I need to set my **video cassette recorder**. There's a great TV show on at eight o'clock that I don't want to miss.
>
> **"REAL SPEAK":** Since I'm not gonna be home tanight, I need da set my **V.C.R.** There's a great TV show on ad aid a'clock th'd I don't wanna miss.

V.D. • venereal disease.

> **EXAMPLE:** If you're going to be sexually intimate with someone, you need to be careful. You don't want to get **V.D.**

> **TRANSLATION:** If you're going to be sexually intimate with someone, you need to be careful. You don't want to get a **venereal disease**.
>
> **"REAL SPEAK":** If y'r gonna be sexually intimate with someone, ya need ta be careful. Ya don't wanna get **V.D.**

V.I.P. • very important person.

> **EXAMPLE:** A **V.I.P.** is coming to our office today. We all need to be on our most professional behavior.
>
> **TRANSLATION:** A **very important person** is coming to our office today. We all need to be on our most professional behavior.
>
> **"REAL SPEAK":** A **V.I.P.**'s coming ta 'ar office taday. We all need ta be on 'ar most pruhfessional behavier.

V.P. • vice president.

> **EXAMPLE:** Congratulations! I heard you were just promoted to **V.P**!
>
> **TRANSLATION:** Congratulations! I heard you were just promoted to **vice president**!
>
> **"REAL SPEAK":** C'ngradjalations! I heard you were just pruhmoded ta **V.P**!

-Y-

Y2K • year 2 thousand (*year 2000*).

> **EXAMPLE:** Everyone thought that when **Y2K** arrived, computers would malfunction. Luckily, nothing major happened.
>
> **TRANSLATION:** Everyone thought that when **the year two thousand** arrived, computers would malfunction. Luckily, nothing major happened.
>
> **"REAL SPEAK":** Ev'ryone thought th't when **Y2K** arrived, c'mpuders would malfunction. Luckily, nothing majer happened.
>
> *Note:* The letter "K" in this abbreviation comes from "*kilo*" which is Greek for "1,000."

LESSON 8 BABYSITTING

"Hey! Cut it out!"

LET'S WARM UP!

MATCH THE PICTURES

As a fun way to get started, see if you can guess the meaning of the new slang words and expressions on the opposite page by using the pictures below and following the context of the sentences.

1. When I found out that my car was destroyed, I **lost it**!
2. Tom and his father are architects. **Like father, like son**.
3. I know you're upset, but try to **keep your cool**.
4. Why are you bothering me? **Cut it out**!
5. I think this gift will **knock your socks off**!
6. You have to be home before midnight or you're going to be punished. I'm **laying down the law**!
7. Benny is already doing chemistry! He's a real **wiz kid**.
8. These kids are making me crazy. I'm **in babysitting hell**!
9. I'm exhausted. I need a **breather**.
10. My mother vacuums every day. She's such a **neat freak**.
11. I'm not sure if I want to go to the movies or hear a concert. It's **a toss up**.
12. Stop **screaming your lungs out** at me! Calm down!
13. David works on the computer all the time. He's turned into a real **computer nerd**.
14. Ernie is always **up to something**. He can't be left alone!

A. stop it
B. child genius
C. excite you
D. cleanliness maniac
E. yelling loudly
F. stating the rules firmly
G. computer enthusiast
H. lost control of my emotions
I. break
J. doing something suspicious
K. the son resembles the father
L. equal
M. having an exhausting time babysitting
N. remain calm

LET'S TALK!

A. DIALOGUE USING SLANG & IDIOMS

The words introduced on the first two pages are used in the dialogue below. See if you can understand the conversation. *Note:* The translation of the words in boldface is on the right-hand page.

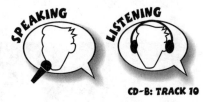

SPEAKING LISTENING

CD-B: TRACK 10

Dennis: You won't believe the night I had. I was in **babysitting hell**. I could have either stayed home and done homework or babysat my sister's eight-year old boy and her baby. It was sort of a **toss up** since neither idea really **knocked my socks off**. Then I figured I could use a **breather** from studying, so I told my sister I'd come over and stay with her kids. What a mistake!

Susie: Why? What happened?

Dennis: After I put the baby to bed, it got really quiet. I figured the older one was **up to something**. When I walked into his bedroom, he was in the middle of lighting a big rocket that he had built! So, I **kept my cool** and told him to **cut it out** right now, but it was too late. It shot through the window and made such a noise that the baby started **screaming his lungs out**. In the middle of all this, my sister, the **neat freak**, came home and when she saw the mess it made, she **lost it**.

Susie: I don't understand something. How did he know how to build a rocket at his age?

Dennis: He's always been a **wiz kid** and a real **computer nerd**. **Like father, like son**.

Susie: If you ever babysit your nephews again, you need to **lay down the law** right from the beginning!

B. DIALOGUE TRANSLATED INTO STANDARD ENGLISH

LET'S SEE HOW MUCH YOU REMEMBER!
Just for fun, bounce around in random order to the words
and expressions in boldface below. See if you can remember
their slang equivalents without looking at the left-hand page!

Dennis: You won't believe the night I had. I was **having an exhausting time babysitting**. I could have either stayed home and done homework or babysat my sister's eight-year old boy and her baby. It was sort of **equal** since neither idea really **excited me**. Then I figured I could use a **break** from studying, so I told my sister I'd come over and stay with her kids. What a mistake!

Susie: Why? What happened?

Dennis: After I put the baby to bed, it got really quiet. I figured the older one was **doing something suspicious**. When I walked into his bedroom, he was in the middle of lighting a big rocket that he had built! So, I **remained calm** and told him to **stop it** right now, but it was too late. It shot through the window and made such a noise that the baby started **screaming excessively**. In the middle of all this, my sister, the **cleanliness maniac**, came home and when she saw the mess it made, she **lost control of her emotions**.

Susie: I don't understand something. How did he know how to build a rocket at his age?

Dennis: He's always been a **child genius** and a real **computer enthusiast**. **He's just like his father**.

Susie: If you ever babysit your nephews again, you need to **state the rules firmly** right from the beginning!

C. DIALOGUE USING "REAL SPEAK"

The dialogue below demonstrates how the slang conversation on the previous page would *really* be spoken by native speakers!

Dennis: You won't believe the nide I had. I w'z 'n **babysidding hell**. I could've either stayed home 'n done homework 'r babysat my sister's eight-year old boy 'n 'er baby. It w'z sord of a **toss up** since neither idea really **knocked my socks off**. Then I figured I could use a **breather** fr'm studying, so I told my sister I'd come over 'n stay with 'er kids. Whad a mistake!

Susie: Why? What happened?

Dennis: After I put the baby da bed, it got really quiet. I figured the older one w'z **up ta something**. When I walked into 'is bedroom, he w'z in the middle of liding a big rocket thad 'e 'ed built! So, I **kept my cool** 'n told 'im da **cud id out** right now, bud it w'z too late. It shot through the window 'n made such a noise that the baby starded **screaming 'is lungs out**. In the middle of all this, my sister, the **neat freak**, came home 'n when she saw the mess it made, she **lost it**.

Susie: I don' understand something. How did 'e know how da build a rocked ad his age?

Dennis: He's always been a **wiz kid** 'n a real **compuder nerd**. **Like father, like son**.

Susie: If ya ever babysit yer nephews again, ya need ta **lay down the law** right fr'm the beginning!

LET'S LEARN!

CD-B: TRACK 11

VOCABULARY

The following words and expressions were used in the previous dialogues. Let's take a closer look at what they mean.

babysitting hell (to be in) *exp.* to be having an exhausting time babysitting.

EXAMPLE: I'd really like to go with you to the movies tonight but I can't. I'm **in babysitting hell**.

TRANSLATION: I'd really like to go with you to the movies tonight but I can't. I'm **having an exhausting time babysitting**.

"REAL SPEAK:" I'd really like ta go with ya da the movies tanight bud I can't. I'm **in babysidding hell**.

Note: Adding the noun **hell** to a particular activity is extremely common in American slang. This popular formula is used to add contempt to an activity. For example: *I was in shopping hell all day;* I was having an exhausting time shopping all day. • *I'm in laundry hell;* I'm having an exhausting time doing laundry.

NOW YOU DO IT:
(Use a sentence with "hell" to add contempt to an activity)

breather (to take a) *exp.* to take a break (and have time to just breath).

EXAMPLE:	I've been working nonstop for the past six hours on this project. I think I need to **take a breather**.
TRANSLATION:	I've been working nonstop for the past six hours on this project. I think I need to **take a break**.
"REAL SPEAK:"	I've been working nonstop fer the pas' six hours on this project. I think I need da **take a breather**.

Synonym 1: **downtime** *n.* • *I need to take some downtime; I need to take a break.*

Synonym 2: **take five/ten (to)** *exp.* to take a five-minute (or ten-minute) break.

NOW YOU DO IT:
(Use "take a breather" in a sentence)

computer nerd (to be a) *exp.* to be a computer enthusiast.

EXAMPLE:	Bill used to be an athlete. Now he spends all of his time in front of the computer. He's turned into a real **computer nerd**!
TRANSLATION:	Bill used to be an athlete. Now he spends all of his time in front of the computer. He's turned into a real **computer enthusiast**!
"REAL SPEAK:"	Bill usta be 'n athlete. Now 'e spends all of 'is time in fronna the c'mpuder. He's turned into a real **c'mpuder nerd**!
Note:	The expression **computer nerd** refers to someone who is not only a computer enthusiast, but who looks like the stereotypical scientist, often with glasses, pens in his shirt pocket, and not at all athletic.

Synonym: **computer geek** *exp.*

NOW YOU DO IT:
(Use "computer nerd" in a sentence)

cut it out (to) *exp.* to stop doing something.

EXAMPLE:	Why are you playing that music so loudly? **Cut it out**! I can't concentrate on my homework!
TRANSLATION:	Why are you playing that music so loudly? **Stop it**! I can't concentrate on my homework!
"REAL SPEAK:"	Why'er you playing that music so loudly? **Cud it out**! I can't concentrade on my homework!

Synonym 1: **All right already!** *exp.* Stop it!

Synonym 2: **cool it (to)** *exp.* • *Cool it!;* Stop it!

Synonym 3: **give it a rest (to)** *exp.* • *Give it a rest!;* Stop it!

Synonym 4: **knock it off (to)** *exp.* • *Knock it off!;* Stop it!

NOW YOU DO IT:
(Use "cut it out" in a sentence)

keep one's cool (to) *exp.* to remain calm.

EXAMPLE: I know you're upset, but try to **keep your cool**. Let's discuss the problem rationally.

TRANSLATION: I know you're upset, but try to **remain calm**. Let's discuss the problem rationally.

"REAL SPEAK:" I know y'r upset, but try da **keep yer cool**. Let's discuss the problem rationally.

Synonym: **keep one's shirt on (to)** *exp.* • *Keep your shirt on!;* Relax! (or "Be patient!")

NOW YOU DO IT:
(Use "keep your cool" in a sentence)

knock someone's socks off (to) *exp.* to thrill someone.

EXAMPLE: For my graduation present, my parents gave me a new car! Their gift really **knocked my socks off**!

TRANSLATION: For my graduation present, my parents gave me a new car! Their gift really **thrilled me**!

"REAL SPEAK:" Fer my graduation present, my parents gam 'e a new car! Their gift really **knocked my socks off**!

Synonym: **blow someone away (to)** *exp.* • **1.** to surprise and thrill someone • **2.** to shock someone with bad news.

NOW YOU DO IT:
(Use "knocked my socks off" in a sentence)

lay down the law (to) *exp.* to state the rules firmly.

EXAMPLE: My son failed his math test, so I **laid down the law** – no more TV until he finishes his homework.

TRANSLATION: My son failed his math test, so I **stated the rules firmly** – no more TV until he finishes his homework.

"REAL SPEAK:" My son failed 'is math test, so I **laid down the law** – no more TV until 'e finishes 'is homework.

Synonym: **put one's foot down (to)** *exp.* to be very firm.

NOW YOU DO IT:
(Use "lay down the law" in a sentence)

Like father, like son *exp.* said of a father and son with similar characteristics.

EXAMPLE: David and his father both have a great sense of humor. **Like father, like son**.

TRANSLATION: David and his father both have a great sense of humor. **The father and son are very similar**.

"REAL SPEAK:" David and 'is father both have a great sense of humor. **Like father, like son**.

Synonym: **the spitting image of someone (to be)** *exp.* said of a son or daughter who looks like one of the parents.

Also: **Like mother, like daughter** *exp.* said of a mother and daughter with similar characteristics.

NOW YOU DO IT:
(Use "Like father, like son" in a sentence)

lose it (to) *exp.* to lose control of one's emotions.

EXAMPLE: When Christina found out that Douglas had been seeing another woman, she **lost it** and told him she never wanted to see him again.

TRANSLATION: When Christina found out that Douglas had been seeing another woman, she **lost control of her emotions** and told him she never wanted to see him again.

"REAL SPEAK:" When Christina found out th't Douglas 'ud been seeing another woman, she **lost it** 'n told 'im she never wan'ed ta see 'im again.

Synonym 1: **come apart at the seams (to)** *exp.*

Synonym 2: **flip out (to)** *exp.*

Synonym 3: **freak [out] (to)** *exp.*

Synonym 4: **unglued (to become)** *exp.*

NOW YOU DO IT:
(Use "lose it" in a sentence)

---

neat freak *n.* a person who is fanatic about cleanliness, cleanliness maniac.

EXAMPLE: My mother never stops cleaning the house. She always has a dust rag in her hands. She's such a **neat freak**!

TRANSLATION: My mother never stops cleaning the house. She always has a dust rag in her hands. She's such a **cleanliness maniac**!

"REAL SPEAK:" My mother never stops cleaning the house. She always has a dust rag 'n 'er hands. She's such a **neat freak**!

Also 1: **spic and span** *exp.* said of something that is very clean and orderly.

Also 2: **neat as a pin** *exp.* said of something that is very clean and orderly.

NOW YOU DO IT:
(Use "neat freak" in a sentence)

---

scream one's lungs out (to) *exp.* to yell extremely loudly.

EXAMPLE: I **screamed my lungs out** during the entire football game. That's why my throat is so sore today!

TRANSLATION: I **yelled extremely loudly** during the entire football game. That's why my throat is so sore today!

"REAL SPEAK:" I **screamed my lungs out** during the entire football game. That's why my throat's so sore daday!

Variation: **scream at the top of one's lungs (to)** *exp.*

Synonym: **scream bloody murder (to)** *exp.*

NOW YOU DO IT:
(Use "scream my lungs out" in a sentence)

toss up (to be a) *exp.* said of two choices that have equal consequences, the same.

EXAMPLE: I could either take my car to a mechanic or fix it myself. **It's a toss up** because the mechanic will be expensive and my time is worth money.

TRANSLATION: I could either take my car to a mechanic or fix it myself. **They both have equal consequences** because the mechanic will be expensive and my time is worth money.

"REAL SPEAK:" I could either take my car do a mechanic 'r fix it myself. **It's a toss up** cuz the mechanic'll be expensive 'n my time's worth money.

Synonym 1: **same difference / same diff.** *exp.*

Synonym 2: **six of one, half a dozen of the other (to be)** *exp.*

NOW YOU DO IT:
(Use "toss up" in a sentence)

up to something (to be) *exp.* to be in the process of doing something suspicious.

EXAMPLE:
– Jack has been in the garage for the past two hours. He must be **up to something**.
– Maybe he's making something for your birthday!

TRANSLATION:
– Jack has been in the garage for the past two hours. He must be **doing something suspicious**.
– Maybe he's making something for your birthday!

"REAL SPEAK:"
– Jack's been in the garage fer the pas' two hours. He must be **up ta something**.
– Maybe 'e's making something fer yer birthday!

Variation: **What [are you • is he • is she • are they] up to?** *exp.* What suspicious activity [are you • is he • is she • are they] doing?

Also: **up to no good (to be)** *exp.* to be in the process of doing something suspicious and wicked.

NOW YOU DO IT:
(Use "up to something" in a sentence)

wiz kid *exp.* a child genius (from the term *wizard*).

EXAMPLE: Nancy's daughter is only four years old and she's already doing algebra! She's a **wiz kid**!

TRANSLATION: Nancy's daughter is only four years old and she's already doing algebra! She's a **child genius**!

"REAL SPEAK:" Nancy's daughter's only four years old 'n she's already doing algebra! She's a **wiz kid**!

Note: **to be a wiz / whiz at something** *exp.* to be an expert at something.

Synonym: **wunderkind** *exp.* (from German – pronounced *vun-dah kint*).

NOW YOU DO IT:
(Use "wiz kid" in a sentence)

LET'S PRACTICE!

A. TRUTH OR LIE (Answers on p. 223)
Read the conversation each person is having on the phone, then read their actual thoughts in the bubble. Decide if the person is telling the truth or a lie by checking the appropriate box.

CD-B: TRACK 12

B. FIND THE DEFINITION *(Answers on p. 223)*
Write the definition of the slang words in boldface
choosing from the word list below.

CD-B: TRACK 13

DEFINITIONS

✔ said of two choices that have equal consequences, the same

✔ to remain calm

✔ to be having an exhausting time babysitting

✔ to be in the process of doing something suspicious

✔ to be a computer enthusiast

✔ to stop doing something

✔ to thrill someone

✔ to lose control of one's emotions

✔ a person who is fanatic about cleanliness, a cleanliness maniac

✔ to yell extremely loudly

✔ to take a break (and have time to just breath)

✔ a genius child

✔ said of a father and son with similar characteristics

✔ to state the rules firmly

---

1. **babysitting hell (to be in)** *exp.* _____.

2. **breather (to take a)** *exp.* _____.

3. **computer nerd (to be a)** *exp.* _____.

4. **cut it out (to)** *exp.* _____.

5. **keep one's cool (to)** *exp.* _____.

6. **knock someone's socks off (to)** *exp.* _____.

7. **lay down the law (to)** *exp.* _____.

8. **Like father, like son** *exp.* _____.

9. **lose it (to)** *exp.* _____.

10. **neat freak** *exp.* _____.

11. **scream one's lungs out (to)** *exp.* _____.

12. **toss up (to be a)** *exp.* _____.

13. **up to something (to be)** *exp.* _____.

14. **wiz kid** *exp.* _____.

CD-B: TRACK 14

C. FIND-THE-WORD GRID *(Answers on p. 223)*

Fill in the blanks with the most appropriate word using the list. Next, find and circle the word in the grid below. The answers may be spelled vertically or horizontally.

SOCKS	CUT	LAW	HELL	LOSE
BREATHER	COOL	LUNGS	WIZ	FREAK

1. I'm tired from working without a break. I'm going to take a ten-minute _____ .

2. I couldn't hear the movie last night because a little baby was screaming his _____ out!

3. Don't hit me on the head any more! _____ it out!

4. The only way to get kids to behave is to lay down the _____.

5. Our house is always clean thanks to my mother. She's a total neat _____.

6. Would you like to visit me at my sister's house? I'm in babysitting _____ and could use help.

7. My five-year old nephew just explained physics to me! He's a real _____ kid!

8. I have some news that's going to knock your _____ off. I'm getting married!

9. I know you're angry, but try to keep your _____.

10. If you don't stop bothering me, I'm going to _____ it!

FIND-THE-WORD GRID

T	N	F	R	E	A	K	C	E	D	G	R	R	E	W	D	S	T	M	A	T
H	C	A	L	L	E	G	R	O	A	O	O	T	A	B	L	E	D	E	M	A
V	W	D	L	R	S	O	S	U	F	C	S	D	F	I	M	C	G	L	O	R
Y	T	J	T	R	E	I	G	H	L	U	E	A	O	C	E	K	O	U	V	V
E	H	O	W	K	C	B	R	E	O	T	H	E	L	O	P	S	H	N	E	E
I	I	U	O	C	O	O	L	H	O	L	A	D	L	R	S	T	A	C	N	T
Q	B	R	A	I	N	S	T	O	R	M	R	M	O	T	I	O	N	H	G	O
U	C	N	K	I	D	L	E	R	D	D	E	I	W	M	C	W	E	O	S	D
E	U	E	W	N	E	T	H	E	R	E	C	O	G	N	I	Z	E	S	O	E
I	T	D	W	D	D	H	T	M	R	E	E	L	O	S	E	Z	O	I	S	A

Fish, Insects & Animals Used in Slang

Everything from the cute and cuddly to the scarey and slimy has been used in the following expressions containing living creatures. Just make sure you **don't have a cow** (get upset) and **chicken out** (lose your courage) on learning these fun expressions when you see this **whale of a** list (enormous). Even if you don't have a **memory like an elephant** (incredible memory), you'll be **in hog heaven** (delighted) as you go through and glance at these very original idioms. It's sure to be **more fun than a barrel of monkeys** (extremely fun)!

ANIMAL

animal *n.* one who is very sexually aggressive.

> **EXAMPLE:** I went out with Ernie last night for the first time. He was an **animal**!

> **TRANSLATION:** I went out with Ernie last night for the first time. He was a **very sexually aggressive person**!

> **"REAL SPEAK":** I wen' out with Ernie las' night fer the firs' time. He w'z 'n **animal**!

party animal *n.* one who loves to go to parties.

> **EXAMPLE:** Dan went to three parties tonight. **He's such a party animal**!

> **TRANSLATION:** Dan went to three parties tonight. **He loves going to parties**!

> **"REAL SPEAK":** Dan went ta three pardies tanight. **He's such a pardy animal**!

ANT

antsy (to be) *adj.* to be restless.

> **EXAMPLE:** I couldn't sleep last night because I was **antsy**. I was worrying about my job.

> **TRANSLATION:** I couldn't sleep last night because I was **restless**. I was worrying about my job.

> **"REAL SPEAK":** I couldn't sleep las' night b'cause I w'z **antsy**. I w'z worrying about my job.

APE

ape over something or someone (to go) *exp.* to go crazy with excitement for something or someone.

> **EXAMPLE:** The moment I met Al, I **went ape over him**. I knew we'd get married some day.

> **TRANSLATION:** The moment I met Al, I **went crazy with excitement over him**. I knew we'd get married some day.

> **"REAL SPEAK":** The moment I met Al, I **went ape over 'im**. I knew we'd get married some day.

BAT

blind as a bat (to be as) *exp.* to be unable to see at all.

> **EXAMPLE:** I'm **as blind as a bat** without my glasses.

> **TRANSLATION:** I'm **unable to see at all** without my glasses.

"REAL SPEAK": I'm **'ez blind 'ez a bat** without my glasses.

like a bat out of hell *exp.* very quickly.

EXAMPLE: The robber ran out of the bank **like a bat out of hell**.

TRANSLATION: The robber ran out of the bank **very quickly**.

"REAL SPEAK": The robber ran oudda the bank **like a bad oudda hell**.

BIRD

birds and the bees (the) exp. the topic of sex.

EXAMPLE: So, when are you going to talk to your son about **the birds and the bees**?

TRANSLATION: So, when are you going to talk to your son about **the topic of sex**?

"REAL SPEAK": So, when'er ya gonna talk ta yer son about **the birds 'n the bees**?

early bird *exp.* a person who gets up early in the morning, an early riser.

EXAMPLE: My mother is a real **early bird**. She gets up at five o'clock every morning.

TRANSLATION: My mother is a real **early riser**. She gets up at five o'clock every morning.

"REAL SPEAK": My mother's a real **early bird**. She gets up 'it five a'clock ev'ry morning.

kill two birds with one stone (to) *exp.* to accomplish two tasks at the same time.

EXAMPLE: If I stay home today, I can do the laundry and prepare dinner. I'll be able to **kill two birds with one stone**.

TRANSLATION: If I stay home today, I can do the laundry and prepare dinner. I'll be able to **accomplish two tasks at the same time**.

"REAL SPEAK": If I stay home taday, I c'n do the laundry 'n prepare dinner. I'll be able da **kill two birds with one stone**.

"The early bird catches the worm" *proverb*
• "The person who gets up early will accomplish more."

EXAMPLE: I love getting up early. After all, **the early bird catches the worm**.

TRANSLATION: I love getting up early. After all, **the person who gets up early will accomplish more**.

"REAL SPEAK": I love gedding up early. After all, **the early bird catches the worm**.

BUCK

buck *n. (extremely popular)* dollar.

EXAMPLE: Can you lend me a few **bucks** for the movies?

TRANSLATION: Can you lend me a few **dollars** for the movies?

"REAL SPEAK": Can ya len' me a few **bucks** fer the movies?

Note: This term refers to the time when native American Indians traded buck skin for merchandise.

pass the buck (to) *exp.* to put the blame on someone else.

EXAMPLE: Quit trying to **pass the buck**. Everyone knows this is your fault.

TRANSLATION: Quit trying to **put the blame on someone else**. Everyone knows this is your fault.

"REAL SPEAK": Quit trying da **pass the buck**. Ev'ryone knows this 'ez yer fault.

BUG

bug *n.* • **1.** virus, cold • **2.** *(short for "computer bug")* a destructive program which infects a computer causing malfunctions.

EXAMPLE 1: I caught a nasty **bug** when I was on vacation. I've never been so sick.

TRANSLATION:	I caught a nasty **cold** when I was on vacation. I've never been so sick.
"REAL SPEAK":	I cod a nasty **bug** wh'n I w'z on vacation. I've never been so sick.
EXAMPLE 2:	My computer keeps freezing all the time. I think my computer has a **bug**.
TRANSLATION:	My computer keeps freezing all the time. I think my computer has **been infected by a destructive program**.
"REAL SPEAK":	My c'mpuder keeps freezing all the time. I think my c'mpuder has a **bug**.

bug someone (to) *exp.* to bother someone.

EXAMPLE:	Stop **bugging** me! Leave me alone!
TRANSLATION:	Stop **bothering** me! Leave me alone!
"REAL SPEAK":	Stop **bugging** me! Lee-me alone!

work out all the bugs (to) *exp.* to remedy all the problems.

EXAMPLE:	I just built my own car. I need to work out all the **bugs**, but it still works great!
TRANSLATION:	I just built my own car. I need to work out all the **problems**, but it still works great!
"REAL SPEAK":	I jus' built my own car. I need ta work oud all the **bugs**, bud it still works great!

BULL

bull *n.* nonsense.

| **EXAMPLE:** | Carla told you she's getting married? That's such **bull**. She doesn't even have a boyfriend. |
| **TRANSLATION:** | Carla told you she's getting married? That's such **nonsense**. She doesn't even have a boyfriend. |

| **"REAL SPEAK":** | Carla told you she's gedding married? That's such **bull**. She doesn' even have a boyfriend. |
| *Note:* | This is a shortened version and euphemism for *"bull shit"* which is vulgar yet *extremely* popular! Another very common euphemism for *"bull shit"* is B.S. |

take the bull by the horns (to) *exp.* to take the initiative.

EXAMPLE:	Don't wait for someone to call you with a job offer. **Take the bull by the horns** and call the companies you want to work for!
TRANSLATION:	Don't wait for someone to call you with a job offer. **Take the initiative** and call the companies you want to work for!
"REAL SPEAK":	Don't wait fer someone ta call you with a job offer. **Take the bull by the horns** 'n call the companies ya wanna work for!

BUTTERFLY

butterflies (to have) *exp.* to be nervous.

EXAMPLE:	I'm giving my presentation in ten minutes to all the executives of our company. **I have butterflies**!
TRANSLATION:	I'm giving my presentation in ten minutes to all the executives of our company. **I'm nervous**!
"REAL SPEAK":	I'm giving my presentation 'n ten minutes ta all the execudives 'ev 'ar company. **I have budderflies**!
Note:	This expression suggests someone whose stomach is jumping from being so nervous that he/she feels like there are butterflies flying around in his/her stomach.

CAMEL

"That's the straw that broke the camel's back!" *exp.* "That's all I can tolerate!"

| **EXAMPLE:** | Our houseguest broke my computer?! **That's the straw that broke the camel's back**. I'm going to tell him to leave right now! |

TRANSLATION: Our houseguest broke my computer?! **That's all I can tolerate**. I'm going to tell him to leave right now!

"REAL SPEAK": 'Ar houseguest broke my c'mpuder?! **That's the straw th't broke the camel's back**. I'm gonna tell 'im da leave right now!

Variation: **"That's the last straw!"** *exp.*

CAT

catnap *n.* a short sleep.

EXAMPLE: I'm going to take a **catnap** before dinner.

TRANSLATION: I'm going to get a **little sleep** before dinner.

"REAL SPEAK": I'm gonna take a **catnap** b'fore dinner.

copycat *n.* one who imitates another person.

EXAMPLE: Laura admired the way Kim was wearing her hair yesterday, so today Laura came to work wearing the same hairstyle. She's such a **copycat**!

TRANSLATION: Laura admired the way Kim was wearing her hair yesterday, so today Laura came to work wearing the same hairstyle. She's such an **imitator**!

"REAL SPEAK": Laura admired the way Kim w'z wearing 'er hair yesterday, so taday Laura came ta work wearing the same hairstyle. She's such a **copycat**!

let the cat out of the bag (to) *exp.* to reveal the secret.

EXAMPLE: How did you know that we were planning a party for you? Who **let the cat out of the bag**?

TRANSLATION: How did you know that we were planning a party for you? Who **revealed the secret**?

"REAL SPEAK": How'd ya know th't we were planning a pardy fer you? Who **let the cad oudda the bag**?

"Look who the cat dragged in!" *exp.* • **1.** a contemptuous remark showing displeasure at seeing someone • **2.** a playful remark said to someone that one has not seen for a long time.

EXAMPLE 1: Oh, no. **Look who the cat dragged in**! Shiela Uppity. I've never liked her.

TRANSLATION: Oh, no. **Look at the awful person who just walked in**! Shiela Uppity. I've never liked her.

"REAL SPEAK": Oh, no. **Look'oo the cat dragged in**! Shiela Uppidy. I've never liked 'er.

EXAMPLE 2: Well, **look who the cat dragged in**! How are you, Jane? It's great to see you again!

TRANSLATION: Well, **what a surprise**! How are you, Jane? It's great to see you again!

"REAL SPEAK": Well, **look'oo the cat dragged in**! How are ya, Jane? It's great ta see ya again!

rain cats and dogs (to) *exp.* to rain heavily.

EXAMPLE: Make sure to take your umbrella. **It's raining cats and dogs**!

TRANSLATION: Make sure to take your umbrella. **It's raining heavily**!

"REAL SPEAK": Make sher da take yer umbrella. **It's raining cats 'n dogs**!

scaredy cat (to be a) *exp.* to be a coward.

EXAMPLE: Don't be such a **scaredy cat**. Just go up to your boss and ask him for a raise.

TRANSLATION: Don't be such a **coward**. Just go up to your boss and ask him for a raise.

"REAL SPEAK": Don't be such a **scaredy cat**. Jus' go up ta yer boss 'n ask 'im fer a raise.

CHICKEN / HEN

chicken *adj.* cowardly.

EXAMPLE: Why won't you go parachuting with me? What are you? **Chicken**?

TRANSLATION:	Why won't you go parachuting with me? What are you? **Cowardly**?
"REAL SPEAK":	Why won'cha go parachuding with me? What are ya? **Chicken**?

chicken out (to) *exp.* to lose one's courage.

EXAMPLE:	I was going to go on the roller coaster, but I **chickened out**. I just don't like fast, scarey rides.
TRANSLATION:	I was going to go on the roller coaster, but I **lost my courage**. I just don't like fast, scarey rides.
"REAL SPEAK":	I w'z gonna go on the roller coaster, b'd I **chickened out**. I jus' don't like fast, scarey rides.

count one's chickens before they're hatched (to) *exp.* to count on something before it's certain.

EXAMPLE:	I know you're supposed to get a big bonus this year, but I wouldn't spend all your money just yet. **Don't count your chickens before they're hatched**.
TRANSLATION:	I know you're supposed to get a big bonus this year, but I wouldn't spend all your money just yet. **Don't count on something before it's certain**.
"REAL SPEAK":	I know y'r supposta ged a big bonus this year, b'd I wouldn' spend all yer money just yet. **Don't coun' cher chickens b'fore they're hatched**.

run around like a chicken with its head cut off (to) *exp.* to try to do more things at one time than one is able.

EXAMPLE:	You're **running around like a chicken with its head cut off**. You need to stop, organize, and do one task at a time.
TRANSLATION:	You're **trying to do more things at one time than you can**. You need to stop, organize, and do one task at a time.
"REAL SPEAK":	Y'r **running around like a chicken with its head cud off**. Ya need ta stop, organize, an' do one task ad a time.
Note:	This expression refers to the fact that after cutting off a chicken's head, the body often continues to run around frantically and aimlessly.

CLAM

clam up (to) *exp.* to become suddenly quiet.

EXAMPLE:	Jody was very talkative until Ken walked in the room. Then she suddenly **clammed up**.
TRANSLATION:	Jody was very talkative until Ken walked in the room. Then she suddenly **stopped talking**.
"REAL SPEAK":	Jody w'z very talkadive until Ken walked 'n the room. Then she suddenly **clammed up**.

clammy *adj.* moist, damp.

EXAMPLE:	Look how nervous I am. My hands are **clammy**.
TRANSLATION:	Look how nervous I am. My hands are **moist**.
"REAL SPEAK":	Look how nervous I am. My hands'er **clammy**.

happy as a clam (to be as) *exp.* to be extremely happy.

EXAMPLE:	David is **as happy as a clam** ever since he met Nora.
TRANSLATION:	David is **extremely happy** ever since he met Nora.
"REAL SPEAK":	David's **'ez happy 'ez a clam** ever since 'e met Nora.

COW

cow (to have a) *exp.* to get extremely upset.

EXAMPLE:	When I told my mother that I couldn't come home for the holidays, she **had a cow**.

TRANSLATION: When I told my mother that I couldn't come home for the holidays, she **got extremely upset**.

"REAL SPEAK": When I told my mother th'd I couldn't come home fer the holidays, she **had a cow**.

Note: The expression *"Don't have a cow!"* is a common expression meaning "Don't get so upset!" It's interesting to note that the equivalent expression in Canada is *"Don't have a bird!,"* and in South Africa it's *"Don't have a puppy!"*

fat cow *exp.* extremely fat person.

EXAMPLE: If you don't stop eating so much chocolate, you're going to turn into a **fat cow**.

TRANSLATION: If you don't stop eating so much chocolate, you're going to turn into a **fat person**.

"REAL SPEAK": If ya don't stop eading so much choc'lite, y'r gonna turn into a **fat cow**.

"Holy cow!" *interj.* an interjection denoting surprise and amazement.

EXAMPLE: Linda is forty years old? **Holy cow**! I thought she was twenty five!

TRANSLATION: Linda is forty years old? **What a surprise**! I thought she was twenty five!

"REAL SPEAK": Linda's fordy years old? **Holy cow**! I thought she w'z twen'y five!

DOG

as sick as a dog (to be) *exp.* to be extremely sick.

EXAMPLE: I was **as sick as a dog** all week. I'm finally doing better today.

TRANSLATION: I was **terribly sick** all week. I'm finally doing better today.

"REAL SPEAK": I w'z **'ez sick 'ez a dog** all week. I'm fin'lly doing bedder taday.

dog *n.* ugly person.

EXAMPLE: Jan's brothers and sisters are so attractive but she's a real **dog**.

TRANSLATION: Jan's brothers and sisters are so attractive but she's a real **ugly person**.

"REAL SPEAK": Jan's brothers 'n sisters'er so attracdive b't she's a real **dog**.

Note: Here is another example where English is often crazy! In English, dogs are known for making the sound "bow-wow" or "woof." Oddly enough, when a person refers to someone by saying, "Bow-wow!" that means the person is ugly. BUT! When a person refers to someone by saying "Woof," it means the opposite – that the person is very good looking and sexy!

dog-eared *exp.* bent at the corner.

EXAMPLE: The pages of this book are all **dog-eared**.

TRANSLATION: The pages of this book are all **bent at the corner**.

"REAL SPEAK": The pages 'a this book'er all **dog-eared**.

doghouse (in the) *exp.* in big trouble.

EXAMPLE: I forgot my wife's birthday! I'm really **in the doghouse**.

TRANSLATION: I forgot my wife's birthday! I'm really **in big trouble**.

"REAL SPEAK": I fergot my wife's birthday! I'm really **'n the doghouse**.

Note: This expression originally referred to a husband who got kicked out of the house and was forced to sleep in the doghouse.

dog-eat-dog *exp.* said of a situation full of fierce competition.

EXAMPLE: It's a **dog-eat-dog world** out there.

TRANSLATION: It's a **fiercely competitive** world out there.

"REAL SPEAK": [no change]

hound someone (to) *exp.* to pester someone.

EXAMPLE: Stop **hounding** me to finish. I'm working as fast as I can.

TRANSLATION: Stop **pestering** me to finish. I'm working as fast as I can.

"REAL SPEAK": Stop **hounding** me da finish. I'm working 'ez fast 'ez I can.

"You can't teach an old dog new tricks"

proverb • "You can't teach an older person anything new."

EXAMPLE: My grandmother doesn't understand how to use a computer and I've tried to explain it to her a hundred times. Well, **you can't teach an old dog new tricks**.

TRANSLATION: My grandmother doesn't understand how to use a computer and I've tried to explain it to her a hundred times. Well, **you can't teach an older person anything new**.

"REAL SPEAK": My gran'mother doesn' understand how da use a c'mpuder 'n I've tried da explain it to 'er a hundred times. Well, **ya can't teach 'n old dog new tricks**.

DUCK

dead duck *exp.* to be in big trouble.

EXAMPLE: There's Carol! If she sees me here, **I'm a dead duck**. I told her I couldn't see her today because I was sick!

TRANSLATION: There's Carol! If she sees me here, **I'm in big trouble**. I told her I couldn't see her today because I was sick!

"REAL SPEAK": There's Carol! If she sees me here, **I'm a dead duck**. I told 'er I couldn't see 'er daday b'cause I w'z sick!

sitting duck *exp.* vulnerable to attack.

EXAMPLE: My car won't start and the storm is almost over us! We're **sitting ducks**!

TRANSLATION: My car won't start and the storm is almost over us! We're **completely vulnerable**!

"REAL SPEAK": My car won't start'n the storm is almost over us! We're **sidding ducks**!

EAGLE

spread eagle (to be) *exp.* to be lying down with arms and legs completely open.

EXAMPLE: When I fell, I landed **spread eagle on the floor**!

TRANSLATION: When I fell, I landed **flat on the floor with my arms and legs completely open**.

"REAL SPEAK": [no change]

ELEPHANT

have a/the memory like an elephant (to) *exp.* to have an exceptional memory.

EXAMPLE: How did you remember her name? You must have **a/the memory like an elephant**.

TRANSLATION: How did you remember her name? You must have **an exceptional memory**.

"REAL SPEAK": How'd ja remember her name? You must have **a/the memory like 'n elephant**.

white elephant *exp.* a possession no longer wanted by its owner and difficult to dispose of.

EXAMPLE: I need to clean out my house. It's full of **white elephants**.

TRANSLATION: I need to clean out my house. It's full of **possessions that I no longer want**.

"REAL SPEAK": I need da clean out my house. It's full 'a **whide elephants**.

FISH

big fish in a small pond (to be a) *exp.* to be a very important person in a small arena.

> **EXAMPLE:** In Mark's town, he was a **big fish in a small pond**. Here in the city, no one knows him.

> **TRANSLATION:** In Mark's town, he was a **very important person**. Here in the city, no one knows him.

> **"REAL SPEAK":** In Mark's town, he w'z a **big fish in a small pond**. Here 'n the cidy, no one knows 'im.

cold fish (to be a) *exp.* to be an unaffectionate and unapproachable person.

> **EXAMPLE:** My new neighbor is a **cold fish**. I went to welcome her to the neighborhood and she didn't even speak to me.

> **TRANSLATION:** My new neighbor is an **unaffectionate and unapproachable person**. I went to welcome her to the neighborhood and she didn't even speak to me.

> **"REAL SPEAK":** My new neighbor's a **cold fish**. I went ta welcome 'er ta the neighberhood 'n she didn' even speak ta me.

fishy *adj.* suspicious.

> **EXAMPLE:** I just found out that John came into the office over the weekend when he was supposed to be out of town. Something's **fishy** around here.

> **TRANSLATION:** I just found out that John came into the office over the weekend when he was supposed to be out of town. Something's **suspicious** around here.

> **"REAL SPEAK":** I jus' found out th't John came inta the office over the weekend when 'e w'z supposta be oudda town. Something's **fishy** around here.

other fish to fry (to have) *exp.* to have other, more important things to do.

> **EXAMPLE:** I can't stay here much longer. I have **other fish to fry**.

> **TRANSLATION:** I can't stay here much longer. I have **other more important things to do**.

> **"REAL SPEAK":** I can't stay here much longer. I have **other fish ta fry**.

"There are plenty of other fish in the sea" *exp.* "There are plenty of other potential mates out there."

> **EXAMPLE:** I'm sorry it didn't work out with you and Marty, but don't worry. **There are plenty of other fish in the sea**.

> **TRANSLATION:** I'm sorry it didn't work out with you and Marty, but don't worry. **There are plenty of other potential mates out there for you**.

> **"REAL SPEAK":** I'm sorry it didn't work out with you 'n Marty, b't don't worry. **There'er plenty 'ev other fish 'n the sea**.

FOX

fox *n.* a sexy person.

> **EXAMPLE:** Did you see my new next door neighbor? What a **fox**!

> **TRANSLATION:** Did you see my new next door neighbor? What a **sexy person**!

> **"REAL SPEAK":** Did'ju see my new nex' door neighbor? Whad a **fox**!

foxy (to be) *adj.* to be sexy.

> **EXAMPLE:** Ellen used to be very plain but lately she's become really **foxy**.

> **TRANSLATION:** Ellen used to be very plain but lately she's become really **sexy**.

> **"REAL SPEAK":** Ellen usta be very plain b't lately she's become really **foxy**.

FROG

have a frog in one's throat (to) *exp.* to have a raspy throat.

EXAMPLE:	Al always sounds like he **has a frog in his throat**, but that's just the way his voice is.
TRANSLATION:	Al always sounds like he **has something in this throat that's making his voice raspy**, but that's just the way his voice is.
"REAL SPEAK":	Al always sounds like 'e **has a frog 'n 'is throat**, b't that's jus' the way his voice is.

GOAT

scapegoat *n.* an object of undeserved blame.

EXAMPLE:	You blame me for everything. I'm tired of being your **scapegoat**.
TRANSLATION:	You blame me for everything. I'm tired of being **the object of undeserved blame for you**.
"REAL SPEAK":	You blame me fer ev'rything. I'm tired 'ev being yer **scapegoat**.

wear kid gloves (to) *exp.* to be very tactful in dealing with someone.

EXAMPLE:	When you give Ernie a suggestion, you need to **wear kid gloves**. He's very sensitive and could get his feelings hurt.
TRANSLATION:	When you give Ernie a suggestion, you need to **be very tactful**. He's very sensitive and could get his feelings hurt.
"REAL SPEAK":	When ya give Ernie a suggestion, ya need ta **wear kid gloves**. He's very sensidive 'n could ged 'is feelings hurt.

Note: A "*kid*" is a young goat and used in slang to refer to a child.

GOOSE

goose someone (to) *exp.* to pinch someone on the buttocks.

EXAMPLE:	When I walked by that old man, he **goosed me**!
TRANSLATION:	When I walked by that old man, he **pinched my buttocks**!
"REAL SPEAK":	When I walked by thad old man, he **goosed me**!

wild goose chase *exp.* a senseless search.

EXAMPLE:	I've been looking all over town for my wallet but I can't find it. I think I'm on a **wild goose chase**.
TRANSLATION:	I've been looking all over town for my wallet but I can't find it. I think I'm on a **senseless search**.
"REAL SPEAK":	I've been looking all over town fer my wallet b'd I can't find it. I think I'm on a **wild goose chase**.

HOG

hog • *1. n.* an overeater • *2. n.* a greedy person • *3. v.* said of someone who does not share.

EXAMPLE 1:	Did you see how much Jim ate last night? What **a hog**!
TRANSLATION:	Did you see how much Jim ate last night? What **an overeater**!
"REAL SPEAK":	Did'ju see how much Jim ate las' night? Whad **a hog**!
EXAMPLE 2:	You didn't leave any food for anyone else! You're **such a hog**!
TRANSLATION:	You didn't leave any food for anyone else! You're **so greedy**!
"REAL SPEAK":	You didn't leave any food fer anyone else! Y'r **such a hog**!
EXAMPLE 3:	Move over! You're **hogging the bed**!
TRANSLATION:	Move over! You're **occupying the entire bed instead of sharing it**!
"REAL SPEAK":	Move over! Y'r **hogging the bed**!

hog heaven (to be in) *exp.* to be in ecstasy.

> EXAMPLE: This massage feels so good. I'm **in hog heaven**!
>
> TRANSLATION: This massage feels so good. I'm **in ecstasy**!
>
> "REAL SPEAK": This massage feels so good. I'm **'n hog heaven**!

hog wild (to go) *exp.* to go crazy with enthusiasm.

> EXAMPLE: When Nancy and Chris saw all the food at the buffet table, they **went hog wild**!
>
> TRANSLATION: When Nancy and Chris saw all the food at the buffet table, they **went crazy with enthusiasm**!
>
> "REAL SPEAK": When Nancy 'n Chris saw all the food 'it the buffet table, they **went hog wild**!

HORSE

beat a dead horse (to) *exp.* to continue to argue a point after it has already been settled.

> EXAMPLE: Tim already said that he won't let you borrow his car, so why are you still bothering him about it? He said no! You're **beating a dead horse**!
>
> TRANSLATION: Tim already said that he won't let you borrow his car, so why are you still bothering him about it? He said no! You're **trying to achieve a result that's already been settled**!
>
> "REAL SPEAK": Tim already said th'd 'e won't let chu borrow 'is car, so why'er ya still bothering 'im aboud it? He said no! Y'r **beading a dead horse**!

eat like a horse (to) *exp.* to eat constantly.

> EXAMPLE: Ever since Kim got pregnant, she's been **eating like a horse**.
>
> TRANSLATION: Ever since Kim got pregnant, she's been **eating constantly.**
>
> "REAL SPEAK": Ever since Kim got pregnant, she's been **eading like a horse.**

from the horse's mouth *exp.* directly from the source.

> EXAMPLE: Steve has decided to break up with Monica and it's not a rumor. I got it **straight from the horse's mouth**.
>
> TRANSLATION: Steve has decided to break up with Monica and it's not a rumor. I got it **directly from the source**.
>
> "REAL SPEAK": Steve's decided ta break up with Monica 'n it's nod a rumer. I god it **straight fr'm the horse's mouth**.

hold one's horses (to) *exp.* to be patient.

> EXAMPLE: **Hold your horses**! I'll be right there!
>
> TRANSLATION: **Be patient**! I'll be right there!
>
> "REAL SPEAK": **Hol'jer horses**! A'll be right there!

horse around (to) *exp.* to play, to fool around.

> EXAMPLE: Would you both stop **horsing around** and help me? We have a lot of work to do.
>
> TRANSLATION: Would you both stop **fooling around** and help me? We have a lot of work to do.
>
> "REAL SPEAK": Would'ju both stop **horsing around** 'n help me? We have a lod 'ev work ta do.

LAMB

gentle as a lamb (to be as) *exp.* to be extremely kind and docile.

> EXAMPLE: My boyfriend is a big bodybuilder, but he's **as gentle as a lamb**.
>
> TRANSLATION: My boyfriend is a big bodybuilder, but he's **extremely kind and docile**.
>
> "REAL SPEAK": My boyfriend's a big bodybuilder, bud 'e's **'ez gen'le 'ez a lamb**.

MOLE

make a mountain out of a molehill (to)

exp. to make a big deal out of nothing.

EXAMPLE:
– I'm furious with Alan because he didn't call me when he said he would.
– You're **making a mountain out of a molehill**. Maybe something unforeseen happened.

TRANSLATION:
– I'm furious with Alan because he didn't call me when he said he would.
– You're **making a big deal out of nothing**. Maybe something unforeseen happened.

"REAL SPEAK":
– I'm furious with Alan b'cause 'e didn' call me when 'e said 'e would.
– Y'r **making a mountain oud 'ev a molehill**. Maybe something unforeseen happened.

MONKEY

make a monkey out of someone (to) *exp.*

to make a fool out of someone.

EXAMPLE:
During our meeting, Jonathan told the executives that my financial report was all wrong. He **made a monkey out of me in front of everyone**.

TRANSLATION:
During our meeting, Jonathan told the executives that my financial report was all wrong. He **made a fool out of me in front of everyone**.

"REAL SPEAK":
During 'ar meeding, Jonathan told the execudives th't my financial report w'z all wrong. He **made a monkey oudda me in fron'ev ev'ryone**.

monkey suit *exp.* tuxedo.

EXAMPLE:
Kim wants me to be part of her wedding party, which means I have to wear a **monkey suit**.

TRANSLATION:
Kim wants me to be part of her wedding party, which means I have to wear a **tuxedo**.

"REAL SPEAK":
Kim wants me da be pard 'ev 'er wedding pardy, which means I hafta ta wear a **monkey suit**.

throw a monkey wrench into the works

(to) *exp.* to stop the process of something by creating an obstacle.

EXAMPLE:
We were about to start rehearsals for the musical but the sponsors **threw a monkey wrench into the works**. They've decided to give us only half the money to produce it!

TRANSLATION:
We were about to start rehearsals for the musical but the sponsors **stopped the process**. They've decided to give us only half the money to produce it!

"REAL SPEAK":
We were about ta start rehearsals fer the musical b't the sponsers **threw a monkey wrench inta the works**. They've decided ta give us only half the money ta pruhduce it!

OWL

night owl *exp.* someone who likes to stay up until late at night.

EXAMPLE:
You watched television until three o'clock in the morning? **You're a real night owl!**

TRANSLATION:
You watched television until three o'clock in the morning? **You really like to stay up late at night!**

"REAL SPEAK":
You watched TV 'til three a'clock 'n the morning? **Y'r a real nide owl!**

PIG

eat like a pig (to) *exp.* to overeat.

EXAMPLE:
I **ate like a pig** on vacation. I need to go on a diet!

TRANSLATION:	I **overate** on vacation. I need to go on a diet!
"REAL SPEAK":	I **ate like a pig** on vacation. I need ta go on a diet!

pig out (to) *exp.* to eat a lot.

EXAMPLE:	We really **pigged out** at Karen's party. You should have seen all the food she served!
TRANSLATION:	We really **ate a lot** at Karen's party. You should have seen all the food she served!
"REAL SPEAK":	We really **pigged out** 'it Karen's pardy. Ya should'ev seen all the food she served!

PIGEON

pigeonhole (to) *v.* to classify or group.

EXAMPLE:	My boss won't promote me in the company because I've been **pigeonholed** as one of their best word processor operators. I can do a lot more than just type!
TRANSLATION:	My boss won't promote me in the company because I've been **classified** as one of their best word processor operators. I can do a lot more than just type!
"REAL SPEAK":	My boss won't pruhmote me 'n the company b'cause I've been **pigeonholed** 'ez one 'a their best word processer operaders. I c'n do a lot more th'n jus' type!

stool pigeon *exp.* informer.

EXAMPLE:	You told the teacher that I cheated on the test?! What **a stool pigeon**!
TRANSLATION:	You told the teacher that I cheated on the test?! What **an informer**!
"REAL SPEAK":	You told the teacher th'd I cheaded on the test?! Whad **a stool pigeon**!

Variation: **stoolie** *n.*

RAT

pour one's money down a rat hole (to)
exp. to spend money worthlessly.

EXAMPLE:	Ken asked you to invest in his time machine? You've got to be kidding! If you invest in that crazy invention, you're **pouring your money down a rat hole**.
TRANSLATION:	Ken asked you to invest in his time machine? You've got to be kidding! If you invest in that crazy invention, you're **wasting your money**.
"REAL SPEAK":	Ken ast'ju da invest 'n 'is time machine? You've godda be kidding! If ya invest 'n that crazy invention, y'r **pouring yer money down a rat hole**.

rat *n.* contemptible person.

EXAMPLE:	That **rat** stole my wallet!
TRANSLATION:	That **contemptible person** stole my wallet!
"REAL SPEAK":	[no change]
Note:	The adjective "dirty" is added to many nouns to add emphasis such as: *You **dirty** rat!;* You horribly contemptible person! • *Mark is a **dirty** liar!;* Mark is a huge liar!

packrat *n. (from the packrat animal which constantly collects food and objects)* someone who collects all sorts of objects and never throws them away.

EXAMPLE:	My mother is a **packrat**. She still has things she's collected from thirty years ago!
TRANSLATION:	My mother is an **avid collector**. She still has things she's collected from thirty years ago!
"REAL SPEAK":	My mother's a **packrat**. She still has things she's collected fr'm thirdy years ago!

rat race *exp.* fast-paced work routine.

EXAMPLE:	I'm tired of the same old **rat race**. One of these days, I'm going to retire.
TRANSLATION:	I'm tired of the same old **fast-paced work routine**. One of these days, I'm going to retire.
"REAL SPEAK":	I'm tired 'a the same ol' **rat race**. One 'a these days, I'm gonna retire.

"Rats!" *interj.* an interjection marking disappointment or frustration.

EXAMPLE:	**Rats**! I forgot to cancel my doctor's appointment today!

TRANSLATION:	**I'm frustrated!** I forgot to cancel my doctor's appointment today!
"REAL SPEAK":	**Rats**! I fergot ta cancel my docter's appointment taday!

smell a rat (to) *exp.* to be suspicious of someone.

EXAMPLE:	What happened to my car?! It has four flat tires! Hmmmm. **I smell a rat**. I wonder if my next door neighbor had anything to do with this.
TRANSLATION:	What happened to my car?! It has four flat tires! Hmmmm. **I'm suspicious of someone**. I wonder if my next door neighbor had anything to do with this.
"REAL SPEAK":	What happen' ta my car?! It has four flat tires! Hmmmm. **I smell a rat**. I wonder if my nex' door neighbor had anything ta do with this.

SNAIL

snail mail *n.* normal postal mail which travels slowly (at a snail's pace) as compared to electronic mail or *Email*, as it's commonly known in Internet jargon.

EXAMPLE:	Since you don't have Email, I'll send you a letter by **snail mail** as soon as I arrive home.
TRANSLATION:	Since you don't have Email, I'll send you a letter by **snail mail** as soon as I arrive home.
"REAL SPEAK":	Since ya don't have Email, a'll send 'ja a ledder by **snail mail** 'ez soon 'ez I arrive home.

SNAKE

snake (to be a real) *exp.* a contemptible and dishonest person.

EXAMPLE:	Don't trust Bill with any personal secrets. He's a real **snake** and will use anything he can against you.
TRANSLATION:	Don't trust Bill with any personal secrets. He's a **real contemptible and dishonest person** and will use anything he can against you.
"REAL SPEAK":	Don't trust Bill with any personal secrets. He's a real **snake** an'll use anything 'e can against you.

Variation: **snake in the grass (to be a)** *exp.*

snake eyes *exp.* said of a pair of dice, each displaying one dot representing the number 1.

EXAMPLE:	In the game of craps commonly played in Las Vegas casinos, the player who **rolls snake eyes** loses.
TRANSLATION:	In the game of craps commonly played in Las Vegas casinos, the player who **throws the dice showing two ones** loses.
"REAL SPEAK":	In the game 'ev craps commonly played in Las Vegas casinos, the player who **rolls snake eyes** loses.

Note: The expression "*to roll*" is commonly used in gambling to mean "to throw the dice."

SHEEP

black sheep of the family (to be the) *exp.* to be the outcast of the family.

EXAMPLE:	Jim has always been **the black sheep of the family** because he gets into so much trouble.
TRANSLATION:	Jim has always been **the outcast of the family** because he gets into so much trouble.
"REAL SPEAK":	Jim's always been **the black sheep 'a the fam'ly** b'cause 'e gets inta so much trouble.

sheepish *adj.* embarrassed about a mistake or misconduct.

EXAMPLE:	Ever since Bill wrongfully accused me of stealing his wallet, he's been very **sheepish** around me.

TRANSLATION: Ever since Bill wrongfully accused me of stealing his wallet, he's been very **embarrassed** around me.

"REAL SPEAK": Ever since Bill wrongfully accused me 'ev stealing 'is wallet, he's b'n very **sheepish** aroun' me.

TURKEY

quit cold turkey (to) *exp.* to end a bad habit instantly.

EXAMPLE: When I found out that smoking could cause cancer, I **quit cold turkey**.

TRANSLATION: When I found out that smoking could cause cancer, I **quit instantly**.

"REAL SPEAK": When I found out th't smoking could cause cancer, I **quit cold turkey**.

WOLF

cry wolf (to) *exp.* to tell people that something is wrong when everything is actually fine as a way to get attention.

EXAMPLE: Ignore his complaining. He's just **crying wolf**.

TRANSLATION: Ignore his complaining. He's just **pretending that something is wrong in order to get our attention**.

"REAL SPEAK": Ignore 'is complaining. He's just **crying wolf**.

wolf down something (to) *exp.* to eat something quickly.

EXAMPLE: I only have time to **wolf down a sandwich**, then I have to leave for the airport.

TRANSLATION: I only have time to **eat a sandwich quickly**, then I have to leave for the airport.

"REAL SPEAK": I only have time ta **wolf down a san'wich**, then I hafta leave fer the airport.

WORM

can of worms *exp.* a source of unpredictable and unexpected problems.

EXAMPLE: When I asked Bret how his job was going, I really **opened up a can of worms**!

TRANSLATION: When I asked Bret how his job was going, I really **opened up a source of problems**!

"REAL SPEAK": When I asked Bret how 'is job w'z going, I really **opened up a can 'ev worms**!

worm out of a situation (to) *exp.* to get out of a situation by giving a lot of excuses.

EXAMPLE: Bonnie was supposed to take me to the airport, but she **wormed out of it**.

TRANSLATION: Bonnie was supposed to take me to the airport, but she **got out of it by giving a lot of excuses**.

"REAL SPEAK": Bonnie w'z sapposta take me da the airport, but she **wormed oud 'ev it**.

worm something out of someone (to) *exp.* to get something from someone by persistent efforts.

EXAMPLE: Eric wasn't going to tell me where he went last night, but I finally **wormed it out of him**.

TRANSLATION: Eric wasn't going to tell me where he went last night, but I finally **got the information by being persistent**.

"REAL SPEAK": Eric wasn't gonna tell me where 'e went las' night, b'd I fin'lly **wormed id oud'ev 'im**.

LESSON 9 AT THE BAKERY

"I freak out over chocolate!"

LET'S WARM UP!

MATCH THE PICTURES *(Answers on p. 224)*

As a fun way to get started, see if you can guess the meaning of the new slang words and expressions on the opposite page by using the pictures below and following the context of the sentences.

1. **What's wrong with this picture**? I'm the only one wearing a tie here.
   Definition: "did you damage that picture"
   ☐ True ☐ False

2. **Get off my back**! I'm working as fast as I can!
   Definition: "stop nagging me"
   ☐ True ☐ False

3. I need to go on a diet. I'm turning into a **tub of lard**.
   Definition: "fat person"
   ☐ True ☐ False

4. Maybe I need to take vitamins. I feel **run down**.
   Definition: "energetic"
   ☐ True ☐ False

5. Miss Pratt loves to eat **junk food**, especially chocolate.
   Definition: "healthful food"
   ☐ True ☐ False

6. I'm feeling tired this morning. I could use **a pick-me-up**!
   Definition: "something to help me sleep at night"
   ☐ True ☐ False

7. David **flips over** sweets! He eats desserts every day.
   Definition: "hates"
   ☐ True ☐ False

8. I've been home in bed sick and **munching out** all day.
   Definition: "eating"
   ☐ True ☐ False

9. If Nancy doesn't get enough sleep, she gets **crabby**!
   Definition: "ill-tempered"
   ☐ True ☐ False

10. You may like Bob, but **from where I sit**, he can't be trusted.
    Definition: "in my opinion"
    ☐ True ☐ False

11. –Where is Noah going?
    – **Beats me**. He left without saying anything.
    Definition: "to beat up someone"
    ☐ True ☐ False

12. After watching the horror movie, Ernie was **wide awake** all night.
    Definition: "completely alert"
    ☐ True ☐ False

13. Phyllis couldn't make up her mind. She was **torn between** staying on her diet and buying a chocolate cake.
    Definition: "conflicted about"
    ☐ True ☐ False

14. Earl is a **couch potato**. He never goes out and gets exercise.
    Definition: "person who prefers lying on the couch all day"
    ☐ True ☐ False

LET'S TALK!

A. DIALOGUE USING SLANG & IDIOMS

The words introduced on the first two pages are used in the dialogue below. See if you can understand the conversation. *Note:* The translation of the words in boldface is on the right-hand page.

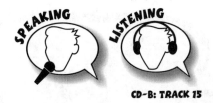

SPEAKING   LISTENING

CD-B: TRACK 15

Irene: Look at all these great desserts! This is just the **pick-me-up** I need!

Jack: I've never seen anyone **flip over** sweets the way you do. I'm not going to get anything. I'm on a diet.

Irene: What?! **What's wrong with this picture**? I must be twenty pounds heavier than you. You don't need to be on a diet. **From where I sit**, you need to eat more!

Jack: **Get off my back**! I hear that all the time. I just don't want to turn into one of those **couch potatoes** who does nothing but **munch out** on horrible **junk food** all day. Besides, when I eat sweets, I feel **run down** all day and then **wide awake** all night. Then the next day, I'm **crabby**! But don't let me stop you from getting something. If you want to become a **tub of lard**, that's your business. So, what are you going to order?

Irene: **Beats me**. I'm **torn between** getting one of those chocolate eclairs and ripping your head off!

B. DIALOGUE TRANSLATED INTO STANDARD ENGLISH

LET'S SEE HOW MUCH YOU REMEMBER!
Just for fun, bounce around in random order to the words
and expressions in boldface below. See if you can remember
their slang equivalents without looking at the left-hand page!

Irene: Look at all these great desserts! This is just the **energy-making food** I need!

Jack: I've never seen anyone **become uncontrollably excited** over sweets the way you do. I'm not going to get anything. I'm on a diet.

Irene: What?! **Why does this not make sense**? I must be twenty pounds heavier than you. You don't need to be on a diet. **In my opinion**, you need to eat more!

Jack: **Stop nagging me**! I hear that all the time. I just don't want to turn into one of those **people who lies around all day** and who does nothing but **eat** horrible **unhealthful food** all day. Besides, when I eat sweets, I feel **tired and slow** all day and then **totally altert** all night. Then the next day, I'm **ill-tempered**! But don't let me stop you from getting something. If you want to become an **extremely fat person**, that's your business. So, what are you going to order?

Irene: **I don't know**. I'm **conflicted about** getting one of those chocolate eclairs and ripping your head off!

C. DIALOGUE USING "REAL SPEAK"

The dialogue below demonstrates how the slang conversation on the previous page would *really* be spoken by native speakers!

Irene: Look 'id all these great desserts! This is jus' the **pick-me-up** I need!

Jack: I've never seen anyone **flip over** sweets the way you do. I'm not gonna ged anything. I'm on a diet.

Irene: What?! **What's wrong with this picture**? I must be twen'y pounds heavier th'n you. You don't need da be on a diet. **Fr'm where I sit**, you need da eat more!

Jack: **Ged off my back**! I hear thad all the time. I jus' don't wanna turn inta one 'a those **couch patadoes** who does nothing b't **munch oud** on horr'ble **junk food** all day. Besides, when I eat sweets, I feel **run down** all day 'n then **wide awake** all night. Then the nex' day, I'm **crabby**! But don't lemme stop you fr'm gedding something. If you wanna become a **tub 'a lard**, that's yer business. So, what'er ya gonna order?

Irene: **Beats me**. I'm **torn between** geddng one 'a those choc'lid eclairs 'n ripping yer head off!

LET'S LEARN!

CD-B: TRACK 16

VOCABULARY

The following words and expressions were used in the previous dialogues. Let's take a closer look at what they mean.

"Beats me" *exp.* "I don't know."

EXAMPLE:
– How much money do you think Eric makes in his job?
– **Beats me**. If you're that curious, why don't you just ask him?

TRANSLATION:
– How much money do you think Eric makes in his job?
– **I don't know**. If you're that curious, why don't you just ask him?

"REAL SPEAK:"
– How much money do ya think Eric makes 'n 'is job?
– **Beats me**. If y'r that curious, why doncha just ask 'im?

Synonym 1: **"I don't have a clue"** *exp.*

Synonym 2: **"I haven't the foggiest idea" / "I haven't the foggiest" exp.**

Synonym 3: **"Don't ask me!"** *exp.*

Synonym 4: **"Who knows?"** *exp.*

NOW YOU DO IT:
(Create a sentence using "Beats me!")

couch potato *exp.* a person who spends hours lying on the couch watching TV, reading, sleeping, etc.

> **EXAMPLE:** When I married Ed, he was very athletic and loved to be outdoors. Now he's turned into a **couch potato**.
>
> **TRANSLATION:** When I married Ed, he was very athletic and loved to be outdoors. Now he's turned into a **person who spends hours lying on the couch**.
>
> **"REAL SPEAK:"** When I married Ed, he w'z very athletic 'n loved da be outdoors. Now 'e's turned into a **couch patado**.
>
> **NOW YOU DO IT:**
> *(Create a sentence using "couch potato")*

crabby (to be) *adj.* to be ill-tempered.

> **EXAMPLE:** I said hello to Nancy this morning and she told me to leave her alone! She's always so **crabby** on Monday mornings.
>
> **TRANSLATION:** I said hello to Nancy this morning and she told me to leave her alone! She's always so **ill-tempered** on Monday mornings.
>
> **"REAL SPEAK:"** I said hello da Nancy this morning 'n she told me da leave 'er alone! She's always so **crabby** on Monday mornings.
>
> *Synonyms:* Since there are so many synonyms for the term "crabby," I'll list many of the most common ones here: **cranky • edgy • to get up on the wrong side of bed • grouchy • grumpy • hot-headed • ready to fly off the handle • touchy**.
>
> **NOW YOU DO IT:**
> *(Create a sentence using "crabby")*

flip over something (to) *exp.* to get extremely excited and enthusiastic about something.

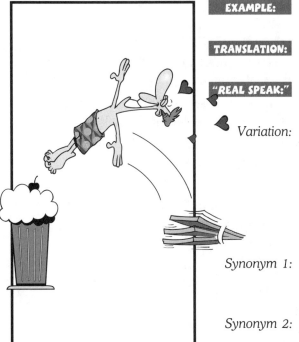

> **EXAMPLE:** The studio **flipped over** my movie idea. In fact, they want to produce it!
>
> **TRANSLATION:** The studio **was extremely excited and enthusiastic about** my movie idea. In fact, they want to produce it!
>
> **"REAL SPEAK:"** The studio **flipped over** my movie idea. In fact, they wanna praduce it!
>
> *Variation:* **flip <u>out</u> over something (to)** *exp.* • **1.** to get extremely excited and enthusiastic about something • *I always flip out over my mother's chocolate cake!*; I always get extremely excited about my mother's chocolate cake! • **2.** to get extremely upset about something • *When Tina heard the bad news, she flipped out over it*; When Tina heard the bad news, she became extremely upset about it.
>
> *Synonym 1:* **freak [out] about something (to)** *exp.* • **1.** to get extremely excited and enthusiastic about something • **2.** to get extremely upset about something.
>
> *Synonym 2:* **wowed by something (to be)** *exp.*
>
> **NOW YOU DO IT:**
> *(Create a sentence using "flipped over")*

"From where I sit..." *exp.* "In my opinion..."

> **EXAMPLE:** Frank says that he loves Christine, but **from where I sit** he's only interested in her money.

> **TRANSLATION:** Frank says that he loves Christine, but **in my opinion** he's only interested in her money.

> **"REAL SPEAK:"** Frank says thad 'e loves Christine, but **fr'm where I sit** he's only int'rested in 'er money.

Synonym 1: **"If you ask me..."** *exp.*

Synonym 2: **"My take on it is that..."** *exp.*

Synonym 3: **"That's my two-cents worth"** *exp.* (added at the end of an opinion) *Frank says that he loves Christine, but he's only interested in her money. That's my two-cents worth.*

> **NOW YOU DO IT:**
> *(Create a sentence using "From where I sit...")*

get off someone's back (to) *exp.* to stop nagging someone.

> **EXAMPLE:** The boss calls me every hour to ask me if I've finished my assignment. I wish he'd **get off my back**!

> **TRANSLATION:** The boss calls me every hour to ask me if I've finished my assignment. I wish he'd **stop nagging me**!

> **"REAL SPEAK:"** The boss calls me ev'ry hour to ask me if I've finished my assignment. I wish 'e'd **ged off my back**!

Variation: **get off someone's case (to)** *exp.*

Synonym 1: **stop bugging someone (to)** *exp.*

Synonym 2: **stop riding someone (to)** *exp.*

> **NOW YOU DO IT:**
> *(Create a sentence using "Get off my back")*

junk food *exp.* unhealthful food (such as food containing a lot of sugar and fat) • (lit.): worthless food.

> **EXAMPLE:** Betty needs to stop eating **junk food** and start exercising if she wants to lose all that weight.

> **TRANSLATION:** Betty needs to stop eating **unhealthful food** and start exercising if she wants to lose all that weight.

> **"REAL SPEAK:"** Betty needs ta stop eading **junk food** 'n stard exercising if she wants ta lose all that weight.

Also 1: **fast food** *exp.* food that is usually prepared in advance, typically high in fat, and able to be purchased quickly.

> *Note:* **fast food restaurant** *exp.* a restaurant that sells *fast food.*

Also 2: **junk food junkie** *exp.* one who is addicted to unhealthful food.

> *Note:* **junkie** *n.* addict.

Also 3: **junk out (to)** *exp.* to eat unhealthful food.

> **NOW YOU DO IT:**
> *(Create a sentence using "junk food")*

munch out (to) *exp.* to eat or snack.

EXAMPLE: Let's go see a movie tonight. We can buy some popcorn and hotdogs and **munch out** during the entire show.

TRANSLATION: Let's go see a movie tonight. We can buy some popcorn and hotdogs and **eat** during the entire show.

"REAL SPEAK:" Let's go see a movie danight. We c'n buy s'm popcorn 'n hotdogs 'n **munch out** during the entire show.

Also: **munchies (to have the)** *exp.* to be hungry for snacks.

Synonym 1: **chow down (to)** *exp.*

Synonym 2: **feed/stuff one's face (to)** *exp.*

Synonym 3: **pig out (to)** *exp.*

Synonym 4: **pork out (to)** *exp.*

Synonym 5: **scarf down (to)** *exp.*

NOW YOU DO IT:
(Create a sentence using "munch out")

pick-me-up (a) *n.* something that helps to increase (or "pick up") one's energy.

EXAMPLE: I'm so tired this morning. I think I need **a pick-me-up**. Do you have any coffee?

TRANSLATION: I'm so tired this morning. I think I need **something that will increase my energy**. Do you have any coffee?

"REAL SPEAK:" I'm so tired th's morning. I think I need **a pick-me-up**. Do ya have any coffee?

Variation: **picker-upper** *n.*

Synonym 1: **lift** *n.* • **1.** something that helps to give one energy • **2.** a ride (to a particular destination).

Synonym 2: **pepper-upper** *n.* (from "to pep up" meaning "to make lively or energetic").

NOW YOU DO IT:
(Create a sentence using "pick-me-up")

run down (to be/feel) *exp.* to have a lack of energy.

EXAMPLE: I think I need to start taking vitamins. By the afternoon, I feel **run down**.

TRANSLATION: I think I need to start taking vitamins. By the afternoon, I feel **a lack of energy**.

"REAL SPEAK:" I think I need da start taking vidam'ns. By the afternoon, I feel **run down**.

Synonym 1: **draggy (to be/feel)** *adj.*

Synonym 2: **feel like one's dragging (to)** *exp.*

Synonym 3: **sluggish (to be/feel)** *adj.*

NOW YOU DO IT:
(Create a sentence using "run down")

torn between something (to be) *exp.* to be conflicted in making a choice.

EXAMPLE:	I'm **torn between** going to Hawaii with Brian and going to Paris with Stan.
TRANSLATION:	I'm **conflicted in making a choice about** going to Hawaii with Brian and going to Paris with Stan.
"REAL SPEAK:"	I'm **torn between** going da Hawaii with Brian or going da Paris with Stan.

NOW YOU DO IT:
(Create a sentence using "torn between")

tub of lard (to be a) *exp.* to be a fat person.

EXAMPLE:	Bert used to be very thin, but he's become a **tub of lard** because he can't stop eating junk food!
TRANSLATION:	Bert used to be very thin, but he's become a **fat person** because he can't stop eating junk food!
"REAL SPEAK:"	Bert usta be very thin, but 'e's become a **tub 'a lard** cuz 'e can't stop eading junk food!

Synonym 1: **fatso/fatty/fat slob (to be a)** *adj.*
Synonym 2: **porker (to be a)** *exp.*

NOW YOU DO IT:
(Create a sentence using "tub of lard")

"What's wrong with this picture?" *exp.* "Why does this not make sense?"

EXAMPLE:	Isn't that John in that limousine? **What's wrong with this picture**? He always tells me he has no money!
TRANSLATION:	Isn't that John in that limousine? **Why does this not make sense**? He always tells me he has no money!
"REAL SPEAK:"	Isn't that John in that limousine? **What's wrong with this picture**? He always tells me he has no money!

Synonym 1: **"What gives?"** *exp.*
Synonym 2: **"What's up with that?"** *exp.*

NOW YOU DO IT:
(Create a sentence using "What's wrong with this picture")

wide awake (to be) *exp.* to be totally alert.

EXAMPLE:	Larry was **wide awake** all night worrying about his new job.
TRANSLATION:	Larry was **totally alert** all night worrying about his new job.
"REAL SPEAK:"	Larry w'z **wide awake** all night worrying about 'is new job.

Antonym: **fast asleep** *exp.* to be in a deep sleep.

NOW YOU DO IT:
(Create a sentence using "wide awake")

LET'S PRACTICE!

A. CREATE YOUR OWN STORY - *(Part 1) (Answers on p. 224)*
Follow the instructions below and write down your answer in the space provided. When you have finished answering all the questions, transfer your answers to the story on the opposite page. Make sure to match the number of your answer with the numbered space in the story. Remember: The funnier your answers, the funnier your story will be!

1. Write down a "thing" *(pencil, potato, toothbrush, etc.)*:
    _____

2. Write down an "adjective" *(big, small, strange, etc.)*:
    _____

3. Write down a "place" *(restaurant, library, market, etc.)*:
    _____

4. Write down a "thing" in plural form *(pencils, potatoes, toothbrushes, etc.)*:
    _____

5. Write down a "thing" *(pencil, potato, toothbrush, etc.)*:
    _____

6. Write down a "thing" in plural form *(pencils, potatoes, toothbrushes, etc.)*:
    _____

7. Write down a "thing" *(pencil, potato, toothbrush, etc.)*:
    _____

8. Write down a "thing" *(pencil, potato, toothbrush, etc.)*:
    _____

9. Write down a "verb" in the first person *(drink, run, type, etc.)*:
    _____

10. Write down a type of "pet" *(cat, dog, hamster, etc.)*:
    _____

11. Write down an "occupation" *(police officer, fire fighter, tailor, etc.)*:
    _____

12. Write down a "thing" in plural form *(pencils, potatoes, toothbrushes, etc.)*:
    _____

B. CREATE YOUR OWN STORY - (Part 2)

Once you've filled in the blanks, read your story aloud. If you've done Part 1 correctly, your story should be hilarious!

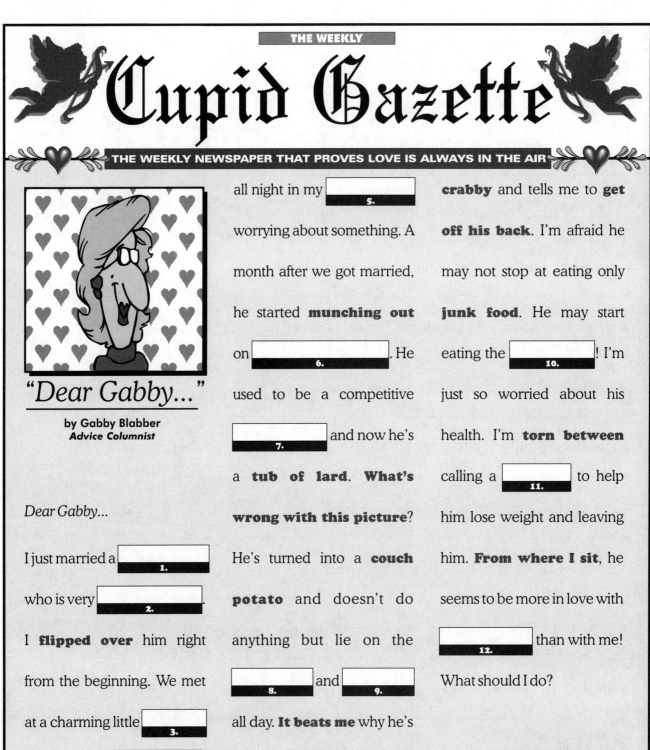

THE WEEKLY

Cupid Gazette

THE WEEKLY NEWSPAPER THAT PROVES LOVE IS ALWAYS IN THE AIR

"Dear Gabby..."

by Gabby Blabber
Advice Columnist

Dear Gabby...

I just married a ___[1.]___ who is very ___[2.]___. I **flipped over** him right from the beginning. We met at a charming little ___[3.]___ known for its ___[4.]___. Well, I've been **wide awake** all night in my ___[5.]___ worrying about something. A month after we got married, he started **munching out** on ___[6.]___. He used to be a competitive ___[7.]___ and now he's a **tub of lard**. **What's wrong with this picture**? He's turned into a **couch potato** and doesn't do anything but lie on the ___[8.]___ and ___[9.]___ all day. **It beats me** why he's changed so much. As soon as I talk about it, he gets crabby and tells me to **get off his back**. I'm afraid he may not stop at eating only **junk food**. He may start eating the ___[10.]___! I'm just so worried about his health. I'm **torn between** calling a ___[11.]___ to help him lose weight and leaving him. **From where I sit**, he seems to be more in love with ___[12.]___ than with me! What should I do?

READING

C. WHAT WOULD YOU DO IF SOMEONE SAID...?

(Answers on p. 224)
What would you do in response to the words in white italics?
Choose your answer by placing an "X" in the box.

CD-B: TRACK 17

#	Phrase	I would...
1.	*I flip over sweets!*	☐ a. offer him some dessert ☐ b. ask him is he's a gymnast ☐ c. ask him if he's a doctor
2.	*Let's go eat some junk food!*	☐ a. suggest going to a fine restaurant ☐ b. offer him some steamed vegetables ☐ c. suggest going to the candy shop
3.	*Get off my back!*	☐ a. leave him alone ☐ b. jump down ☐ c. ask a lot of questions
4.	*You're turning into a tub of lard!*	☐ a. go to the bank and get more money ☐ b. borrow a tub of lard from a neighbor ☐ c. go on a diet immediately
5.	*I'm feeling run down.*	☐ a. suggest he take a nap ☐ b. give him some new clothes ☐ c. get the license of the car that hit him
6.	*I'm feeling crabby today.*	☐ a. leave her alone ☐ b. pester her more ☐ c. offer her a larger variety of shellfish
7.	*It beats me where your car keys are!*	☐ a. thank him for finding my keys ☐ b. ask why he beat up someone ☐ c. continue to search on my own
8.	*I need a pick-me-up.*	☐ a. offer to give him a relaxing massage ☐ b. lift him over my head ☐ c. offer him a strong cup of coffee
9.	*I'm torn between staying on my diet and getting dessert.*	☐ a. offer to mend his shirt ☐ b. help him make a decision ☐ c. try to cheer him up
10.	*Let's go munch out somewhere.*	☐ a. suggest we go to the movies ☐ b. suggest we go to a restaurant ☐ c. suggest we go to the bank.

D. "ACROSS" WORD PUZZLE (Answers on p. 224)
Fill in the crossword puzzle by choosing the correct word from the list below.

WRITING

CD-B: TRACK 18

TORN	CRABBY	MUNCH
POTATO	RUN	FLIP
PICK	BACK	WIDE

1. Steve spends hours watching TV. He's such a couch ⬜⬜⬜⬜ .

2. If I don't get enough sleep I get ⬜⬜⬜⬜⬜⬜ .

3. I'm hungry. Let's go ⬜⬜⬜⬜⬜ out at my house.

4. The movie was great! You're going to ⬜⬜⬜⬜ over it!

5. I'm ⬜⬜⬜⬜ between getting the ice cream and the cake.

6. I was ⬜⬜⬜⬜ awake all night. That's why I'm so tired.

7. Stop bothering me! Get off my ⬜⬜⬜⬜ !

8. I feel ⬜⬜⬜ down. I think I need a cup of coffee as a ⬜⬜⬜ -me-up.

195

Numbers Used in Slang

This list will help you **zero in** (*focus on*) on many useful expressions containing numbers. Once you have a good understanding of this next category, you should be in **seventh heaven** (*ecstatic*)!

(ZERO)

zero in on someone or something (to) *exp*. to find, to aim directly at, to focus on either **1.** someone, or **2.** something.

> **EXAMPLE 1:** (*someone*) I tried to hide from Maggie, but she **zeroed in on me**.
>
> **TRANSLATION:** I tried to hide from Maggie, but she **found me**.
>
> **"REAL SPEAK":** I tried ta hide fr'm Maggie, but she **zeroed in on me**.
>
> **EXAMPLE 2:** (*something*) Scientists are trying to **zero in on** a cure for AIDS.
>
> **TRANSLATION:** Scientists are trying **to find** a cure for AIDS.
>
> **"REAL SPEAK":** Scientists'er trying da **zero in on** a cure fer AIDS.

(ONE / ONCE / FIRST)

back to square one (to go) *exp*. to go back to the beginning.

> **EXAMPLE:** Unfortunately, our strategy didn't work, so we'll need to **go back to square one** and try again.
>
> **TRANSLATION:** Unfortunately, our strategy didn't work, so we'll need to **go back to the beginning** and try again.
>
> **"REAL SPEAK":** Unfortunately, 'ar strategy didn't work, so we'll need ta **go back ta square one** 'n try again.

first come, first served *exp*. • the first people who arrive will be the first people served.

> **EXAMPLE:** My mechanic doesn't take appointments. **First come, first served**.
>
> **TRANSLATION:** My mechanic doesn't take appointments. **The first people who arrive first will be the first people served**.
>
> **"REAL SPEAK":** My mechanic doesn' take appointments. **Firs' come, firs' served**.

first things first *exp*. the most important things must be done first.

> **EXAMPLE:** Ok. **First things first**. We need to compile all our notes. Then we can enter them in the word processor.
>
> **TRANSLATION:** Ok. **We need to do the most important things first**. We need to compile all our notes. Then we can enter them in the word processor.
>
> **"REAL SPEAK":** Ok. **Firs' things first**. We need da c'mpile all 'ar notes. Then we c'n enter th'm in the word processer.

give someone the once over (to) *exp*. to scrutinize someone.

> **EXAMPLE:** When I met Linda's parents for the first time, they both **gave me the once over**.
>
> **TRANSLATION:** When I met Linda's parents for the first time, they both **scrutinized me**.
>
> **"REAL SPEAK":** When I met Linda's parents fer the firs' time, they both **gamme the once over**.

look out for number one (to) *exp.* to take care of oneself.

> **EXAMPLE:** Good luck with your negotiations. Just remember **to look out for number one**.

> **TRANSLATION:** Good luck with your negotiations. Just remember **to look out for yourself**.

> **"REAL SPEAK":** Good luck with yer negoshiations. Just remember **da look out fer number one**.

not to know the first thing about something *exp.* not to know anything at all about something.

> **EXAMPLE:** My mother **doesn't know the first thing about** computers.

> **TRANSLATION:** My mother **doesn't know anything at all about** computers.

> **"REAL SPEAK":** My mother **doesn' know the firs' thing about** c'mpuders.

one-track mind (to have a) *exp.* to be obsessed with only one thought.

> **EXAMPLE:** Jerry talks about work all the time. He **has a one-track mind**.

> **TRANSLATION:** Jerry talks about work all the time. He's **obsessed with just one thought**.

> **"REAL SPEAK":** [no change]

put all one's eggs into one basket (to) *exp.* to risk everything by counting on only one thing out of many.

> **EXAMPLE:** I know your job interview went well, but you shouldn't stop interviewing. It's not wise to **put all your eggs into one basket**.

> **TRANSLATION:** I know your job interview went well, but you shouldn't stop interviewing. It's not wise to **risk everything by counting on only one thing out of many**.

> **"REAL SPEAK":** I know yer job in'erview went well, but ya shouldn't stop in'erviewing. It's not wise ta **pud all yer eggs inta one basket**.

(TWO / SECOND)

get one's second wind (to) *exp.* to get energized again.

> **EXAMPLE:** I was so tired an hour ago, but now I'm getting **my second wind**.

> **TRANSLATION:** I was so tired an hour ago, but now I'm getting **energized again**.

> **"REAL SPEAK":** I w'z so tired 'n hour ago, b't now I'm gedding **my secon' wind**.

have second thoughts about something (to) *exp.* to develop doubts about something.

> **EXAMPLE:** I thought it was a good idea to start a business but I'm **getting second thoughts**. It may be too expensive.

> **TRANSLATION:** I thought it was a good idea to start a business but I'm **developing doubts**. It may be too expensive.

> **"REAL SPEAK":** I thod it w'z a good idea da stard a bizness b'd I'm **gedding secon' thoughts**. It may be too expensive.

on second thought *exp.* as I think it over again.

> **EXAMPLE:** I think we should leave for the airport at noon. **On second thought**, there may be traffic, so we should probably leave at eleven o'clock.

> **TRANSLATION:** I think we should leave for the airport at noon. **As I think it over again**, there may be traffic, so we should probably leave at eleven o'clock.

> **"REAL SPEAK":** I think we should leave fer the airport 'it noon. **On secon' thought**, there may be traffic, so we should prob'ly leave 'id eleven a'clock.

put one's two cents [worth] in (to) *exp.* to give one's opinion.

> **EXAMPLE:** I don't think you should hire him. He doesn't seem to have enough experience. Thank you for letting me **put in my two cents [worth]**.

| **TRANSLATION:** | I don't think you should hire him. He doesn't seem to have enough experience. Thank you for letting me **give my opinion**. |
| **"REAL SPEAK":** | I don't think ya should hire 'im. He doesn' seem da have anuf experience. Thank you fer ledding me **pud in my two cents [worth]**. |

put two and two together (to) *exp.* to solve the mystery, to arrive at a correct conclusion.

EXAMPLE:	I just **put two and two together**. David not only works with Shelly, but they're also married!
TRANSLATION:	I just **figured out the mystery**. David not only works with Shelly, but they're also married!
"REAL SPEAK":	I jus' **put two 'n two dagether**. David nod only works with Shelly, b't they're also married!

second nature (to be) *exp.* to be instinctive.

EXAMPLE:	Cooking is **second nature to** me.
TRANSLATION:	Cooking is **instinctive for** me.
"REAL SPEAK":	Cooking's **secon' nature da** me.

stand on one's own two feet (to) *exp.* to be self-supporting.

EXAMPLE:	Ed's parents used to pay for everything. Now that he's in school, he has to **stand on his own two feet**.
TRANSLATION:	Ed's parents used to pay for everything. Now that he's in school, he has to **be self-supporting**.
"REAL SPEAK":	Ed's parents usta pay fer ev'rything. Now th'd 'e's 'n school, he hasta **stand on 'is own two feet**.

tell someone a thing or two (to) *exp.* to tell someone how one truly feels.

EXAMPLE:	Mindy borrowed my sweater and ruined it. When she gets home, I'm going to **tell her a thing or two**.
TRANSLATION:	Mindy borrowed my sweater and ruined it. When she gets home, I'm going to **tell her how I feel**.
"REAL SPEAK":	Mindy borrowed my sweader 'n ruined it. When she gets home, I'm gonna **tell 'er a thing 'r two**.

"There are no two ways about it" *exp.* "It's absolutely certain."

EXAMPLE:	**There are no two ways about it**. Frank has been dishonest with us.
TRANSLATION:	**It's absolutely certain**. Frank has been dishonest with us.
"REAL SPEAK":	**There'er no two ways aboud it**. Frank's been dishonest with us.

(THREE / THIRD)

get the third degree (to) *exp.* to get interrogated.

EXAMPLE:	As soon as I got home, my mother **gave me the third degree**. She wanted to know why I was out so late.
TRANSLATION:	As soon as I got home, my mother **interrogated me**. She wanted to know why I was out so late.
"REAL SPEAK":	As soon 'ez I got home, my mother **gamme the third degree**. She wan'ed ta know why I w'z out so late.

(SIX)

six of one, half a dozen of the other (to be) *exp.* to amount to the same thing.

EXAMPLE:	We could either meet at the restaurant or I could pick you up. It's **six of one, half a dozen of the other**.
TRANSLATION:	We could either meet at the restaurant or I could pick you up. It's **the same to me**.
"REAL SPEAK":	We could either meed 'it the resterant 'r I could pick you up. It's **six 'ev one, half a dozen 'a the other**.

(SEVEN / SEVENTH)

seventh heaven (to be in) *exp.* to be in ecstasy.

EXAMPLE:	My vacation to Hawaii was wonderful. I was in **seventh heaven** the entire time!
TRANSLATION:	My vacation to Hawaii was wonderful. I was in **ecstasy** the entire time!
"REAL SPEAK":	My vacation ta Hawaii w'z wonderful. I w'z 'n **seventh heaven** the entire time!

(NINE)

cloud nine (to be on) *exp.* to be extremely happy, euphoric.

EXAMPLE:	Ever since I met David, I've been **on cloud nine**.
TRANSLATION:	Ever since I met David, I've been **euphoric**.
"REAL SPEAK":	[no change]

nine-to-five *exp.* a full-time job.

EXAMPLE:	I used to have a **nine-to-five**. Now I'm a consultant with flexible hours.
TRANSLATION:	I used to have a **full-time job**. Now I'm a consultant with flexible hours.
"REAL SPEAK":	I usta have a **nine-da-five**. Now I'm a c'nsultant with flexible hours.

the whole nine yards (to go) *exp.* to go to the limit.

EXAMPLE:	Mark's party was fantastic. He served food and drinks, had a band, and decorated his entire house. He really went **the whole nine yards**.
TRANSLATION:	Mark's party was fantastic. He served food and drinks, had a band, and decorated his entire house. He really **went to the limit**.
"REAL SPEAK":	Mark's pardy w'z fantastic. He served food 'n drinks, had a band, an' decoraded 'is entire house. He really went **the whole nine yards**.

(TEN)

ten (to be a) *exp.* to be first-rate.

EXAMPLE:	I met the greatest guy yesterday. He's **a ten**!
TRANSLATION:	I met the greatest guy yesterday. He's **first-rate**!
"REAL SPEAK":	I met the greadest guy yesderday. He's **a ten**!

top ten *exp.* the ten most popular.

EXAMPLE:	David's song just **made the top ten**!
TRANSLATION:	David's song just **became one of the ten most popular**!
"REAL SPEAK":	David's song jus' **made the top ten**!

(TWENTY-TWO)

catch twenty-two *exp.* a frustrating situation where alternative solutions contradict each other.

| EXAMPLE: | At my job interview, they told me I didn't have enough experience. I'm really frustrated. I need experience in order to get a job, but I need a job in order to get experience! This is **such a catch twenty-two**! |
| TRANSLATION: | At my job interview, they told me I didn't have enough experience. I'm really frustrated. I need experience in order to get a job, but I need a job in order to get experience! This is **a frustrating situation where alternative solutions contradict each other**! |

"REAL SPEAK": At my job in'erview, they told me I didn' have anuf experience. I'm really frus'drated. I need experience in order da ged a job, b'd I need a job in order da ged experience! This is **such a catch twen'y-two**!

(EIGHTY-EIGHT)

eighty-eight (the) *n.* piano (due to its eighty-eight keys).

EXAMPLE: I've been playing **the ol' eighty-eight** since I was a little boy.

TRANSLATION: I've been playing **my faithful piano** since I was a little boy.

"REAL SPEAK": I've been playing **the ol' aidy-eight** since I w'z a liddle boy.

Note: The adjective "old," commonly reduced to *ol'*, is popularly used to mean "faithful" and is often used when referring to "the eighty-eight."

(ONE THOUSAND)

"If I've told you once, I've told you a thousand times..." *exp.* "I've repeated this to you over and over again..."

EXAMPLE: If I've told you once, I've told you a thousand times, you can't borrow my car!

TRANSLATION: I've told you over and over again, you can't borrow my car!

"REAL SPEAK": If I've tol'ju once, I've tol'ju a thousan' times, ya can't borrow my car!

(ONE MILLION)

feel like a million bucks (to) *exp.* to feel great.

EXAMPLE: I had a good night's sleep and now I **feel like a million bucks**!

TRANSLATION: I had a good night's sleep and now I **feel great**!

"REAL SPEAK": I had a good night's sleep 'n now I **feel like a million bucks**!

Note: **buck** *n.* (extremely popular – from "buckskin" which used to be traded by the Indians) dollar.

million of them (a) *exp.* a repertory of a million stories and jokes.

EXAMPLE: I'm glad you liked that joke. I've got **a million of them**!

TRANSLATION: I'm glad you liked that joke. I've got **a million more stories and jokes**!

"REAL SPEAK": I'm glad ja liked that joke. I've god **a million of 'em**!

Note: The phrase "I've got a million of them" is almost always reduced to *"I got a million of 'em!"*

never in a million years *exp.* absolutely never.

EXAMPLE: **Never in a million years did I think** I'd see you again!

TRANSLATION: **I absolutely never thought** I'd see you again!

"REAL SPEAK": **Never 'n a million years did I think** I'd see you again!

one-in-a-million (to be) *exp.* to be rare.

EXAMPLE: Debbie is always there if I need her. She's **one-in-a-million**.

TRANSLATION: Debbie is always there if I need her. She's **rare**.

"REAL SPEAK": Debbie's always there if I need 'er. She's **one-'n-a-million**.

LESSON 10 — ON THE PHONE

"You hit the nail on the head!"

LET'S WARM UP!

MATCH THE PICTURES *(Answers on p. 224)*

As a fun way to get started, see if you can guess the meaning of the new slang words and expressions on the opposite page by using the pictures below and following the context of the sentences.

1. Greg is a scientist? I didn't know he was such a **brain**!
   - ❏ boring person
   - ❏ genius

2. What's **eating** you? You look worried about something.
   - ❏ entertaining
   - ❏ upsetting

3. I'm **in the dark** about what happened last night!
   - ❏ well informed
   - ❏ uninformed

4. When you called Bob a liar, you **hit the nail on the head**.
   - ❏ were absolutely correct
   - ❏ were absolutely incorrect

5. Dan kept me **on hold** for twenty minutes!
   - ❏ waiting outside
   - ❏ waiting on the phone

6. What did you **dig up** about Cecily?
   - ❏ discover
   - ❏ say

7. **A little birdie told me** that Gina is dating Steve!
   - ❏ a secret informant
   - ❏ a small bird

8. I **feel like a fish out of water** here. I'm leaving.
   - ❏ am very thirsty
   - ❏ don't belong

9. I think Karen **has the hots for me** but I don't like her!
   - ❏ is sexually interested in me
   - ❏ is suffering from the heat

10. The new boss is very strict. Now it's **sink or swim**!
    - ❏ time to leave for the day
    - ❏ about survival

11. Ed gave the boss a gift! He's really trying to **kiss up**.
    - ❏ insult him
    - ❏ flatter him

12. Ann is weird. I don't think she's **cooking on all four burners**.
    - ❏ completely rational
    - ❏ very pretty

13. If you lie, you may **paint yourself into a corner**.
    - ❏ get paint on yourself
    - ❏ get in a difficult situation

14. I have to work this weekend. My boss is a **slave driver**!
    - ❏ relentlessly demanding boss
    - ❏ lenient boss

15. I'm **working like mad** in order to leave on time today!
    - ❏ working slowly
    - ❏ working as fast as possible

LET'S TALK!

A. DIALOGUE USING SLANG & IDIOMS

The words introduced on the first two pages are used in the dialogue below. See if you can understand the conversation. *Note:* The translation of the words in boldface is on the right-hand page.

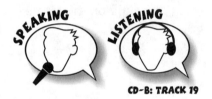

CD-B: TRACK 19

Chris: Sorry to keep you **on hold** but the boss has been looking over everyone's shoulder this morning.

Debbie: I know. He's been a **slave driver** all week.

Chris: Luckily he just left for lunch. So, tell me. What did you **dig up on** the new guy? What was **eating him** yesterday? I'm totally **in the dark**!

Debbie: Well, at first I assumed he was hired because he's such a **brain**, but now I'm starting to think he's **not cooking on all four burners**. I think he has a problem telling the truth. In fact, I bet he lied to get this job.

Chris: I think you **hit the nail on the head**. That explains why he seems like **a fish out of water** here.

Debbie: Well, he obviously lied and told the boss he had years of experience so he'd get a huge assignment. Now he's **painted himself into a corner** and knows it's **sink or swim**. I **work like mad** to get my assignments done and he just **kisses up to** the boss in order to get excused! And I just found out that Gladys in the accounting department **has the hots for him**!

Chris: You've got to be kidding! How do you know all this?

Debbie: Let's just say **a little birdie told me**.

B. DIALOGUE TRANSLATED INTO STANDARD ENGLISH

LET'S SEE HOW MUCH YOU REMEMBER!
Just for fun, bounce around in random order to the words
and expressions in boldface below. See if you can remember
their slang equivalents without looking at the left-hand page!

Chris: Sorry to keep you **waiting on the phone** but the boss has been watching us closely
            this morning.

Debbie: I know. He's been a **relentlessly demanding boss** all week.

Chris: Luckily he just left for lunch. So, tell me. What did you **find out about** the new guy?
            What was **bothering him** yesterday? I'm totally **uninformed**!

Debbie: Well, at first I assumed he was hired because he's such a **genius**, but now I'm starting
            to think he's **not completely rational**. I think he has a problem telling the truth. In
            fact, I bet he lied to get this job.

Chris: I think you **reached a correct conclusion**. That explains why he seems like **he
            doesn't belong** here.

Debbie: Well, he obviously lied and told the boss he had years of experience so he'd get a huge
            assignment. Now he's **gotten himself into a difficult situation** and knows it's
            about survival. I **work very hard** to get my assignments done and he just
            flatters the boss in order to get excused! And I just found out that Gladys in the
            accounting department **is sexually attracted to him**!

Chris: You've got to be kidding! How do you know all this?

Debbie: Let's just say **an unknown source told me**.

C. DIALOGUE USING "REAL SPEAK"

The dialogue below demonstrates how the slang conversation
on the previous page would *really* be spoken by native speakers!

Chris: Sorry da keep ya **on hold** b't the boss'ez been looking over ev'ryone's shoulder this morning.

Debbie: I know. He's been a **slave driver** all week.

Chris: Luckily 'e jus' left fer lunch. So, tell me. Whad'ja **dig up on** the new guy? What w'z **eading 'im** yesderday? I'm todally **in the dark**!

Debbie: Well, at first I assumed 'e w'z hired cuz 'e's such a **brain**, b't now I'm starding da think 'e's **not cooking on all four burners**. I think 'e has a problem telling the truth. In fact, I bet 'e lied ta get this job.

Chris: I think ya **hit the nail on the head**. That explains why 'e seems like **a fish oudda water** here.

Debbie: Well, 'e obviously lied 'n told the boss 'e had years of experience so 'e'd ged a huge assignment. Now 'e's **pain'ed 'imself into a corner** 'n knows it's **sink 'r swim**. I **work like mad** da get my assignments done 'n he jus' **kisses up ta** the boss 'n order da get excused! An' I jus' found out th't Gladys 'n the accoun'ing department **has the hots for 'im**!

Chris: You've godda be kidding! How do ya know all this?

Debbie: Let's jus' say **a liddle birdie told me**.

LET'S LEARN!

CD-B: TRACK 20

VOCABULARY

The following words and expressions were used in the previous dialogues. Let's take a closer look at what they mean.

"A little birdie told me" *exp.* "A secret informant told me."

EXAMPLE:
– Who told you that Mark got fired?
– We'll just say **a little birdie told me**.

TRANSLATION:
– Who told you that Mark got fired?
– We'll just say **a secret informant told me**.

"REAL SPEAK:"
– Who told'ja th't Mark got fired?
– We'll jus' say **a liddle birdie told me**.

Note: The term *birdie* is actually children's language for "bird."

NOW YOU DO IT. COMPLETE THE PHRASE ALOUD:

A little birdie told me that...

brain (to be a) *n.* to be an extremely smart person, a genius.

> **EXAMPLE:** You got an "A" on the math final? Wow! You're really a **brain**!
>
> **TRANSLATION:** You got an "A" on the math final? Wow! You're really a **genius**!
>
> **"REAL SPEAK:"** You god 'n "A" on the math final? Wow! Y'r really a **brain**!
>
> *Also:* **brainy** *adj.* extremely smart.
>
> **NOW YOU DO IT. COMPLETE THE PHRASE ALOUD:**
> *I think ...is a real brain because...*

cooking on all four burners (not to be) *exp.* said of someone who is crazy or irrational.

> **EXAMPLE:** My new neighbor talks to imaginary people! I don't think he's **cooking on all four burners**.
>
> **TRANSLATION:** My new neighbor talks to imaginary people! I don't think he's **completely rational**.
>
> **"REAL SPEAK:"** My new neighbor talks to amaginary people! I don't think he's **cooking on all four burners**.
>
> *Synonym 1:* **both oars in the water (not to have)** *exp.*
>
> *Synonym 2:* **the elevator doesn't go all the way up to the top** *exp.* said of someone who is crazy or irrational.
>
> **NOW YOU DO IT. COMPLETE THE PHRASE ALOUD:**
> *I don't think... is cooking on all four burners because...*

dig up something on someone (to) *exp.* to find information about someone.

> **EXAMPLE:** You won't believe what I **dug up on** Gina. She works as a clown in the evenings!
>
> **TRANSLATION:** You won't believe what I **found out about** Gina. She works as a clown in the evenings!
>
> **"REAL SPEAK:"** You won't believe whad I **dug up on** Gina. She works as a clown 'n the evenings!
>
> *Note:* **dirt** *n.* information or gossip about someone • *So what's the **dirt** on Gina?; So what's the gossip about Gina?*
>
> **NOW YOU DO IT. COMPLETE THE PHRASE ALOUD:**
> *You won't believe what I dug up about...*

feel like a fish out of water (to) *exp.* to feel out of place, as if you don't belong.

> **EXAMPLE:** Everyone at this party is a professor except for me! I **feel like a fish out of water**.
>
> **TRANSLATION:** Everyone at this party is a professor except for me! I **feel like I don't belong here**.
>
> **"REAL SPEAK:"** Ev'ryone 'it this pardy's a prafesser except fer me! I **feel like a fish oudda wader**.
>
> **NOW YOU DO IT. COMPLETE THE PHRASE ALOUD:**
> *I always feel like a fish out of water when...*

have the hots for someone (to) *exp.* to be sexually attracted to someone.

EXAMPLE: Carol keeps following me! I think she **has the hots for me**. What should I do? I don't like her!

TRANSLATION: Carol keeps following me! I think she **is romantically interested in me**. What should I do? I don't like her!

"REAL SPEAK:" Carol keeps following me! I think she **has the hots fer me**. What should I do? I don't like 'er!

Note: **hot** *adj.* sexy • *Pat is* **hot***!*; Pat is sexy!

NOW YOU DO IT. COMPLETE THE PHRASE ALOUD:
I have the hots for...

hit the nail on the head (to) *exp.* to reach a correct conclusion.

EXAMPLE: – I think Ron is insecure about his height.
– **You hit the nail on the head**!

TRANSLATION: – I think Ron is insecure about his height.
– **You reached a correct conclusion**!

"REAL SPEAK:" – I think Ron's insecure aboud 'is height.
– **You hit the nail on the head**!

Synonym: **Bingo!** *exp. (from the popular game of Bingo where the winner yells "Bingo!" when he/she has won).*

NOW YOU DO IT. COMPLETE THE PHRASE ALOUD:
You hit the nail on the head when you said...

in the dark (to be) *exp.* to be unaware.

EXAMPLE: How is Tom after his operation? His family has been keeping me **in the dark**!

TRANSLATION: How is Tom after his operation? His family has been keeping me **uninformed**!

"REAL SPEAK:" How's Tom after 'is operation? His family's been keeping me **in the dark**!

Synonym: **keep someone guessing (to)** *exp.*

NOW YOU DO IT. COMPLETE THE PHRASE ALOUD:
Why did you keep me in the dark about...

kiss up to someone (to) *exp.* to flatter someone in order to get something.

EXAMPLE: Bob always **kisses up to** the boss. The only reason he does that is because he wants a raise.

TRANSLATION: Bob always **flatters** the boss. The only reason he does that is because he wants a raise.

"REAL SPEAK:" Bob always **kisses up ta** the boss. The only reason 'e does thad is cuz 'e wants a raise.

Synonym 1: **butter someone up (to)** *exp.*
Synonym 2: **lay it on thick (to)** *exp.*
Synonym 3: **sweet talk someone (to)** *exp.*

NOW YOU DO IT. COMPLETE THE PHRASE ALOUD:
...always kisses up to... because...

on hold (to be) *exp.* to be kept waiting on the telephone.

EXAMPLE: I was **on hold** for twenty minutes until someone finally took my call!

TRANSLATION: I was **kept waiting** for twenty minutes until someone finally took my call!

"REAL SPEAK:" I w'z **on hold** fer twen'y minutes until someone fin'lly took my call!

Synonym: **put someone on hold (to)** *exp.* to make someone wait on the phone.

NOW YOU DO IT. COMPLETE THE PHRASE ALOUD:

I was on hold for... minutes when I called...

paint oneself into a corner (to) *exp.* to get oneself into a difficult situation or predicament.

EXAMPLE: To impress Connie, Bill told her that he was a doctor. Now she wants him to be her parents' doctor! He really **painted himself into a corner**!

TRANSLATION: To impress Connie, Bill told her that he was a doctor. Now she wants him to be her parents' doctor! He really **got himself into a difficult situation**!

"REAL SPEAK:" To impress Connie, Bill told 'er th't he w'z a docter. Now she wants 'im da be 'er parents' docter! He really **pain'ed 'imself into a corner**!

Note 1: There are many slang synonyms for "a difficult situation" or "predicatment." For example: **a tight spot • a tight squeeze • a fine how do you do** (*old-fashioned, yet heard in jest*) **• a can of worms • a fine mess**.

Note 2: There are many slang synonyms for "to be in a difficult situation" or "in a predicament." For example: **in a jam • in a pickle • in hot water • up a creek • up a creek without a paddle • in a fix**.

NOW YOU DO IT. COMPLETE THE PHRASE ALOUD:

I painted myself in a corner when I...

sink or swim (to) *exp.* to die or survive.

EXAMPLE: This is my last chance to show my boss that he needs me in his company. It's **sink or swim**!

TRANSLATION: This is my last chance to show my boss that he needs me in his company. It's **die or survive**!

"REAL SPEAK:" This is my las' chance ta show my boss thad 'e needs me in 'is company. It's **sink 'r swim**!

Synonym: **do or die (to)** *exp.*

NOW YOU DO IT:

Use "sink or swim" in a sentence.

slave driver *n.* a boss who is extremely demanding often to the point of being unreasonable.

EXAMPLE: My new boss insists that we work one day each weekend. He's a **slave driver**!

TRANSLATION: My new boss insists that we work one day each weekend. He's a **demanding boss**!

"REAL SPEAK:" My new boss insis' th't we work one day each weekend. He's a **slave driver**!

NOW YOU DO IT. COMPLETE THE PHRASE ALOUD:
I think my boss is a real slave driver because...!

"What's eating him/her/you/them/etc?" *exp.* "What's bothering him/her/you/etc.?"

EXAMPLE: I asked Eric how he was doing today and he told me to leave him alone! I wonder **what's eating him**.

TRANSLATION: I asked Eric how he was doing today and he told me to leave him alone! I wonder **what's bothering him**.

"REAL SPEAK:" I asked Eric how 'e w'z doing taday an' 'e told me da leave 'im alone! I wonder **what's eading him**?.

Synonym 1: **"What's bugging him/her/you/them/etc.?"** *exp.*
Synonym 2: **"What's his/her/your/their/etc. deal?"** *exp.*
Synonym 3: **"What's up with him/her/you/them/etc.?"** *exp.*

NOW YOU DO IT. COMPLETE THE PHRASE ALOUD:
What's eating...?

work like mad (to) *exp.* to work with great intensity.

EXAMPLE: I need **to work like mad** in order to get this assignment done by four o'clock!

TRANSLATION: I need **to work with great intensity** in order to get this assignment done by four o'clock!

"REAL SPEAK:" I need **da work like mad** 'n order da get this assignment done by four a'clock!

Synonym 1: **cook (to)** *exp.*
Synonym 2: **hustle (to)** *exp.*
Synonym 3: **slave away (to)** *exp.*
Synonym 4: **work like crazy (to)** *exp.*
Synonym 5: **work one's head off (to)** *exp.*

NOW YOU DO IT:
Use "work like mad" in a sentence.

LET'S PRACTICE!

CD-B: TRACK 21

A. CORRECT OR INCORRECT? *(Answers on p. 224)*

Decide whether or not the words in boldface have been used correctly or incorrectly by checking the appropriate box.

1. Bonnie follows Carl everywhere. I think she **has the hots for** him!
   ❑ CORRECT   ❑ INCORRECT

2. I'm totally **in the dark**. I know everything that happened yesterday.
   ❑ CORRECT   ❑ INCORRECT

3. Patricia is so stupid. What a **brain**!
   ❑ CORRECT   ❑ INCORRECT

4. You're right. You **hit the nail on the head**!
   ❑ CORRECT   ❑ INCORRECT

5. Stop **looking over my shoulder**. I'll show you my work when it's finished.
   ❑ CORRECT   ❑ INCORRECT

6. You'd better **work like mad** if you want to finish before five o'clock!
   ❑ CORRECT   ❑ INCORRECT

7. I didn't want to go to Steve's party tonight, so I told him I was sick. Now today I'm supposed to go to a lunch party and Steve's going to be there! I really **painted myself into a corner**!
   ❑ CORRECT   ❑ INCORRECT

8. I'm really hungry. I feel like **a fish out of water**.
   ❑ CORRECT   ❑ INCORRECT

9. I was **on hold** for an hour in the swimming pool.
   ❑ CORRECT   ❑ INCORRECT

10. What's **eating you**? You seem upset about something.
    ❑ CORRECT   ❑ INCORRECT

11. Nancy is **kissing up to** the boss because she's hoping for a raise.
    ❑ CORRECT   ❑ INCORRECT

12. So tell me about Jill? What did you **dig up on** her?
    ❑ CORRECT   ❑ INCORRECT

13. My boss is very relaxed. He's a real **slave driver**.
    ❑ CORRECT   ❑ INCORRECT

14. That guy is talking to himself. Obviously, he's **not cooking on all four burners**.
    ❑ CORRECT   ❑ INCORRECT

15. Don't worry if you fail the assignment. It's **sink or swim**. You can always try again.
    ❑ CORRECT   ❑ INCORRECT

B. BLANK-BLANK *(Answers on p. 224)*

Fill in the blank with the correct word(s)
from Column B.

CD-B: TRACK 22

COLUMN A	COLUMN B
1. Sorry to keep you on _____. The phones have been so busy today.	**birdie**
2. – How did you know I got the job? – A little _____ told me.	**in the dark**
3. What a predicament! You really painted yourself _____ this time!	**eating**
4. Trish is a rocket scientist? Wow! She must really be a _____!	**the hots**
5. I heard that Paul and Don had a big fight! What happened? I'm totally _____!	**on all four burners**
6. What's _____ you today? You seem really upset about something.	**hold**
7. I hate the way Eric _____ up to the boss. You know that it's only because he wants a raise.	**slave driver**
8. You're right! You _____ on the head!	**hit the nail**
9. Did you see the way Larry looks at me in class? I think he has _____ for me.	**like mad**
10. My history teacher isn't cooking _____. He thinks he's really George Washington!	**kisses**
11. My boss wants me to work all weekend again. What a _____!	**into a corner**
12. So, tell me. What did you _____ on Janet? I hear that she used to be an actress!	**dig up**
13. If you want to leave in time for the movie, you'd better work _____ to finish early.	**water**
14. I'm not comfortable here. I feel like a fish out of _____.	**brain**

CD-B: TRACK 23

C. TRUE OR FALSE *(Answers on p. 224)*

Decide whether or not the definition of the words in boldface is true or false by checking an "X" in the correct box.

1. **"A little birdie told me"** *exp.* "A secret informant told me."
   ❏ TRUE ❏ FALSE

2. **"What's eating him/her/you/etc?"** *exp.* "What's bothering him/her/you/etc.?"
   ❏ TRUE ❏ FALSE

3. **work like mad (to)** *exp.* to be angry about having to work late.
   ❏ TRUE ❏ FALSE

4. **hit the nail on the head (to)** *exp.* to reach a correct conclusion.
   ❏ TRUE ❏ FALSE

5. **dig up something on someone** *exp.* to find information about someone
   ❏ TRUE ❏ FALSE

6. **have the hots for someone (to)** *exp.* to be very angry at someone.
   ❏ TRUE ❏ FALSE

7. **in the dark (to be)** *exp.* to be unaware.
   ❏ TRUE ❏ FALSE

8. **slave driver** *n.* a boss who is extremely demanding often to the point of being unreasonable.
   ❏ TRUE ❏ FALSE

9. **kiss up to someone (to)** *exp.* to try to be romantic with someone.
   ❏ TRUE ❏ FALSE

10. **paint oneself into a corner (to)** *exp.* to be in a hurry.
    ❏ TRUE ❏ FALSE

11. **brain** *n.* an extremely smart person, a genius.
    ❏ TRUE ❏ FALSE

12. **feel like a fish out of water (to)** *exp.* to be extremely thirsty.
    ❏ TRUE ❏ FALSE

13. **cooking on all four burners (not to be)** *exp.* said of someone who is crazy or irrational.
    ❏ TRUE ❏ FALSE

14. **sink or swim (to)** *exp.* to die or survive.
    ❏ TRUE ❏ FALSE

15. **on hold (to be)** *exp.* to be kept waiting on the telephone.
    ❏ TRUE ❏ FALSE

THE SLANGMAN FILES

Colors Used in Slang Expressions

What better way to add color to a phrase than by actually using a color in the expression itself! If you're **green** (*lacking experience*) in the area of expressions using colors, you'll be **tickled pink** (*delighted*) to know that you can learn them here right now. It just takes using a little **grey matter** (*brain power*)!

BLACK

black out (to) *exp.* to faint.

> **EXAMPLE:** My fever got so high that I **blacked out**.
>
> **TRANSLATION:** My fever got so high that I **fainted**.
>
> **"REAL SPEAK":** My fever got so high th'd I **blacked out**.
>
> *Also:* **black out** *n.* an interruption in electric power causing the lights to go out • *Everyone was concerned that on January 1, 2000, there would be a blackout;* Everyone was concerned that on January 1, 2000, there would be an interruption in electric power.

blackballed (to be) *exp.* to be prevented from being hired or accepted to a specific group.

> **EXAMPLE:** Jeff can't find a job anywhere. He's being **blackballed** because he has a bad reputation.
>
> **TRANSLATION:** Jeff can't find a job anywhere. He's being **prevented from being hired** because he has a bad reputation.
>
> **"REAL SPEAK":** Jeff can't find a job anywhere. He's being **blackballed** b'cause 'e has a bad reputation.

blacklisted (to be) *exp.* to prevent someone from being hired or accepted to a specific group.

> **EXAMPLE:** Many TV and movie writers couldn't get work in Hollywood because they were **blacklisted** due to suspicion of being communists.

> **TRANSLATION:** Many TV and movie writers couldn't get work in Hollywood because they were **prevented from working** due to suspicion of being communists.
>
> **"REAL SPEAK":** Many TV 'n movie wriders couldn' get work 'n Hollywood b'cause they were **blacklisted** due da suspicion 'ev being communists.
>
> *Note:* This expression comes from the McCarthy period when those who were thought to be communists or communist sympathizers were put on a list (later termed the "blacklist") and targeted for discrimination.

give someone a black eye (to) *exp.* to bruise someone's eye usually through a punch.

> **EXAMPLE:** When my girlfriend found out that I was seeing someone else, she **gave me a black eye**.
>
> **TRANSLATION:** When my girlfriend found out that I was seeing someone else, she **punched me in the eye and bruised it**.
>
> **"REAL SPEAK":** When my girlfrien' found out th'd I w'z seeing someone else, she **gamme a black eye**.

in the black *exp.* said of a company that is making a profit.

> **EXAMPLE:** This year our company is finally in **the black**!
>
> **TRANSLATION:** This year our company is finally **making a profit**!
>
> **"REAL SPEAK":** This year 'ar company's fin'lly in **the black**!

Note: Ledger sheets show positive numbers in black ink and negative numbers in red.

See: **in the red**, *p. 216.*

little black book *exp.* a "secret" little address book containing names and phone numbers of people for dating.

EXAMPLE: Once Sam and Diane got married, Diane tried to find Sam's **little black book** and burn it!

TRANSLATION: Once Sam and Diane got married, Diane tried to find Sam's **secret address book of potential dates** and burn it!

"REAL SPEAK": Once Sam 'n Diane got married, Diane tried ta fin' Sam's **liddle black book** 'n burn it!

"That's the pot calling the kettle black!" *exp.* "You're accusing someone of having the same flaw as you!"

EXAMPLE: You think I'm stubborn?! Well, **that's the pot calling the kettle black!**

TRANSLATION: You think I'm stubborn?! Well, **you're accusing me of having the same flaw as you!**

"REAL SPEAK": You think I'm stubborn?! Well, **that's the pot calling the keddle black!**

BLUE

blues (the) *n.pl.* • **1.** a style of jazz, evolved from southern American Negro songs usually distinguished by a slow tempo and often melancholy or *"blue"* (which is slang for "depressing") • **2.** depression.

EXAMPLE 1: No one could sing **the blues** like Bessie Smith. She sang with so much feeling!

TRANSLATION: No one could sing **melancholy songs** like Bessie Smith. She sang with so much feeling!

"REAL SPEAK": No w'n could sing **the blues** like Bessie Smith. She sang with so much feeling!

EXAMPLE 2: I have the **blues** today.

TRANSLATION: I'm **depressed** today.

"REAL SPEAK": I have the **blues** taday.

blue (to feel) *adj.* depressed and sad.

EXAMPLE: I'm feeling **blue** today. It's my birthday and no one remembered.

TRANSLATION: I'm feeling **depressed** today. It's my birthday and no one remembered.

"REAL SPEAK": I'm feeling **blue** daday. It's my birthday 'n no w'm remembered.

Note: A popular song in the mid 1900s was *"Red roses for a blue lady"* meaning "red roses for a sad lady."

once in a blue moon *exp.* rarely.

EXAMPLE: My entire family will be together this holiday. That happens **once in a blue moon** because we all live so far from each other.

TRANSLATION: My entire family will be together this holiday. That happens **rarely** because we all live so far from each other.

"REAL SPEAK": My entire fam'ly'll be dagether this holiday. That happens **once 'n a blue moon** b'cause we all live so far fr'm each other.

out of the blue *exp.* without warning.

EXAMPLE: I didn't even see the driver who hit me. He appeared **out of the blue!**

TRANSLATION: I didn't even see the driver who hit me. He appeared **without warning!**

"REAL SPEAK": I didn' even see the driver who hit me. He appeared **oudda the blue!**

Variation: **out of the clear blue** *exp.*

swear up a blue streak (to) *exp.* to swear a lot.

EXAMPLE: Nancy can really **swear up a blue streak** when she's angry.

TRANSLATION: Nancy can really **swear a lot** when she's angry.

"REAL SPEAK": Nancy c'n really **swear up a blue streak** when she's angry.

talk until one is blue in the face (to) *exp.* to talk until one has nothing left to say.

EXAMPLE: You can **talk** to Tina **until you're blue in the face.** She's very stubborn and won't listen to anyone else's opinion.

TRANSLATION: You can talk to Tina **until you have nothing else to say**, but she'll ignore you. She's very stubborn and won't listen to anyone else's opinion.

"REAL SPEAK": You c'n **talk** ta Tina **'til y'r blue 'n the face**. She's very stubbern 'n won't listen ta anyone else's apinion.

"What in blue blazes?!" *interj.* an interjection of surprise or annoyance.

EXAMPLE: **What in blue blazes** is that?! I've never seen anything like it in my life!

TRANSLATION: **Wow! What** is that?! I've never seen anything like it in my life!

"REAL SPEAK": **What'n blue blazes** is that?! I've never seen anything like id in my life!

GRAY

gray area *exp.* an unclear or uncertain issue.

EXAMPLE: I'm not sure how to answer that question because it's **a gray area**.

TRANSLATION: I'm not sure how to answer that question because it's **an unclear issue**.

"REAL SPEAK": I'm not sure how da answer that question b'cause it's **a gray area**.

gray matter *exp.* intelligence, "brains."

EXAMPLE: Ted keeps making mistakes in his job. I don't think he has a lot of **gray matter**.

TRANSLATION: Ted keeps making mistakes in his job. I don't think he has a lot of **intelligence**.

"REAL SPEAK": Ted keeps making mistakes 'n 'is job. I don't think 'e has a lod 'a **gray madder**.

GREEN

get the green light (to) *exp.* to get approval.

EXAMPLE: We just got the **green light** to begin the project.

TRANSLATION: We just got the **approval** to begin the project.

"REAL SPEAK": We jus' got the **green light** ta b'gin the project.

green (to be) *adj.* to be a novice.

EXAMPLE: I don't want him to perform the operation on me. He's still **green**.

TRANSLATION: I don't want him to perform the operation on me. He's still **a novice**.

"REAL SPEAK": I don't wan' 'im ta perform the operation on me. He's still **green**.

Note: This describes someone who is still immature or "unripened" like a green piece of fruit.

green thumb (to have a) *exp.* to have a talent for gardening and making plants grow.

EXAMPLE: Your plants are beautiful! You must really have a **green thumb**.

TRANSLATION: Your plants are beautiful! You must really have a **talent for gardening**.

"REAL SPEAK": Yer plants'er beaudif'l! You must really have a **green thumb**.

green with envy (to be) *exp.* to be extremely jealous.

EXAMPLE: John was **green with envy** when he saw my new car.

TRANSLATION: John was **extremely jealous** when he saw my new car.

"REAL SPEAK": John w'z **green with envy** when 'e saw my new car.

the grass is always greener on the other side *exp.* other situations always seem better than the present ones.

EXAMPLE: I was tired of the earthquakes in Los Angeles, so I moved to New York. But the winters in New York are so cold! I guess **the grass is always greener on the other side**.

TRANSLATION: I was tired of the earthquakes in Los Angeles, so I moved to New York. But the winters in New York are so cold! I guess **other situations always seem better than the present ones**.

"REAL SPEAK": I w'z tired 'a the earthquakes 'n L.A., so I moved ta New York. But the winters 'n New York'er so cold! I guess **the grass 'ez always greener on the other side**.

Variation: **The grass is always greener**
exp. (a common shortened variation).

PINK

in the pink (to be) *exp.* to be enjoying good health (exhibited by a healthy pink color of one's skin).

| EXAMPLE: | I was sick for a week, but I'm finally **in the pink**. |

| TRANSLATION: | I was sick for a week, but I'm finally **healthy again**. |

| "REAL SPEAK": | I w'z sick fer a week, b'd I'm fin'lly **in the pink**. |

pinky *n.* one's little finger.

| EXAMPLE: | Natalie is very elegant. Whenever she drinks, she holds her glass with her **pinky** sticking up. |

| TRANSLATION: | Natalie is very elegant. Whenever she drinks, she holds her glass with her **little finger** sticking up. |

| "REAL SPEAK": | Natalie's very elegant. Whenever she drinks, she holds 'er glass with 'er **pinky** sticking up. |

tickled pink (to be) *exp.* delighted.

| EXAMPLE: | I was **tickled pink** when I heard that you're getting married. Congratulations! |

| TRANSLATION: | I was **delighted** when I heard that you're getting married. Congratulations! |

| "REAL SPEAK": | I w'z **tickled pink** when I heard th't cher gedding married. C'ngrats! |

RED

beet red *exp.* extremely red (like a beet).

| EXAMPLE: | Laura **turned beet red** when she ripped her dress in public. |

| TRANSLATION: | Laura **became extremely red** when she ripped her dress in public. |

| "REAL SPEAK": | Laura **turned beet red** when she ripped 'er dress 'n public. |

catch someone red-handed (to) *exp.* to discover someone in the process of committing a sneaky act.

| EXAMPLE: | I **caught** John **red-handed** stealing money. |

| TRANSLATION: | I **caught** John **in the act of** stealing money. |

| "REAL SPEAK": | [no change] |

in the red *exp.* said of a company that is losing money.

| EXAMPLE: | If our company doesn't **get out of the red** soon, we're going to have to go out of business. |

| TRANSLATION: | If our company doesn't **stop losing money** soon, we're going to have to go out of business. |

| "REAL SPEAK": | If 'ar company doesn't **ged oudda the red** soon, w'r gonna hafta go oudda bizness. |

| *Note:* | Ledger sheets show positive numbers in black ink and negative numbers in red. |

See: **in the black**, *p. 213.*

not to be worth a red cent *exp.* to be absolutely worthless.

| EXAMPLE: | That painting **isn't worth a red cent**. |

| TRANSLATION: | That painting **is absolutely worthless**. |

| "REAL SPEAK": | That pain'ing **isn't worth a red cent**. |

paint the town red (to) *exp.* to go into town and have a great time (going to the movies, to dinner, etc.).

| EXAMPLE: | To celebrate the new year, let's go into the city and **paint the town red**. |

| TRANSLATION: | To celebrate the new year, let's go into the city and **have some fun**. |

| "REAL SPEAK": | Ta celebrate the new year, let's go inta the cidy 'n **paint the town red**. |

red cent (not to have a) *exp.* not to have a single coin, to be broke.

| EXAMPLE: | I spent all my money buying gifts for Christmas. I **don't have a red cent** left. |

| TRANSLATION: | I spent all my money buying gifts for Christmas. I **don't have any money at all** left. |

"REAL SPEAK": I spen' all my money buying gif's fer Chris'mas. I **don't have a red cent** left.

Note: This expression can *only* be used in the negative. It would be incorrect to say: "*I have a red cent.*"

red neck *exp.* *(derogatory)* racist, one with bigoted ideas.

EXAMPLE: My uncle doesn't believe in equal rights. He's **such a red neck**.

TRANSLATION: My uncle doesn't believe in equal rights. He's **so bigoted**.

"REAL SPEAK": My uncle doesn't b'lieve 'n equal rights. He's **such a red neck**.

Note: This expression pertains to the southern rural working class which is said to be intolerant of any race other than white. The term originated because rural people are associated with sunburned necks from working outside.

red tape *exp.* excessive and seemingly unnecessary procedures.

EXAMPLE: There **was so much red tape** I had to go through in order to get a new passport.

TRANSLATION: There **were so many excessive and seemingly unnecessary procedures** I had to go through in order to get a new passport.

"REAL SPEAK": There **w'z so much red tape** I had ta go through 'n order da ged a new passport.

roll out the red carpet for someone (to) *exp.* to give someone first-rate treatment.

EXAMPLE: When the new boss arrives, let's make sure to **roll out the red carpet for her**.

TRANSLATION: When the new boss arrives, let's make sure to **give her first-rate treatment**.

"REAL SPEAK": When the new boss arrives, let's make sher da **roll out the red carpet for her**.

Note: When dignitaries or celebrities arrive to a special event, it is customary to roll out an actual red carpet for them to walk on so as not to dirty their shoes on the ground.

Variation: **give someone the red-carpet treatment (to)** *exp.* to give someone first-rate treatment.

see red (to) *exp.* to be furious.

EXAMPLE: When I walked out of the restaurant and noticed that my car had been stolen, I **saw red**!

TRANSLATION: When I walked out of the restaurant and noticed that my car had been stolen, I **was furious**!

"REAL SPEAK": When I walked oudda the resterant 'n noticed th't my car'ed been stolen, I **saw red**!

WHITE

white as a ghost (to be as) *exp.* to be extremely pale, usually due to fear.

EXAMPLE: You look **as white as a ghost**! What happened?

TRANSLATION: You look **terribly pale**! What happened?

"REAL SPEAK": You look **'ez white 'ez a ghost**! What happened?

Variation: **white as a sheet (to be as)** *exp.*

white-bread (to be) *adj.* to be stereotypically/ caricaturistically American (white Anglo-Saxon Protestant, middle class).

EXAMPLE: Connie has blond hair, goes to church every Sunday, is a cheerleader, and dresses conservatively. She's so **white-bread**!

TRANSLATION: Connie has blond hair, goes to church every Sunday, is a cheerleader, and dresses conservatively. She's so **stereotypically American**!

"REAL SPEAK": Connie has blond hair, goes ta church ev'ry Sunday, is a cheerleader, an' dresses conservadively. She's so **white-bread**!

Note: This adjective equates someone with white bread since it was considered the typical bread in the homes of most Americans in the mid-1900s.

white-knuckle *exp.* describes something filled with tension and fear.

> **EXAMPLE:** Mimi shouldn't be allowed to drive a car. I was her passenger today and it was **a white-knuckle ride**.
>
> **TRANSLATION:** Mimi shouldn't be allowed to drive a car. I was her passenger today and it was **really scary**.
>
> **"REAL SPEAK":** Mimi shouldn't be allowed ta drive a car. I w'z 'er passenger daday an' it w'zh **a white-knuckle ride**.
>
> *Note:* The expression "*white-knuckle*" refers to ones knuckles as they turn white from being clutched.

white lie *exp.* a small lie which is used to get someone out of a difficult situation or to spare someone's feelings.

> **EXAMPLE:** I didn't want to go to Tom's party, so I told him a **white lie**. I said that I wasn't feeling well.
>
> **TRANSLATION:** I didn't want to go to Tom's party, so I told him a **small lie**. I said that I wasn't feeling well.
>
> **"REAL SPEAK":** I didn't wanna go da Tom's pardy, so I told 'im a **white lie**. I said th'd I wasn' feeling well.

ANSWERS TO LESSONS 1-10

LESSON ONE – AT WORK
LET'S WARM UP!

1. failing to do his job
2. reprimanded me
3. lunatic
4. agree
5. get smarter and more aware
6. playing stead of working
7. report
8. an undesirable surprise
9. seen doing something wrong
10. made mistakes with

LET'S PRACTICE!
A. CHOOSE THE RIGHT WORD

1. eye to eye
2. rude
3. carpet
4. blew
5. up
6. wacko
7. clue
8. off
9. act
10. wheel

B. CONTEXT EXERCISE

1. doesn't make sense
2. makes sense
3. doesn't make sense
4. makes sense
5. doesn't make sense
6. makes sense
7. makes sense
8. doesn't make sense
9. makes sense

C. CREATE YOUR OWN SENTENCE (SUGGESTIONS FOR ANSWERS)

1. He got called on the carpet this morning.
2. He fell asleep at the wheel.
3. Someone blew the whistle on me.
4. Yes. I caught her in the act!
5. Because she goofs off all the time.
6. She botched it up!
7. Yes. He needs to get a clue.
8. One of these days, she's going to have a rude awakening.
9. Yes. They don't seem to see eye to eye.
10. Yes. He's a wacko!

D. COMPLETE THE PHRASE

1. called on the carpet
2. eye to eye
3. get a clue
4. act
5. wacko
6. blow the whistle
7. rude
8. wheel
9. goofing off

LESSON TWO – AT THE MALL
LET'S WARM UP!

1. broken
2. severe headache
3. dishonest
4. had all I can tolerate
5. intellectually arrogant person
6. cheated
7. fool
8. suspicious
9. very upset
10. excessively high

LET'S PRACTICE!
A. FIND THE MISSING WORDS

Tom: I hate car shopping. It always give me a **splitting** headache.

Pat: Me, too I hate having to talk with those **slimy** car salespeople who try to cheat you.

Tom: And some of them talk to you like you're a moron. I've really **had** it with being treated like a **birdbrain** just because I don't know a lot about cars.

Pat: I know what you mean. Also, there's something I don't understand. The prices are all through the **roof** on the cars on the other side of the lot. But the cars over here are all relatively inexpensive. Doesn't that seem **fishy**?

Tom: That's probably because the cars on this side are all used and will go on the **fritz** within a week.

Pat: If that happens to my new car, I'm going to be beside **myself**! I'm so tired of being **burned** every time I buy something. No matter what price you pay for something, it should work!

Tom: Oh, no. Here comes a salesperson. Great. He'll probably give us a lecture all about cars and act like a total **know-it-all**.

B. CREATE YOUR OWN NEWSPAPER COLUMN

Remember, be as creative as your own imagination!

C. MATCH THE SENTENCES

1.	D	3.	H	5.	G	7.	B	9.	J
2.	C	4.	E	6.	F	8.	A	10.	I

LESSON THREE – HOUSEGUEST
LET'S WARM UP!

1.	H	3.	J	5.	B	7.	I	9.	G
2.	A	4.	F	6.	D	8.	C	10.	E

LET'S PRACTICE!
A. WHAT DOES IT MEAN?

1. a surprise
2. extremely nervous
3. to leave quickly
4. to get worse
5. everything possible
6. to have an easy life
7. to collapse
8. extremely drunk
9. to eat everything
10. to eat quickly

B. COMPLETE THE FAIRY TALE

Once upon a time, there was a little girl named Goldilocks who wandered into a small house in the woods. The house was wonderful and had everything you could ever want. Whoever lived there certainly had it **made**. Little did Goldilocks realize that soon she was going to be in for a **shocker**!

She noticed some food on the table and picked up a spoon and tasted the porridge in the big bowl, but it was too hot. She tasted the porridge in the medium size bowl, but that porridge was too cold. Then she tasted the porridge in the tiny little bowl. "Mmmmmm," she said. "This porridge is just right!" so she **wolfed** it down! But she didn't stop there. She went into the kitchen and ate everything but the **kitchen sink**!

Then Goldilocks saw three chairs in the living room. She climbed into the big chair but it was too hard. Then she sat in the medium size chair but it was too soft. Next, she sat in Baby Bear's little chair. "Ahhhh," she said. "This chair is just right!" Just then there was a loud CRACK! and the little chair broke!"

Then she climbed upstairs to the bedroom, yawned, and said, "I'm feeling sleepy." So she pulled down the covers and climbed into the big bed to **crash** for a while, but it was too hard. Then she tried the medium size bed but it was too soft. So she climbed into Baby Bear's little bed. It was just right and she fell asleep!

Later the Three Bears returned from the local bar. Things were about to go **downhill** for Goldilocks. Suddenly Papa, who was completely **plastered** from drinking too much, cried out, "Someone's been eating my porridge!" Then Mamma cried out, "Someone's been eating MY porridge!" And Baby Bear cried out, "Someone's been eating MY porridge. And they've eaten it all up!" Someone was eating them out of **house and home**.

Then the Three Bears saw their chairs in the living room. "Someone's been sitting in my chair!" Papa Bear said. "Someone's been sitting in MY chair!" Mamma Bear said. "Someone's been sitting in MY chair," Baby Bear cried. "And now it's broken!"

Then the Three Bears went upstairs to the bedroom. "Someone's been sleeping in my bed!" Papa Bear shouted. "Someone's been sleeping in MY bed!" Mamma Bear exclaimed. "Someone's been sleeping in MY bed," Baby Bear squeaked. "...And there she is!" Suddenly Goldilocks woke up and Baby Bear screamed, "**Beat** it!" She was such a nervous **wreck** that she didn't know what to do! Finally, she ran down the stairs and out the door. She didn't stop until she was all the way back home. And the Three Bears never saw Goldilocks again!

C. CONTEXT EXERCISE

1.	D	6.	C
2.	J	7.	E
3.	B	8.	H
4.	I	9.	F
5.	A	10.	G

D. COMPLETE THE PHRASE

Cecily: How is it going with your houseguest?

Lee: It's going **downhill**. Every day he **crashes** in front of the television for hours. All he ever does is sleep and eat us out of **house and home**. You should have seen the sandwich he **wolfed** down this morning. He put everything on it but the **kitchen sink**. He has it **made** here.

Cecily: Why don't you just tell him to **beat it**?

Lee: He was my roommate in college and it's only for another two days. I just hope that I don't turn into a nervous **wreck** by the time he leaves. He even came home late last night totally **plastered**!

Cecily: Maybe you should just lock the front door so he can't come back in! Wouldn't he be in for a **shocker**?!

LESSON FOUR – AT THE PARK
LET'S WARM UP!

1. angry
2. passionate about
3. disgusts me
4. go ahead
5. become aware of what's really happening
6. let's not talk about this subject
7. persistently annoying thought
8. at just the right moment
9. foolish and weak-looking person
10. find girls for an intimate encounter
11. bruised eye
12. has changed his attitude

LET'S PRACTICE!

A. CROSSWORD PUZZLE

B. CHOOSE THE RIGHT WORD

1.	nick	4.	nagging	7.	go	10.	tune
2.	out	5.	black	8.	off	11.	geek
3.	up	6.	out	9.	crazy	12.	up

C. MATCH THE COLUMN

1.	F	4.	D	7.	K	10.	E
2.	B	5.	A	8.	J	11.	G
3.	L	6.	C	9.	I	12.	H

LESSON FIVE – THE BIRTHDAY PARTY

LET'S WARM UP!

1.	False	4.	True	7.	True	10.	False
2.	True	5.	True	8.	True	11.	True
3.	True	6.	False	9.	False	12.	False

LET'S PRACTICE!

A. YOU'RE THE AUTHOR

Jennifer: I finally had it **out** with Carol for telling me that my house is ugly and too artsy-**fartsy**. She really **bugs** me big **time**! I've had a **bone** to pick with her for a long time about her insults. Getting her to pay a compliment is like pulling **teeth**!

Louise: She told you that *you* have bad taste?! I have a hard time **swallowing** that because she has the worst taste of anyone I've ever met. I mean, look at her! Her clothes are all old and **cheesy** and she always looks like she's having a bad hair **day**. And I have to tell you that I'm head over **heels** with the way you've decorated your house. I think she's just blind as a **bat** and can't see how pretty your house really is! You need to stop inviting her to your parties, although it won't matter. She'll probably just **crash** them!

B. I KNOW THE ANSWER, BUT WHAT'S THE QUESTIONS?

1. Did you see Nancy's new furniture?
2. Was it easy getting Mike to drive you to the airport?
3. Did you and Steve ever become friends again?
4. Did you invite Louise to your party?
5. Did you like the movie?
6. Was your mother ever able to get a driver's license?

C. FIND YOUR PERFECT MATCH

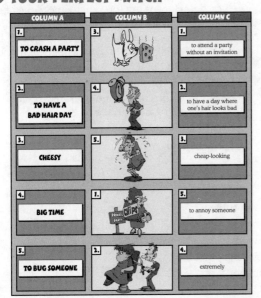

D. IMAGINE THAT...

In this section, you could have many possible answers. Remember, respond to each situation by making a complete sentence using one of the groups of words in the word list AND using each group only once. Be as creative as you'd like!

LESSON SIX – IN THE SUBWAY
LET'S WARM UP!

1. crazy
2. extremely scared
3. give that to me
4. destined to die
5. ridicule you
6. was completely unexpected
7. thief
8. robbed
9. stole it right in front of me
10. person who prefers to stay home
11. vulnerable to attack
12. flirted with you

LET'S PRACTICE!

A. THE UNFINISHED CONVERSATION (SUGGESTIONS FOR ANSWERS)

1. It's true. He's not playing with a full deck!
2. Everyone made fun of me!
3. I told him to hand it over.
4. He made a pass at me!
5. I was held up on my way to the market!

B. CHOOSE THE RIGHT WORD

1. stiff
2. ducks
3. up
4. home
5. crook
6. nose
7. deck
8. fun
9. pass
10. goner
11. blue
12. Hand

C. COMPLETE THE STORY

You're probably going to *make fun of me* for being so stupid, but I walked home late last night and was *held up* by a *crook*. I should have known I'd be a *sitting duck* in that neighborhood. At first I just thought it was some guy trying to *make a pass* at me; then I realized he wasn't *playing with a full deck*. He *came out of the blue* and told me to *hand over* my money. I was *scared stiff*! I really thought I was a *goner*. After an experience like that, I think I'm going to become more of a *homebody*.

D. CREATE YOUR OWN SENTENCE (SUGGESTIONS FOR ANSWERS)

1. I was help up!
2. Someone swiped it right from under my nose!
3. Yes. It came from out of the blue.
4. I was scared stiff!
5. Yes. I thought I was a goner.
6. Yes. He made a pass at me!
7. Yes. We're sitting ducks out here.
8. He was making fun of your shirt.
9. No. He's not playing with a full deck.
10. Yes. He's a crook.

LESSON SEVEN – ACHES & PAINS
LET'S WARM UP!

1. D
2. C
3. N
4. J
5. F
6. B
7. M
8. G
9. I
10. H
11. K
12. L
13. E
14. A

LET'S PRACTICE!

A. YOU'RE THE AUTHOR

Joe: I'm not **myself** today. I **tweaked** my back yesterday lifting some heavy boxes. I've been wanting to clean the basement for months and I needed to move some big boxes upstairs. So, I thought, "No **sweat**!" I'm in tip-**top** shape. But I guess I **overdid** it. I used to be so **buff** when I worked out every day. Now I'm such a **wimp**. It really gets me **down**. My plans for cleaning the basement this month just went up in **smoke**.

Doug: The most important thing is that you rest. Once when I hurt my back, I went to a back specialist who wanted me to go under the **knife** right away! What a **quack**! I knew if I could just **hang** in there for a couple of weeks, I'd be up at and at **them** soon. Besides, it was actually fun watching the **tube** all day!

B. CROSSWORD PUZZLE

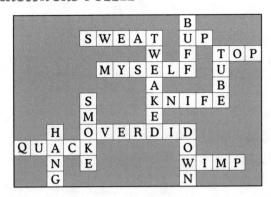

D. CREATE YOUR OWN SENTENCE (SUGGESTIONS FOR ANSWERS)

1. I'm going to stay <u>home</u> and watch a <u>movie</u> on the <u>tube</u>.

2. I <u>tweaked</u> my <u>back</u> and had to stay in <u>bed</u>.

3. Yes. I want to be <u>buff</u>, so I go to the <u>gym</u> often. I don't want to become a <u>wimp</u>.

4. <u>No sweat</u>. I'd be <u>glad</u> to <u>help</u>.

5. Yes. I'm going <u>under the knife</u> to get my <u>leg</u> repaired. I hope I don't get a <u>quake</u> to do the surgery!

6. Don't let it <u>get you down</u>. You'll be <u>up and at them</u> soon. Just try to <u>hang in there</u>.

C. TRUE OR FALSE

1.	False	6.	True
2.	False	7.	True
3.	False	8.	False
4.	False	9.	True
5.	True	10.	True

LESSON EIGHT – BABYSITTING
LET'S WARM UP!

1.	H	4.	A	7.	B	10.	D	13.	G
2.	K	5.	C	8.	M	11.	L	14.	J
3.	N	6.	F	9.	I	12.	E		

LET'S PRACTICE!
A. TRUTH OR LIE

1.	lie	3.	lie	5.	lie
2.	lie	4.	truth	6.	truth

B. FIND THE DEFINITION

1. to be having an exhausting time babysitting
2. to take a break (and have time to just breath)
3. to be a computer enthusiast
4. to stop doing something
5. to remain calm
6. to thrill someone
7. to state the rules firmly
8. said of a father and son with similar characteristics
9. to lose control of one's emotions
10. a person who is fanatic about cleanliness; cleanliness maniac
11. to yell extremely loudly
12. said of two choices that have equal consequences; the same
13. to be in the process of doing something suspicious
14. a genius child (from the term *wizard*)

C. FIND-THE-WORD GRID

1. breather
2. lungs
3. cut
4. law
5. freak
6. hell
7. wiz
8. socks
9. cool
10. lose

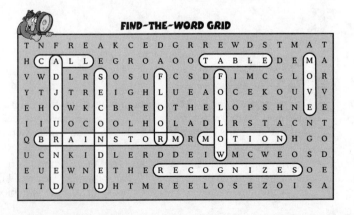

FIND-THE-WORD GRID

LESSON NINE – AT THE BAKERY
LET'S WARM UP!

1. False
2. True
3. True
4. False
5. False
6. False
7. False
8. True
9. True
10. True
11. False
12. True
13. True
14. True

LET'S PRACTICE!
A. & B. CREATE YOUR OWN STORY

In this section, you could have many possible answers. Remember, the more creative you are, the funnier your story will be!

C. WHAT WOULD YOU DO IF SOMEONE SAID...

1. a
2. c
3. a
4. c
5. a
6. a
7. c
8. c
9. b
10. b

D. "ACROSS" WORD PUZZLE

1. potato
2. crabby
3. munch
4. flip
5. torn
6. wide
7. back
8. run / pick

LESSON TEN – ON THE PHONE
LET'S WARM UP!

1. genius
2. upsetting
3. uninformed
4. were absolutely correct
5. waiting on the phone
6. discover
7. a secret informant
8. don't belong
9. is sexually interested in me
10. about survival
11. flatter him
12. completely rational
13. get in a difficult situation
14. relentlessly demanding boss
15. working as fast as possible

LET'S PRACTICE!
A. CORRECT OR INCORRECT?

1. correct
2. incorrect
3. incorrect
4. correct
5. correct
6. correct
7. correct
8. incorrect
9. incorrect
10. correct
11. correct
12. correct
13. incorrect
14. correct
15. incorrect

B. BLANK-BLANK

1. hold
2. birdie
3. into a corner
4. brain
5. in the dark
6. eating
7. kisses
8. hit the nail
9. the hots
10. on all four burners
11. slave driver
12. dig up
13. like mad
14. water

C. TRUE OR FALSE

1. true
2. true
3. false
4. true
5. true
6. false
7. true
8. true
9. false
10. false
11. true
12. false
13. true
14. true
15. true

INDEX

WHAT'S NEW FROM...

SLANGMAN® INC.
"If you don't know slang & idioms, you don't know the language!"

dba Slangman Publishing / dba Slangman Education Essentials

STREET SPEAK 1
THE COMPLETE COURSE IN AMERICAN SLANG & IDIOMS

This book is full of popular slang and idioms used every day by Americans — and it is very easy to use. You will be more confident and have fun using English when you learn the "real" English spoken by Americans.

Book: 144 pages — ISBN: 1891888-080 • US $18.95

This 2-Audio CD set presents the dialogues, exercises, and vocabulary sections. (Requires the book)

2-Audio CD set — ISBN: 1891888-293 • US $35.00

This 2-Audio Cassette set presents the dialogues, exercises, and vocabulary sections. (Requires the book)

2-Audio Cassette set — ISBN: 1891888-307 • US $25.00

STREET SPEAK 2
THE COMPLETE COURSE IN AMERICAN SLANG & IDIOMS

Expensive classes won't teach you the "real" language spoken by Americans. With our Slangman books, learn popular slang and idioms spoken by every American through entertaining dialogues, activities, and games. Learn as few or as many words as you want. (There are over 500 in the book!)

Book: 232 pages — ISBN: 1891888-604 • US $21.95

This 2-Audio CD set presents the dialogues, exercises, and vocabulary sections. (Requires the book)

2-Audio CD set — ISBN: 1891888-315 • US $35.00

This 2-Audio Cassette set presents the dialogues, exercises, and vocabulary sections. (Requires the book)

2-Audio Cassette set — ISBN: 1891888-323 • US $25.00

STREET SPEAK 3
THE COMPLETE COURSE IN AMERICAN SLANG & IDIOMS

This book contains entertaining dialogues, activities and games to help you learn more popular slang and idioms used constantly in American movies, music, relationships, and in daily American life. This book will give you more confidence when you speak to Americans!

Book: 240 pages — ISBN: 1891888-226 • US $21.95

This 2-Audio CD set presents the dialogues, exercises, and vocabulary sections. (Requires the book)

2-Audio CD set — ISBN: 1891888-331 • US $35.00

This 2-Audio Cassette set presents the dialogues, exercises, and vocabulary sections. (Requires the book)

2-Audio Cassette set — ISBN: 1891888-34X • US $25.00

DIRTY ENGLISH
A GUIDE TO POPULAR OBSCENITIES IN ENGLISH

This humorous book will teach you the most popular dangerous words and expressions used in the English language. It's also easy to understand and fun to read, even for the beginning English learner. It contains over 1,000 dangerous expressions used every day in American conversations. We will even show you which American movies, TV shows, and songs use these kinds of words. In addition, you will find over 2,400 sentences written as Americans really speak! These phrases will definitely help you communicate with Americans and understand our culture.

Book: 240 pages — ISBN: 1891888-234 • US $21.95

BIZ SPEAK 1
SLANG, IDIOMS & JARGON USED IN BUSINESS ENGLISH

If you do business with Americans, this book is for you! If you don't know the essential American slang and idioms used by all business professionals, you risk embarrassment, loss of respect, and loss of money. Entertaining dialogues, activities and games will quickly help put you "get the inside track"...that's slang for "get the advantage"!

Book: 240 pages — ISBN: 1891888-145 • US $21.95

This 2-Audio CD set presents the dialogues, exercises, and vocabulary sections. (Requires the book)

2-Audio CD set — ISBN: 1891888-358 • US $35.00

This 2-Audio Cassette set presents the dialogues, exercises, and vocabulary sections. (Requires the book)

2-Audio Cassette set — ISBN: 1891888-366 • US $25.00

BIZ SPEAK 2
SLANG, IDIOMS & JARGON USED IN BUSINESS ENGLISH

Don't be confused or embarrassed when doing business with Americans! Learn more popular slang words and idioms used in almost every American company. Entertaining dialogues, activities, and games will help you understand the real language spoken in American businesses.

Book: 240 pages — ISBN: 1891888-153 • US $21.95

This 2-Audio CD set presents the dialogues, exercises, and vocabulary sections. (Requires the book)

2-Audio CD set — ISBN: 1891888-374 • US $35.00

This 2-Audio Cassette set presents the dialogues, exercises, and vocabulary sections. (Requires the book)

2-Audio Cassette set — ISBN: 1891888-382 • US $25.00

PRICES/AVAILABILITY SUBJECT TO CHANGE

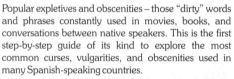

ORDER FORM

SLANGMAN INC.
"If you don't know slang & idioms, you don't know the language!"

dba Slangman Publishing
12206 Hillslope Street
Studio City, CA 91604 - USA

INTERNATIONAL:
1-818-769-1914

TOLL FREE (US/Canada):
1-877-SLANGMAN (752-6462)

WORLDWIDE FAX:
1-413-647-1589

EMAIL:
info@slangman.com

Preview chapters and shop online at:
WWW. SLANGMAN .COM

SHIPPING

Domestic Orders

SURFACE MAIL
(Delivery time 5-7 days).
Add $5 shipping/handling for the first item,
$1 for each additional item.

RUSH SERVICE
Available at extra charge. Contact us for details.

International Orders

SURFACE MAIL
(Delivery time 6-8 weeks).
Add $5 shipping/handling for the first item,
$2 for each additional item. Note that shipping to some countries may be more expensive. Contact us for details.

AIRMAIL
Available at extra charge. Contact us for details.

TITLE	ISBN	QTY	PRICE	TOTAL
The Slangman Guide To **STREET SPEAK 1**	Book: 1891888-080		$18.95	
	CDs: 1891888-293		$35.00	
	Cassettes: 1891888-307		$25.00	
The Slangman Guide To **STREET SPEAK 2**	Book: 1891888-064		$21.95	
	CDs: 1891888-315		$35.00	
	Cassettes: 1891888-323		$25.00	
The Slangman Guide To **STREET SPEAK 3**	Book: 1891888-226		$21.95	
	CDs: 1891888-331		$35.00	
	Cassettes: 1891888-34X		$25.00	
The Slangman Guide To **BIZ SPEAK 1**	Book: 1891888-145		$21.95	
	CDs: 1891888-358		$35.00	
	Cassettes: 1891888-366		$25.00	
The Slangman Guide To **BIZ SPEAK 2**	Book: 1891888-153		$21.95	
	CDs: 1891888-374		$35.00	
	Cassettes: 1891888-382		$25.00	
The Slangman Guide To **DIRTY ENGLISH**	Book: 1891888-234		$21.95	
STREET SPANISH 1	Book: 1471179-701		$16.95	
	Cassette: 1891888-188		$12.50	
STREET SPANISH 2	Book: 0471179-71X		$16.95	
	Cassette: 1891888-196		$12.50	
STREET SPANISH 3	Book: 0471179-728		$16.95	
	Cassette: 1891888-20X		$12.50	
STREET SPANISH SLANG DICTIONARY & THESAURUS	Book: 0471168-343		$17.95	
STREET FRENCH 1	Book: 0471138-983		$16.95	
	Cassette: 1891888-005		$12.50	
STREET FRENCH 2	Book: 0471138-991		$16.95	
	Cassette: 1891888-013		$12.50	
STREET FRENCH 3	Book: 0471138-009		$17.95	
	Cassette: 1891888-021		$12.50	
STREET FRENCH SLANG DICTIONARY & THESAURUS	Book: 0471168-068		$17.95	
STREET ITALIAN 1	Book: 0471384-380		$15.95	

Total for Merchandise		
Sales Tax *(California residents only add applicable sales tax)*		
Shipping *(See left)*		
ORDER TOTAL		

Prices/availability subject to change

Name _____

(School/Company) _____

Street Address _____

City _____ State/Province _____ Postal Code _____

Country _____ Phone _____

Email _____

Method of Payment (Check one):

☐ Personal Check or Money Order
(Must be in U.S. funds and drawn on a U.S. bank.)

☐ VISA   ☐ Master Card   ☐ Discover   ☐ American Express   ☐ JCB

Credit Card Number · · · · · · Expiration Date

_____
Signature